KU-184-088

fertility DeMYSTiFieD

Susan Warhaus, M.D.

New York   Chicago   San Francisco   Lisbon   London   Madrid   Mexico City
Milan   New Delhi   San Juan   Seoul   Singapore   Sydney   Toronto

The **McGraw·Hill** Companies

Copyright © 2007 by The McGraw-Hill Companies, Inc. All rights reserved. Printed in the United States of America. Except as permitted under the United States Copyright Act of 1976, no part of this publication may be reproduced or distributed in any form or by any means, or stored in a database or retrieval system, without the prior written permission of the publisher.

1 2 3 4 5 6 7 8 9 10 11 12 13 14 15 16 17 18 19 20 21 22 23 24 25 26 27 28 29 30 31   DOC/DOC   0 9 8 7

ISBN-13: 978-0-07-147922-6
ISBN-10:   0-07-147922-8

McGraw-Hill books are available at special quantity discounts to use as premiums and sales promotions, or for use in corporate training programs. For more information, please write to the Director of Special Sales, Professional Publishing, McGraw-Hill, Two Penn Plaza, New York, NY 10121-2298. Or contact your local bookstore.

This book is printed on acid-free paper.

To the many women and men who long to become parents—
may your loving dreams come true.

CONTENTS

FOREWORD

Fertility Demystified is a great resource for women and their partners who want to become parents but are having difficulty because of fertility issues. As a practicing fertility specialist, I deal with patients and their fertility challenges every day. Most of them have great hope of becoming parents but also feel the emotional frustration and apprehension of attempting to determine their diagnosis and treatment options. This book is designed to put those of you needing fertility assistance more at ease and to provide you with some insight into what you may expect as you start or continue your journey through the sometimes confusing and seemingly overwhelming fertility process.

This book was written and reviewed as a collaboration between two doctors: an OB/GYN physician and a fertility specialist. Our goal as physicians is to provide you with the best information available so you can have the knowledge you need to make the best decisions for your individual condition.

Fertility is a complicated field of medicine that is constantly evolving as scientific breakthroughs and emerging techniques are discovered. Because it's easy to feel overwhelmed, this book has been written in a manner that is easy to understand. *Fertility Demystified* takes a logical and systematic approach to the field of fertility, which could otherwise seem difficult and complex. This book examines the potential causes of infertility and explains the various tests, procedures, and fertility drugs that you may encounter. It also provides a straightforward look at female and male anatomy to help you better understand the reproductive process. Current and emerging fertility technologies are explained in an easy to follow manner.

The book is arranged so that each major fertility topic has its own chapter. At the end of each chapter, you'll notice a summary that emphasizes the key points discussed within the chapter. You can use these summaries to refresh your memory, or you may choose to use them as an introduction to see if a specific chapter is relevant to your needs right now.

Once you have completed this book, keep it handy as a quick and practical reference guide. You may even want to take notes and/or bring it with you to your doctor appointments. That way you can ask your own fertility specialist how a condition or treatment relates to your own particular situation.

I hope that you enjoy this book and find it to be a useful guide and resource. I wish you the very best success on your journey toward parenthood.

Nathaniel Zoneraich, M.D.
Reproductive Endocrinology and Infertility

ACKNOWLEDGMENTS

Back in the day, my college roommate Cathy and I were best of friends. Like so many good friends during our late teens and 20s, we shared our thoughts and emotions over relationships, career choices, and our own self-worth. We both married, and I was able to get pregnant easily. But Cathy and her husband really struggled and endured much turmoil surrounding their diagnosis of infertility. Thankfully, she and her husband eventually became parents to a beautiful baby girl. Now, some 18 years later as I write this book, thoughts of my old friend Cathy are once again in the forefront of my mind. Cathy, I want to acknowledge to you that I finally understand the difficulties that you endured during your fertility treatments. I'm so happy that you were able to realize your dreams of becoming a wonderful and loving mother.

I want to also thank my wonderful husband, Larry. Thank you so much for proofreading this book to make sure it is easy to understand and makes common sense. You continue to amaze me as you do things for me that are far above and beyond my expectations. What a gift it is to have you as my life partner.

Thanks also to those responsible for helping me write this book. Dr. Nathaniel Zoneraich is an outstanding reproductive endocrinologist and fertility specialist. Dr. Nate, I so appreciate your expertise in the writing of this book to ensure its accuracy and relevance. Also, thank you to my editor at McGraw-Hill, Johanna Bowman. You have done a terrific job of putting everything together and making this book come to life!

CHAPTER 1

The Causes of Infertility

Many couples who want to become pregnant often find that it's more difficult than they originally believed. Sadly, this problem is common. According to the American College of Obstetricians and Gynecologists, approximately 15 percent of couples in the United States may be infertile. This means that of the more than 40 million couples of childbearing age living together in the United States today, about 6 million of them may be affected by infertility issues. So if you are reading this book and have concerns about becoming pregnant, please know that you are not alone and that you have reason to feel optimistic and hopeful.

Medical research has shown that if you are a healthy young couple and have sexual intercourse a couple of times each week, your chances are about one in five (that is 20 percent) of becoming pregnant during any one menstrual cycle. This figure starts to decline in a woman's late 20s and early 30s and decreases even more after age 35. A man's fertility also declines with age, but not as early.

Many women today choose to delay parenthood because of career, finances, or other important personal reasons. Unfortunately, since they are somewhat older, they may experience problems conceiving. But regardless of your age or particular situation, current diagnosis and treatments offer great expectations for you to successfully become a parent.

The Definition of Infertility

The medical world defines infertility as not being able to conceive after 12 months of having regular heterosexual intercourse without the use of birth control. If you are unable to become pregnant after one year of unprotected sex, talk with your doctor about an infertility evaluation for you and your partner. If you are older than 35 or have certain medical conditions, the evaluation should be done sooner than one year. In many cases, tests can be performed to determine the cause of the infertility. Based upon those test results, treatment can be tailored to your specific needs and your infertility can be treated. Lifestyle changes, medication, surgery, or assisted reproductive technologies may be recommended.

The Roller Coaster of Emotions

Finding out that you or your partner may be facing fertility problems is often difficult to handle from an emotional standpoint. It's normal to feel depressed and discouraged at times. Many couples describe their emotions as ranging from fear and stress to hope and joy. Only couples who have experienced the problem of infertility can truly understand its devastating emotional and physical impacts. Infertility evaluation and treatment can be stressful and will require a big commitment from both you and your partner. That's why the two of you should work together with a knowledgeable, compassionate doctor and medical team who are considerate and sensitive to your emotional needs.

Potential Causes of Infertility

Many factors can cause or contribute to reduced fertility. Fertility concerns may be attributed to an issue with the woman, the man, the couple, or their lifestyle. That's why you and your partner should be evaluated and treated as a couple. Some causes may be easily found and treated, while others are more complex. In rare instances, no cause can be found at all.

Roughly speaking, about one-third of infertility cases may be attributable to the woman and another third to the man, while the last third either has to do with problems involving both partners or remains unexplained.

For women, infertility may be caused by a combination of many issues, including the following possibilities:

- Health and lifestyle choices
- Ovulation problems
- Hormonal imbalances
- Anatomical problems
- Genetic abnormalities
- Serious infections

Infertility issues for men include:

- Health and lifestyle habits
- Anatomical abnormalities and blockages
- Genetic and hormonal factors

The type of treatment you receive depends on what may be causing the infertility.

This chapter will take a closer look at the various causes of infertility and will help you determine where to focus your concerns.

Causes of Infertility: Health and Lifestyle Concerns for Women

Infertility may be caused by a variety of physical conditions and lifestyle choices. Sometimes, you can change your lifestyle habits and improve your own fertility.

ADVANCING AGE

The current social trend seems to be for women to wait longer before starting a family. Advantages to waiting to start a family include established career, financial security, and overall maturity. However, there may also be a price to pay for delayed childbearing. Many women find it more difficult to become pregnant than they expected. That's because, from a hormonal standpoint, most women reach their reproductive peak between the ages of 20 and 25. As you age, various changes within the reproductive system occur that may reduce your fertility. For example, fewer eggs are capable of forming a viable embryo. Also, the follicles, which are saclike structures surrounding each egg and are supposed to rupture and release the egg during ovulation, may not be as sturdy as they were when you were younger and thus may not be capable of effective ovulation. The quality of your eggs is one of the major determinants of whether you can become pregnant.

It's known that the release of reproductive hormones diminishes after a woman's 20s, and therefore most women will ovulate less reliably. Consequently, most women over the age of 35 have fewer viable eggs and may ovulate less regularly. In addition, the incidence of pelvic disorders, such as endometriosis or uterine fibroids, seems to increase as a woman gets older. Endometriosis may reduce your fertility. Uterine fibroids that are located inside of your uterus and compromise your uterine cavity may also limit your fertility.

SMOKING

Virtually all scientific studies conclude that smoking is detrimental to your fertility. The American Society for Reproductive Medicine states that the best available scientific data indicates cigarette smoking strongly contributes to infertility and should be discouraged for both male and female partners. Tobacco appears to impinge on your fertility by reducing your ovarian reserve and also to contribute to fetal chromosomal abnormalities. Furthermore, women who smoke have an increased risk of miscarriage or stillbirth.

ALCOHOL

There is some controversy about the relationship between alcohol and the ability to conceive. According to RESOLVE: The National Infertility Association, even moderate alcohol consumption (five drinks per week) can impair conception. Other studies state that no definite link exists between moderate alcohol intake and the ability to become pregnant. Medical research studies have shown that women who partake in heavy alcohol consumption, more than six drinks per day, are more likely to suffer from irregular menstrual cycles and ovulation abnormalities. Heavy drinking has been shown to disrupt the normal menstrual cycle and reproductive function ranging from infertility and increased risk for miscarriage to impaired fetal growth and development, according to a 1993 study published by the National Institutes of Health.

It is also well recognized that alcohol can adversely affect the developing unborn baby. Therefore, most health professionals agree that it is best to avoid alcohol completely when considering pregnancy.

ILLICIT DRUG USE

Marijuana can interfere with ovulation in women. Other street drugs, such as cocaine, heroin, and ecstasy, have also been shown to dramatically diminish female fertility. Women who use these drugs may experience irregular menstrual cycles and abnormal ovulation.

PRESCRIPTION MEDICATIONS

Certain prescription medications can have a negative impact on your fertility. For example, steroids (such as cortisone or prednisone) taken in high doses can prevent your pituitary gland from producing proper amounts of hormones. The resulting hormonal imbalance may interfere with your ovulation. It may also interrupt your normal menstrual cycle.

Also, certain tranquilizers and several older types of blood pressure medications (such as Largactil) have been shown to raise a woman's level of prolactin hormone. Prolactin is the hormone that stimulates breast milk production and blocks ovulation. This shift in prolactin hormone can therefore interfere with your normal ovulation function.

RECENT OR PAST USE OF CONTRACEPTION

Many women are concerned about how past use of contraception might affect their future fertility. In almost all cases, your fertility is returned to normal within a short time of discontinuing the contraception.

Birth control pills prevent pregnancy by stopping the ovulation process. Almost always, birth control pills do not affect your future fertility. That's especially true if your menstrual periods were normal prior to beginning the pill. However, a few women who stop taking birth control pills experience some difficulty getting pregnant. A medical investigation may be a good idea if you have gone off birth control pills and still don't have normal menstrual periods within six months.

Another type of contraception is the Depo-Provera hormone injection, which works by stopping ovulation. One shot is supposed to prevent pregnancy for three months. Unfortunately, many women who want to become pregnant often find that it takes between 6 and 16 months for their menstrual cycle and ovulation process to return to normal.

NUTRITION

What you eat may affect your menstrual cycle, ovulation, and overall hormonal balance. That's why you should consume a healthy and well-balanced diet. Plus, diets that are either too high or low in calories can significantly affect your overall body weight. Extreme weight loss or weight gain may affect your menstrual cycle and fertility.

EXERCISE

Regular and vigorous exercise can change your menstrual cycle. In extreme cases, your menstrual periods may stop completely. This problem seems to be especially common among long-distance runners. However, women who exercise to excess and dramatically reduce their body weight and fat content may also experience a lack of menstrual periods. And without your menstrual cycle, you will not be able to ovulate and conceive.

BODY WEIGHT

Being overweight by even 10 to 15 percent above normal can overload your body with estrogen. This extra estrogen is produced within the fatty tissue and can dramatically change your hormone balance. In many cases, obese women ovulate irregularly, if at all.

Lack of body fat may also result in irregular periods and infertility. A woman who is underweight by 10 to 15 percent has less fat storage and therefore less estrogen. Although it may vary from woman to woman, most medical experts agree that a woman needs a body fat content of approximately 22 percent to allow for the normal hormonal balance and subsequent ovulation process. This topic is covered in more depth in Chapter 5.

CHRONIC DISEASE

Medical conditions such as lupus, diabetes, thyroid disease, and rheumatoid arthritis have been shown to reduce your fertility. If you have one of these medical conditions, it's imperative that you take your prescribed medication and be under the care of a qualified health care provider. This is especially true when you are trying to become pregnant.

Cancer may or may not affect fertility. However, the cancer treatments, such as chemotherapy or radiation, almost always will. If possible, talk with a fertility expert before starting your chemotherapy or radiation. It's often possible to work with your team of doctors and come up with a plan to safeguard or at least improve your future fertility.

ENVIRONMENTAL AND OCCUPATIONAL FACTORS

Prolonged exposure to emotional stress, high temperatures, chemicals, radiation, or electromagnetic or microwave emissions may reduce your fertility. Various occupational hazards also exist within certain work environments. For example, the rubber, leather, and dry-cleaning industries use the solvent benzene, which may adversely affect your fertility. Flight attendants are exposed to radiation and high altitudes, which may reduce fertility. Doctors, nurses, and other hospital employees may be exposed to anesthesia, chemicals, and radiation, all of which can have a harmful effect. Even people who work nights or irregular shifts may be adversely affected in their fertility because of changes in their internal clock and natural biorhythms.

PITUITARY GLAND TUMORS

The pituitary gland is considered your body's master gland because it is responsible for orchestrating all of the hormones in your body. So it stands to reason that a tumor within the pituitary gland may be associated with abnormal hormone production. For example, pituitary tumors often cause elevated levels of prolactin hormone. In addition, pituitary gland tumors can sometimes cause other hormonal imbalances, such as interrupting the release of follicle-stimulating hormone (FSH) and luteinizing hormone (LH). FSH and LH are both hormones that are made by the pituitary gland and help with the growth and development of your eggs and your ovulation process. This shift of these hormones may negatively impact your ovulation and fertility.

ADRENAL GLAND PROBLEMS

Your body contains two adrenal glands, one located on top of each kidney. Their function is to produce hormones that control your metabolism, heart rate, blood pressure, and other important body functions. Problems within the adrenal gland can cause increased levels of male hormones (also known as androgens). Even a slight increase of male hormone can interfere with the ovulation process and thus fertility. Signs of increased male hormone include excessive facial hair, hair on the lower abdomen, hair on the big toe, and extra hair around the anus. Acne and oily skin may also be associated with excessive male hormone.

LIFE'S NOT FAIR

You probably already know that life's not always fair. But here's just another reason that you can add to your list. When a female is born, she's born with her lifetime supply of eggs already inside her ovaries. However, a man generates a new supply of sperm about every three months. Therefore, any drugs, alcohol, or medications you take, or environmental elements you are exposed to can potentially damage all the eggs that you'll ever produce. In contrast, because a man generates a new sperm supply about every three months, his potentially damaged sperm are replaced with healthy new sperm every few months. It's easy to see how disease and toxic substances can have a much more severe and long-lasting effect on a woman than on a man. Not fair!

Figure 1.1 illustrates normal female anatomy.

Figure 1.1.   Anatomy of the Female Abdomen

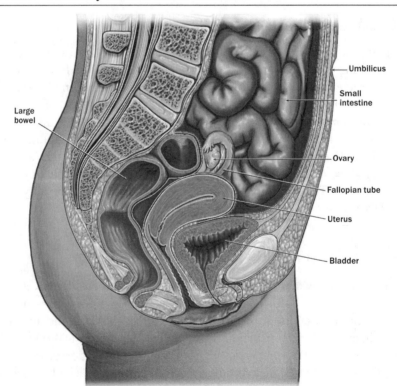

Illustration copyright © Nucleus Medical Art, all rights reserved, nucleusinc.com.

Specific Causes of Infertility for Women

Certain medical conditions can lead to infertility. Proper diagnosis and treatment may restore or improve your fertility.

POLYCYSTIC OVARY SYNDROME (PCOS)

The medical condition known as polycystic ovary syndrome (PCOS) causes your ovaries to act abnormally and leads to irregular or lack of menstrual periods, abnormal or absent ovulation, and, therefore, infertility. PCOS is a common cause of infertility and occurs in about 5 to 10 percent of reproductive-age women.

Symptoms of PCOS do not typically show up until after puberty, when menstruation begins. In some women, hormonal changes may begin as early as the very first menstrual cycle. In most women with PCOS, changes occur gradually, over time.

Symptoms of PCOS may include:

- Increased body and facial hair (also known as hirsutism)
- Acne
- Darkened color of the skin along the neck, armpits, groin, and inner thighs
- Obesity
- Irregular menstrual periods or no periods
- Vaginal yeast infections

What Does PCOS Do? How Does It Affect My Fertility?

The circumstance that causes PCOS usually originates in your pituitary gland. The pituitary gland is considered your body's master gland because it triggers the release of hormones for your entire body. Instead of the normal reproductive hormonal balance, PCOS causes your hormones to become out of sync. PCOS also causes higher concentrations of male hormones (androgens). The result of this complex hormonal imbalance is that ovulation occurs irregularly, if at all.

In a normal ovary with normal ovulation function, one follicle matures and an egg is released each month, and this corresponds to rising progesterone levels. In a polycystic ovary, there are many follicles, but they do not mature and, therefore, no egg is released. Because the eggs are not released, progesterone levels remain low and out of sync with the other hormone counterparts, androgen and estrogen. This results in irregular periods and continues the cycle of PCOS hormonal imbalance.

In addition, many women with PCOS produce too much insulin or the insulin they produce doesn't work properly. Insulin is a hormone that controls your body's use of sugar (glucose) but also usually plays a role in PCOS. Insulin interrupts the normal growth of the follicle in the ovaries. The affected ovaries contain such a large number of immature egg follicles; that they become abnormally enlarged and function abnormally. (See Figure 1.1.)

Who Is at Risk? What Causes PCOS?

Women with PCOS often have a family member with the condition. In fact, PCOS is considered a genetic disorder. This means that if you have PCOS, most likely you were born with the condition. Remember that PCOS might also be passed to your female children.

How Is PCOS Diagnosed?

To diagnose PCOS, your doctor will ask you questions about your health, your menstrual cycle, and your family history. The doctor will also perform a physical examination and order blood tests to check your hormone levels. If PCOS is suspected, a pelvic ultrasound may be performed to closely view your ovaries.

How Is PCOS Treated?

Treatment depends on your symptoms and your desire for pregnancy. A low carbohydrate diabetic diet along with regular exercise may be prescribed to lower your insulin levels. Additionally, research has shown that approximately 75 percent of women with PCOS respond well to fertility medication. In some cases, laparoscopic surgery is required to remove ovarian cysts that resulted from PCOS.

Women with PCOS should be aware of potential long-term health risks. They are at an increased risk of developing uterine cancer and are at risk of developing diabetes. PCOS has also been linked to heart disease, abnormal lipid profile, and high blood pressure. Because of these increased health risks, women with PCOS should be evaluated carefully by their doctor on an annual or more frequent basis.

PCOS is a condition that you are born with, so you can never truly be cured. However, with proper treatment, your symptoms can be relieved and you can live a healthy and normal life. Becoming pregnant is certainly possible but may require some advance planning and treatments to be determined between you and your doctor.

ENDOMETRIOSIS

Endometriosis is a medical condition where the tissue that lines the inside of your uterus (also called the endometrium) spreads to other areas of your body, usually to your pelvic organs. Endometrial tissue found on your fallopian tubes or ovaries can lead to scarring, adhesions, and blockages within your pelvis. (See Figure 1.2.)

Figure 1.2. Endometrial Lesions

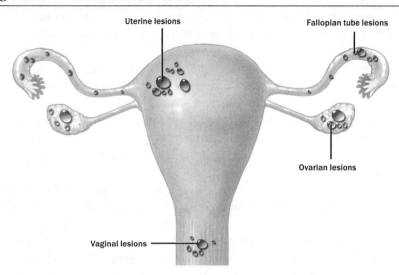

Illustration copyright © Nucleus Medical Art, all rights reserved, nucleusinc.com.

Endometriosis is estimated to affect about 7 percent of women of childbearing age. However, endometriosis is found in approximately one-third of infertile women. Therefore, endometriosis is a major factor when considering the causes of female fertility problems.

The main symptom of endometriosis is pelvic pain. The pain and cramping occurs most often just before and during your menstrual cycle. The pain sometimes occurs during sexual intercourse, urination, or bowel movements. The amount of pain does not always tell you the severity of your condition. For example, some women with slight pain may have a severe case of endometriosis. However, those with significant pain may actually have mild endometriosis. And some women with endometriosis have absolutely no symptoms. In many situations, endometriosis is only diagnosed as part of an infertility evaluation, after a woman has been unable to conceive on her own.

What Does Endometriosis Do? How Does It Affect My Fertility?

It's important to understand exactly what endometriosis does and how it affects your fertility. Under normal circumstances, the only place that endometrial tissue can be found is the inside of your uterus. However, if you have endometriosis, that means endometrial tissue is also growing somewhere else within your body. It most often appears in various places within your pelvis, such as the ovaries, fallopian tubes, outside surface of the uterus, space behind the uterus, bowel and rectum, and bladder. It may occasionally be found in more distant parts of the body, though this is rare.

Wherever endometrial tissue is found within your body, it basically still acts the same as that found within your uterus. Endometrial tissue is very responsive to changes in your hormones. So during your menstrual period, the tissue breaks down and bleeds, just the same way that the lining of your uterus does. This bleeding can cause pain, especially just before and during your period. The breakdown and bleeding of the endometrial tissue located throughout your pelvic organs can cause scar tissue and adhesions.

Oftentimes the scarring and adhesions cause various pelvic organs to bind together and distort the normal pelvic anatomy. This could cause the ovaries to become anchored in an awkward position so that the egg cannot properly reach the opening of the fallopian tube. In another case, the scarring and adhesions may block the fallopian tubes so that an egg cannot pass from the ovary into the uterus. Endometrial tissue may grow within an ovary and cause a cyst, usually called a chocolate cyst or endometrioma. The affected ovary and cyst may not be able to ovulate and function normally. Sometimes an ovary cannot properly release an egg because the egg is trapped within the follicle by scarring on the ovary's surface.

Endometriosis may also reduce fertility in other ways besides the scarring and adhesions already discussed. For example, toxic substances may be released by the endometrial tissue scattered about your pelvis. In this case, even if the egg is successfully released from the ovary and passes to the fallopian tube, the toxins might diminish the egg's ability to become fertilized. In addition, endometriosis can lessen fertility by giving off an immune response. That means that the endometrial tissue outside the uterus sends a signal to release destructive cells within the pelvis that can destroy eggs, sperm, and even an embryo.

Who Is at Risk? What Causes Endometriosis?

No one is certain of the cause of endometriosis, but several good theories exist. Some believe that menstrual cycle flow can go backward from the uterus, move up through the fallopian tubes, and spill into the pelvis. Others suggest that endometrial cells can be carried through the blood and lymph vessels to various parts of the body. Still others suggest a more complex method involving antibodies and changes at the cellular and hormonal level.

Endometriosis seems to occur most commonly in women who are in their 30s and 40s. It also occurs more frequently in women who have never had children. Endometriosis appears to have a genetic component. In fact, women with a mother, sister, or daughter who have endometriosis are more likely to have it themselves.

How Is Endometriosis Diagnosed?

First, your doctor will take a detailed medical history and perform a physical exam, including a pelvic exam. If you and your doctor are suspicious that you may have endometriosis, your doctor may perform a laparoscopy to view the inside of your pelvic cavity. If endometriosis is found, your doctor will determine the extent of the disease and in some cases also destroy or remove the tissue at the same time.

How Is Endometriosis Treated?

Treatment for endometriosis depends on the extent of the disease, your symptoms, and whether you want to have children. Endometriosis can be treated with medication, surgery, or a combination of both. You should be aware that treatments may temporarily relieve pain and infertility, but the symptoms will most likely eventually return. That's because whatever process caused the endometriosis in the first place is probably still taking place within your body.

In some cases of endometriosis, medications are prescribed to relieve pain and cramping discomfort. Nonsteroidal anti-inflammatory (NSAID) medications such as Motrin, Advil, Aleve, or Anaprox may be recommended. Various hormones, such as birth control pills, gonadotropin-releasing hormone (GnRH), progestin, and danazol, are sometimes prescribed. Such hormones may relieve pain and also help to slow the growth of the endometrial tissue and new adhesions. These hormonal medications almost always prevent pregnancy and therefore are not used when a woman is trying to become pregnant.

In many cases of endometriosis, surgery is the best choice for treatment. Surgery is usually performed via laparoscopy. During the laparoscopy procedure, the endometrial tissue is either destroyed or removed. After surgery, you may have relief from pain and your doctor will be able to discuss your fertility chances. Some studies have shown that pregnancy rates after surgery for women with moderate endometriosis can be as high as 47 percent. Rates for those with severe endometriosis may be about 38 percent. These rates may not seem great, but they are much better than the chances of conceiving without treatment.

PELVIC INFLAMMATORY DISEASE (PID)

Pelvic inflammatory disease (PID) is a serious infection of your pelvic reproductive organs, such as fallopian tubes and ovaries. In most cases, the infection is caused by a sexually transmitted disease (STD) such as gonorrhea or chlamydia.

Unfortunately, PID is fairly common in the United States, being diagnosed in more than 1 million women each year. In fact, it is estimated that PID is the cause of about 20 percent of all infertility problems, and the incidence seems to be increasing.

Symptoms of PID can vary greatly from severe pain, fever, and discomfort to no symptoms at all. The more common symptoms of PID are as follows:

- Abnormal vaginal discharge
- Pain in the pelvis or abdomen
- Abnormal menstrual bleeding
- Fever and chills
- Painful urination
- Nausea and vomiting
- Painful sexual intercourse

If you have one or more of these symptoms, that doesn't necessarily mean that you have PID. However, you should see your doctor for an evaluation. Even with no symptoms, PID is capable of causing severe damage to a woman's reproductive organs. Sadly, most cases of PID are undetected until a woman presents for an infertility evaluation.

What Does PID Do? How Does It Affect My Fertility?

PID can cause infertility by infecting, damaging, and scarring your pelvic reproductive organs. The fallopian tubes are especially vulnerable to PID and can become severely scarred and completely or partially blocked. If your fallopian tubes are completely blocked, the sperm and egg can never get together. If your tubes are partially blocked, the egg and the sperm may meet, but the fertilized egg may not be able to reach the uterus for implantation. In this situation, a tubal (ectopic) pregnancy will result. In a tubal pregnancy, the fertilized egg grows within the fallopian tube, instead of moving into the uterus as planned. This can lead to fallopian tube rupture, internal bleeding, and often emergency surgery. Unfortunately, tubal pregnancies are never viable, healthy pregnancies.

In some cases of blocked fallopian tubes, pus collects within the tube and causes the tube to expand. Over time, the pus is absorbed and replaced by a clear straw-colored fluid. The result is a fluid-filled, swollen, and often useless fallopian tube, called a hydrosalpinx (water in the tube). Medical research has shown that this fluid, which contains dead cells and other harmful products, may be toxic to egg and sperm.

PID can lead to serious long-term problems, such as infertility, ectopic pregnancy, and chronic pelvic pain. You have a greater risk of infertility if you experience multiple cases of PID or if the infections are especially severe.

Who Is at Risk? What Causes PID?

PID can occur in any sexually active women, but it's most common among young women. Here's a list that shows who is at an increased risk for developing PID:

- If you have STDs, especially gonorrhea or chlamydia infection
- If you have more than one sex partner
- If your sex partner has more than one sex partner
- If you have had a case of PID in the past
- If you are a sexually active woman who douches frequently
- If you have an intrauterine device (IUD), such as Paragard or Mirena

Since PID is an infection, it is caused by various types of germs and bacteria. Almost all cases stem from sexually transmitted diseases (STDs), such as gonorrhea or chlamydia. Without proper antibiotic treatment, the STD infection can move upward from the vagina and cervix, eventually finding its way into the uterus, fallopian tubes, and ovaries.

See your doctor right away if you think you may have an STD or a PID. The earlier you receive proper antibiotic treatment, the better you will feel and your fertility will be better preserved.

How Is PID Diagnosed?

PID is sometimes difficult to diagnose. One reason is that the uterus, fallopian tubes, and ovaries are within your pelvic cavity and not as easy to examine as are your genitals on the outside of your body. Another reason is that the symptoms of PID can vary greatly. PID often mimics other serious medical conditions, such as appendicitis or ectopic pregnancy, so it may take a while for your doctor to properly diagnose your condition.

If you or your doctor suspects PID, your doctor will discuss your detailed medical history, sexual habits, birth control methods, and symptoms. Your temperature will be taken to see if you have a fever. The doctor will perform a pelvic exam to determine whether your pelvic organs are tender. Your vagina and cervix will be swabbed and cultured to check for STDs. Sometimes blood tests are also done.

If your diagnosis is still uncertain, the doctor may order further tests or procedures. Additional tests sometimes used to diagnose PID include ultrasound, endometrial biopsy, and laparoscopy.

How Is PID Treated?

PID is treated with antibiotic medications. Antibiotic pills are usually prescribed for two entire weeks. Even if you are feeling better after a few days, you must take all of the medication prescribed. That's the only way to make sure the infection is gone. Your doctor may schedule a visit several days after antibiotic treatment begins to see how you are doing. If your condition hasn't improved, you may need to be treated in a hospital with intravenous antibiotics. Early treatment is vital to prevent long-term problems, such as infertility.

Your sex partner needs to see his doctor because he will need to be treated for STD infection also. You can still pass STDs to your partner even while you are being treated. That's why it's best to avoid sexual intercourse until both you and your partner have completed your antibiotics treatment regimens and been cleared by your doctors.

DIETHYLSTILBESTROL (DES) ABNORMALITIES OF THE FEMALE REPRODUCTIVE ORGANS

Diethylstilbestrol (DES) was a widely prescribed medication during the late 1950s and early 1960s. Its purpose was to attempt to prevent miscarriages. Unfortunately, DES was later found to cause side effects in the mother's children, especially the female children. If your mother took DES during her pregnancy with you, you might have reproductive abnormalities that could decrease your fertility. DES has been associated with abnormal pelvic anatomy and also abnormal cervical mucus production. DES daughters are also at risk for a very rare type of vaginal and cervical cancer called clear cell adenocarcinoma, which occurs in about 1 in 1,000 DES daughters. This cancer is virtually nonexistent among premenopausal women not exposed to DES.

Only about 20 percent of these DES daughters experience problems with their reproductive tract and infertility.

Symptoms of DES exposure can vary. Some women with DES abnormalities experience irregular menstrual periods. However, most women have no symptoms and don't realize that they have a problem until they try to become pregnant.

What Do DES Abnormalities Do? How Do They Affect My Fertility?

Women whose mothers took DES during pregnancy are often referred to as DES daughters. DES daughters may have a variety of reproductive tract anatomical abnormalities. Table 1.1 highlights possible DES-associated abnormalities and how they might affect your fertility.

Table 1.1. Effects of DES

Pelvic Organ	How DES Can Change Your Body	How DES Might Affect Fertility
Vagina	The upper part of your vagina may have glandular tissue, usually absent in normal vaginas.	This particular abnormality should not affect your fertility.
Cervix	The outer part of your cervix may have increased glandular tissue. The cervical canal is usually long and somewhat distorted.	These cervical malformations often lead to reduced cervical mucus. If you don't produce the proper amounts of cervical mucus, sperm may not be able to pass safely into your uterus.
Uterus	DES daughters classically possess an abnormally shaped uterus, called T-shaped. It has a very small and distorted inner uterine cavity. The muscle wall of the uterus tends to be more fibrous than usual.	This small uterine cavity and fibrous muscle tissue cause lack of stretch and flexibility of the uterus. They may be responsible for higher incidence of premature births within DES daughters.
Fallopian tubes	The fallopian tubes are usually shorter than regular tubes. The inner lining of the tubes are often irregular and distorted.	These tubal abnormalities explain the increased tubal (ectopic) pregnancy rate associated with DES daughters.
Ovaries	The ovaries are not affected by DES because they are formed from a different origin than the other organs already discussed.	The ovaries almost always are not affected. They usually appear and function normally.

Who Is at Risk? What Causes DES Abnormalities?

Daughters of women who took DES during pregnancy may have reproductive abnormalities that could reduce fertility.

The medication was a powerful hormone that had numerous side effects. Subsequently, DES is no longer prescribed in the United States today.

How Are DES Abnormalities Diagnosed?

If you are able, ask your mother if she took DES during her pregnancy with you. If you suspect that your mother might have taken DES during her pregnancy, be sure to talk with your physician.

Suspecting an exposure to DES will help your doctor diagnose this potential set of problems. Even without considering DES, your doctor might notice that your cervix appears abnormal during a routine Pap and pelvic examination. To diagnose uterine and fallopian tube abnormalities, you will have to undergo more tests. A hysterosalpingogram (HSG) is usually performed to evaluate the shape of the uterine cavity and also to determine if the fallopian tubes are blocked. In this test, a fluid with dye is injected through your cervix and into your uterus and the fluid's pathways are monitored with x-ray. DES daughters typically reveal a T-shape or butterfly-shape uterus on HSG rather than the normal rounded pear shape. The HSG will also test for fallopian tube length and openness but may not detect irregularities within the inner fallopian tube lining, as this is more difficult.

How Are DES Abnormalities Treated?

Depending on the nature and extent of the abnormalities, various treatments will be considered. For example, inadequate cervical mucus may be treated by the use of estrogens or perhaps intrauterine insemination. Surgical correction may be needed for a severely misshapen uterus. Various assisted reproductive technologies may be called upon if the fallopian tubes are a problem.

ASHERMAN'S SYNDROME

Asherman's syndrome is an acquired condition recognized by the formation of adhesions and scar tissue within the uterine cavity. In most cases, the adhesions are so severe that the front and back walls of the uterus stick to one another.

The primary symptom is lack of any menstrual periods. Sometimes patients with Asherman's syndrome do experience light vaginal spotting.

What Does Asherman's Syndrome Do? How Does It Affect My Fertility?

The severe adhesions and scarring of the inner uterine cavity usually causes collapse and also blocks the opening between the uterus and the fallopian tubes. In some cases, one or both tubes may remain open to the uterus. However, even if a fertilized egg is able to successfully travel from the tube and into the uterus, proper implantation within the scarred, collapsed uterine cavity is rarely possible.

Who Is at Risk? What Causes Asherman's Syndrome?

Only women who have had a prior uterine surgery are at risk for Asherman's syndrome. Asherman's syndrome occurs most often after a dilation and curettage (D&C) that may have been performed because of a miscarriage or retained placenta after delivery. However, Asherman's syndrome may also occur in other situations, such as after an abortion or Cesarean section.

How Is Asherman's Syndrome Diagnosed?

If you have had a D&C, an abortion, or any other type of surgery to your uterus, be sure to talk with your doctor. Being suspicious for the possibility of Asherman's syndrome will help with the diagnosis. The best way to diagnose these uterine adhesions and scarring is through a procedure called hysteroscopy. For this procedure, your doctor places a thin telescope-like device into your vagina and through your cervix. The doctor advances the device into your inner uterine cavity for optimal viewing. Scarring, adhesions, and blockages can then be seen.

How Is Asherman's Syndrome Treated?

Treatment involves the hysteroscopy procedure used for diagnosis just discussed. While the hysteroscope is still in place within the uterus, the doctor uses a special scissorlike instrument to remove the adhesions. The objective is to remove as much scar tissue as possible and free any adhesions along the walls of the uterine cavity. After the hysteroscopy, a small balloon is placed in the uterine cavity for a few days to prevent the recurrence of adhesions. Many doctors also prescribe estrogen after the surgery, because estrogen will stimulate the new growth of uterine tissue and promote healing.

According to a publication from the National Institutes of Health (NIH), Asherman's syndrome can be cured in most women with surgery; however, more than one surgery is sometimes needed. The NIH estimates that approximately 70 to 80 percent of women who are infertile because of Asherman's syndrome will have a successful pregnancy after treatment.

Causes of Infertility:
Health and Lifestyle Concerns for Men

Low sperm count, or oligospermia, is the main cause of male infertility. Under normal circumstances, between 60 to 100 million sperm are delivered with each ejaculation. Many of those sperm are killed by vaginal secretions or destroyed during their journey toward the fallopian tubes. Therefore, a man who begins with a lower than average sperm count may find he has fertility difficulties.

Sperm production may be influenced by a whole host of lifestyle choices, health issues, and environmental factors.

SMOKING

Smoking reduces the motility of the sperm and lowers the average sperm count by approximately 15 percent. The American Society for Reproductive Medicine states that men who smoke cigarettes have a lower sperm count, impaired sperm movement (motility), and increased abnormalities in sperm shape and function. All of these factors can dramatically reduce a couple's chances of conceiving.

ALCOHOL

Consuming alcohol of more than one or two drinks per day can affect the quality and quantity of sperm, lower testosterone levels, and contribute to impotence. A 1996 research study from Finland showed that moderate alcohol consumption can kill off some sperm-producing cells within the testicles and also may cause abnormal sperm shapes. A normally shaped sperm should resemble a streamlined tadpole with an oval head and long tail. Abnormally shaped sperm vary in appearance and may have two tails, a tapered head, a crooked kinky shape, or an unusually large or small head. Any of these abnormalities make it so that the sperm is unable to penetrate the surface of the egg and therefore unable to successfully fertilize the egg. Men who partake in heavy alcohol consumption—that is, more than six drinks per day—are more likely to suffer from low sperm count, poor sperm motility, and abnormal sperm shape.

ILLICIT DRUG USE

A medical research study conducted in 2003 showed that regular smoking of marijuana can have detrimental effects on male fertility. It was shown that marijuana is linked to lowered sperm count and poor sperm motility. In addition, the sperm that are able to enter the vagina tend to be slowed and weakened, making it almost impossible for them to penetrate the egg's outer shell for fertilization to occur. It is generally accepted by medical experts that heavy marijuana or cocaine use may temporarily reduce the number and quality of sperm by as much as 50 percent. Other street drugs, including heroin and ecstasy, have also been shown to dramatically diminish male fertility. Men who use these drugs may suffer from reduced sex drive, abnormally shaped sperm, and low sperm count.

PRESCRIPTION MEDICATIONS

Certain prescription medications can diminish a man's fertility. High doses of anabolic steroids often reduce sperm count. Additionally, these anabolic steroids can also lead to abnormal sperm, erectile dysfunction, and atrophy of the testicles.

Prescription drugs that are known to interfere with sperm production include the antibiotics tetracycline and nitrofurantoin, the antiulcer medication cimetidine, the anticolitis medication Salazopyrin, and the antigout medication allopurinol.

Impotence can become a factor for men who take a beta-blocking medication. Beta-blockers are sometimes prescribed to control blood pressure and for certain heart conditions. Examples of beta-blockers include atenolol, propranolol, and nadolol.

NUTRITION

Good nutrition is important for men also. In fact, researchers report that crash diets have a tendency to lower sperm count. The better a man's nutritional status, the healthier his sperm will be and the more easily the woman will conceive.

A man's diet should be similar to that of his female counterpart, taking into consideration that his calorie intake may be altered based on age, body structure, and activity level. He should consume healthy foods and key nutrients, such as vitamin C, vitamin E, selenium, zinc, calcium, and vitamin D. These vitamins and minerals have been identified as having a positive role in sperm production.

BODY WEIGHT

Medical research studies are uncertain about the role of male body weight with infertility issues. Some studies have found an association between obesity in men with infertility. However, other research studies have shown no such correlation.

CHRONIC DISEASE

Cancer may or may not affect fertility. However, cancer treatment with chemotherapy or radiation almost always reduces sperm production. If possible, talk with a fertility expert before starting chemotherapy or radiation. It's often possible to come up with a plan to safeguard or improve your future fertility.

PREVIOUS ILLNESS: MUMPS

A history of mumps may be another cause of male infertility. If a male gets the mumps during or just after puberty, he is at risk for the virus attacking the testicles. In severe cases, the man will have an increased risk of fertility problems later in life.

INJURY

A scrotal injury may contribute to male fertility problems. That's especially true if the injury interferes with the testicular blood flow and sperm transportation.

ENVIRONMENTAL AND OCCUPATIONAL FACTORS

Exposure to toxic substances, such as lead, cadmium, mercury, hydrocarbons, pesticides, and radioactivity, may negatively impact the sperm count and quality.

Warmer temperatures tend to hinder sperm production. That's because the temperature in the scrotum must be below the rest of the body for the testicles to produce healthy sperm. Exposing the male genitals to heat, such as the frequent use of saunas, steam rooms, hot tubs, whirlpools, and hot baths, can temporarily lower sperm count. Men who wear tight clothing may be lowering their sperm count as well. That's because the testicles are pressed closely to the body and become warmer than if they were able to hang freely within the scrotal sac. Males with infertility difficulties are often advised not to wear tight-fitting pants or underwear.

Emotional stress may interfere with sperm count and also lead to premature ejaculation or even impotence.

PITUITARY GLAND ABNORMALITIES

Pituitary gland abnormalities are a rare cause for male infertility. In such circumstances, the pituitary gland fails to release hormones necessary to promote sperm production. The pituitary gland in the man produces two important hormones for sexual reproduction: luteinizing hormone (LH) and follicle-stimulating hormone (FSH). The primary function of LH is to act on specialized cells within the testicles to manufacture the male hormone testosterone. FSH has the main purpose of stimulating the production of sperm. In most cases of pituitary gland abnormalities, either LH or FSH or both are greatly reduced. This drop in hormones results in lowered testosterone levels and also reduced sperm production.

Specific Causes of Infertility for Men

Men may experience fertility problems because of a variety of abnormal physical conditions.

SEXUALLY TRANSMITTED DISEASES (STDs)

Blockage of the sperm ducts may be caused by STDs. STDs, such as chlamydia, have also been linked to low sperm count. Antibiotic treatment usually treats this condition.

OBSTRUCTION OF THE VAS DEFERENS OR EPIDIDYMIS

Normally, the vas deferens and the epididymis transport sperm. An obstruction along these tracts will result in a sperm count of zero. Surgical treatment is usually required.

VARICOCELE

A varicocele is a collection of dilated veins within the scrotum that look like varicose veins. It lessens a man's fertility by producing a slightly higher temperature in the testicles. A varicocele occurs in about 15 percent of all men and accounts for as much as 40 percent of male infertility problems.

Varicoceles are treated surgically. The most common type of procedure is microsurgery, which is done on an outpatient basis under spinal anesthesia. The enlarged veins are repaired surgically, and regular blood flow is restored to improve sperm quality. Some physicians also prescribe fertility medications, such as Clomid, after the surgery to stimulate sperm production. The success rate of the surgery varies, but approximately 80 percent of men have an increased sperm count following this surgery.

PREVIOUS VASECTOMY

A vasectomy is a voluntary surgery to block the sperm ducts for the purpose of contraception. Sometimes, for various personal reasons, the man wishes to have his vasectomy reversed. In fact, approximately 10 percent of vasectomized men eventually request vasectomy reversal in the United States.

While it is usually possible to surgically reconnect the tubes after vasectomy, some men remain infertile because their body has developed an immune reaction against their own sperm. That means they develop antibodies that automatically destroy or immobilize their own sperm. This is more often the case when the vasectomy occurred more than 10 years earlier.

Additionally, the average patency (openness) rate of vasectomy reversal is about 90 percent, but the pregnancy rate is closer to 60 percent. This means that 90 percent of the time the sperm flow in the vas tube is restored, but pregnancy successfully occurs only 60 percent of the time because of antibodies and various other unrelated fertility problems.

DIETHYLSTILBESTROL (DES) ABNORMALITIES OF THE MALE REPRODUCTIVE ORGANS

Unfortunately, it is not just DES daughters who are affected; if the woman who took the DES was pregnant with a male child, her son may experience fertility difficulties as well. According to the Centers for Disease Control and Prevention (CDC), the most common research finding for DES sons is that they have an increased risk for benign (noncancerous) growths on their testicles. Sons of women who took this drug have been found to have abnormal sperm type and motility. They also occasionally have testicular abnormalities. If you suspect that your partner has been exposed to DES, please alert your fertility specialist.

GENETICS: INHERITED FERTILITY PROBLEMS

In rare cases, male infertility may be inherited. This is usually diagnosed through blood samples and by performing chromosomal analysis. For example, a man with cystic fibrosis may have missing or obstructed vas deferens, the tubes that carry sperm. Another example is Klinefelter's syndrome, where the man is born with two X and one Y chromosomes (the normal is one X and one Y). In this situation, the man has had abnormally developed testicles since puberty but possesses other normal male physical characteristics. A more common genetic disorder is polycystic kidney disease, a condition where large cysts form on the kidneys and other organs and may cause infertility if a cyst develops in the man's reproductive tract.

Treatment is difficult and must be tailored to the particular problem, such as surgical repair or specific medical therapy.

Unexplained Infertility

For 10 to 15 percent of all infertile couples, a definite cause of the infertility cannot be identified. Such cases are referred to as unexplained infertility. However, some good news is that as many as 60 percent of these couples will eventually conceive without treatment within three years.

Treatment for unexplained infertility presents a challenge for both the couple and the fertility specialist. Some fertility doctors recommend a treatment of Clomid, gonadotropin, or both to stimulate egg follicle production. This is followed by sexual intercourse at the time of ovulation or artificial insemination with the partner's sperm. If pregnancy still does not occur, then various assisted reproductive technologies, such as in vitro fertilization (IVF), may be performed.

Conclusion

While this chapter has spent a fair amount of time discussing what is possibly wrong with your or your partner's fertility, please do not despair. There is great hope for you to become parents and very soon!

Right now is the best time to be embarking on your journey of fertility and parenthood. That's because medical technology is continuing to advance and has come so far that you have many choices and options. As you read further in this book, you'll learn about basic male and female anatomy and how they work, various tests and procedures, and medications you may be offered. If practical, you may want to try a natural approach to fertility first; we'll discuss natural ways to conceive with nutrition choices, lifestyle changes, and alternative techniques. Of course, the assisted reproductive technologies are discussed in detail. These techniques are explained in plain English so that you'll feel comfortable understanding the ins and outs of IVF and other important technologies. So many new and emerging fertility technologies exist today that anyone who dreams of becoming a mommy or daddy has good reason to feel hopeful and optimistic.

Additionally, fertility issues have come out of the closet and people are talking openly about them. Thank goodness people are finally realizing that fertility dilemmas are nothing to be ashamed of and it helps to share your experiences and thoughts with others. It's perfectly normal for you to feel a wide range of emotions, from crying to jumping with joy. Some days you'll thirst for knowledge and read this book and devour information readily. Other days, frankly, you'll be sick of the whole thing and just need to take a break—go shopping or take a bubble bath or do something else entirely. These are completely normal and natural feelings.

The most important thing is that you are smart and taking the time to learn about your body and your options. That means you'll be able to make the best choices and decisions for you and your unborn baby when those situations present themselves. And they are about to do so—very soon.

Summary

Here is a summary of key facts and concepts discussed in this chapter.

Overview and Important Facts

- Approximately 15 percent of couples in the United States may be infertile.
- Infertility is defined as not being able to conceive after 12 months of having regular heterosexual intercourse without the use of birth control.
- Facing fertility problems is often difficult to handle and can have devastating emotional and physical effects on you and your partner.
- About one-third of infertility cases may be attributable to the woman and another third to the man, while the last third either has to do with problems involving both partners or remains unexplained.

Causes of Infertility: Health and Lifestyle Concerns for Women

- Advancing age—especially women over the age of 35
- Smoking
- Alcohol
- Illicit drug use
- Certain prescription medications
- Recent or past use of contraception
- Diet, exercise, and weight
- Certain disease and medical conditions
- Environmental and occupational factors
- Gland and hormone problems

Specific Causes of Infertility for Women

- Polycystic ovary syndrome (PCOS)
- Pelvic inflammatory disease (PID)
- Diethylstilbestrol (DES) abnormalities
- Asherman's Syndrome

Causes of Infertility: Health and Lifestyle Concerns for Men

- Smoking
- Alcohol

- Illicit drug use
- Certain prescription medications
- Nutrition and weight
- Disease and injury
- Environmental occupational factors
- Gland and hormonal imbalance

Specific Causes of Infertility for Men

- Sexually transmitted disease (STD)
- Obstruction
- Varicocele
- Prior vasectomy
- Diethylstilbestrol (DES)
- Genetics

Unexplained Infertility

- For between 10 and 15 percent of all infertile couples, a definite cause of the infertility cannot be identified.
- As many as 60 percent of these couples will eventually conceive without treatment within three years.

CHAPTER 2

Miscarriage and Other Early Pregnancy Loss

This chapter is dedicated to those of you who have experienced early pregnancy loss. You are part of a distinct group of women who have felt the happiness and joy of conceiving, only to have your hopes and dreams shattered by the loss of your pregnancy. What a challenging ordeal you've endured. Not only have you had to go through the physical pains and hormonal swings, but you've also faced the emotional ups and downs of losing your baby during the early stages of pregnancy.

Introduction to Early Pregnancy Loss

A normal pregnancy is supposed to last approximately 40 weeks. Pregnancy loss prior to 20 weeks is referred to as an early pregnancy loss. In most cases, the early pregnancy loss is a miscarriage. Sometimes the loss is an ectopic pregnancy, which is a pregnancy located outside of your uterus. Rarely, the loss is an unusual type of pregnancy called molar pregnancy, which is a condition that results in growth of placenta-like abnormal tissue within your uterus.

The loss of a pregnancy usually involves more than the loss of the baby. It also triggers a tremendous emotional impact, including feelings of sadness, guilt, and grief.

Miscarriage

If you have experienced a miscarriage, you are well aware of the physical and emotional difficulties that come with it. Chances are you were delighted when that first pregnancy test showed up as positive. You might have shared the good news with friends and family. However, within a short time, you started to bleed and cramp. A visit to the doctor revealed a miscarriage. With shock and disappointment, you must come to terms with the grief of miscarriage.

WHAT IS MISCARRIAGE? WHAT HAPPENS TO MY BODY?

A miscarriage is a pregnancy that is lost prior to 20 weeks of pregnancy. When you stop and consider all of the complex steps involved in forming a human being, it's very sad but not surprising that sometimes not all the steps go as planned. The fertilization process of combining the male sperm and the female egg is very detailed and intricate. If any one step doesn't occur exactly right, miscarriage may occur. For this reason, many medical professionals believe that a miscarriage is the body's way of dealing with a fetus that is probably abnormal. Even so, this is not much consolation to a woman who is experiencing the heartbreak of miscarriage.

The two primary symptoms of miscarriage are vaginal bleeding and cramping in the lower abdomen or back. While bleeding is certainly something to have checked out by your doctor, it does not necessarily mean you are miscarrying. In fact, the majority of women who experience light bleeding during the first trimester continue their pregnancies and deliver healthy babies. However, sometimes the bleeding is quite heavy, and you may even pass some fetal tissue. If so, try to collect the fetal tissue in a clean container and bring it to the doctor for evaluation.

Remember to call your doctor right away if you experience bleeding or cramping. Your doctor will want to examine you and find out exactly what is happening to your body.

WHO IS AT RISK? WHAT CAUSES MISCARRIAGE?

Miscarriage is the most common type of pregnancy loss, occurring in about 15 to 20 percent of all pregnancies. Most miscarriages happen during the first three months of pregnancy.

Miscarriage is a sad event, and many women look to blame themselves or search to find a reason for the miscarriage. In most situations, you won't find an answer because the cause of miscarriage is usually not known. It has been estimated that more than half of all miscarriages are due to problems with the chromosomes of the fetus. These chromosomal problems occur randomly. When the egg and sperm combine, thousands of steps must be accomplished to form a normal fetus, and if a problem occurs with the number of chromosomes or the structure of a chromosome, then miscarriage may occur. The American College of Obstetricians and Gynecologists states that most aspects of daily life do not increase the risk of miscarriage. They go on to say that no proof exists that activities such as work, exercise, or sex cause miscarriage. Most falls do not result in miscarriage either. Likewise, fright, stress, and morning sickness do not lead to miscarriage.

Do not blame yourself. Most miscarriages seem to happen by chance and not because of something you did or didn't do. In most cases when you have experienced a miscarriage, it's not likely to happen with future pregnancies.

HOW IS MISCARRIAGE DIAGNOSED?

Sometimes it is difficult to tell if your pregnancy is going to miscarry or not. You and your doctor need to be extra attentive during the first few months of your pregnancy. If concerns such as bleeding and cramping arise, you may be asked to reduce your physical activity and perhaps even rest in bed. It's also important to avoid sexual intercourse during this time. These precautions may not necessarily prevent a miscarriage, but they may reduce your discomfort and may also provide you with peace of mind, knowing that you did everything within your power to avoid miscarriage.

Your doctor will probably do a pelvic exam to see if your cervix has opened and fetal tissue is passing. In addition, your doctor will likely perform an ultrasound to view the pregnancy. If a developing fetus with a heartbeat is seen, that's an encouraging sign. However, if no heartbeat is noted, more concern and evaluating are warranted.

If it is still uncertain whether you are miscarrying, your doctor may draw your blood to check your pregnancy hormone levels. During early pregnancy, the pregnancy hormone human chorionic gonadotropin (hCG) rises in a certain pattern. In the case of miscarriage, the hCG level typically does not rise. Therefore, your doctor may draw your hCG level one day and recheck it a few days later to establish a pattern.

Within a few days, after pelvic examination, ultrasound, and hormonal level testing, the diagnosis of miscarriage may be confirmed.

HOW IS MISCARRIAGE TREATED?

Once the diagnosis of miscarriage has been made, treatment is largely based on whether tissue is still present in your uterus. If all of the tissue has been passed, the miscarriage is considered complete and no further treatment is needed.

Oftentimes some tissue remains within your uterus. This tissue must be removed to avoid future problems with bleeding and infection. In most cases, your doctor will recommend a dilation and curettage (D&C). During this procedure, your cervix is dilated and the tissue is then removed from within your uterus. Anesthesia is typically required, so the D&C is performed in an operating room. In most cases, you may go home within a few hours after the procedure. It's normal to experience some spotting and mild cramping for several days afterward.

Follow-up care after a miscarriage is very important. Your doctor will want to check on you within a couple of weeks to ensure that you have no remaining problems.

Most doctors recommend that you wait about three months before trying to get pregnant again. This time period allows your body to get back into its regular cycle. It also gives you a few months to deal with your emotions from this difficult ordeal.

About 90 percent of women who miscarry will become pregnant again. However, there is still the normal 15 to 20 percent chance of having another miscarriage. Therefore, you should see your doctor right away when you become pregnant again.

Recurrent Miscarriages

Having one prior miscarriage should not affect your ability to have normal pregnancies in the future. But if you have experienced two or more miscarriages in a row, you may need some special medical attention. Your doctor may want to investigate for possible underlying medical problems.

About half of recurrent miscarriage cases have no underlying cause. For the remaining half, certain risk factors have been identified. It's possible that recurrent miscarriage may be caused by particular lifestyle factors, chromosomal problems, low progesterone, abnormalities of the uterus, or your own medical condition.

Diagnostic tests can be performed to help you and your doctor determine if you have one of these health concerns. In many cases, treatment is available and you can avoid problems in future pregnancies.

Enduring recurrent miscarriages is extremely difficult, both from a physical and an emotional standpoint. Keep in mind that even if you have experienced recurrent miscarriages, you still have a good chance to have a baby.

POTENTIAL CAUSES OF RECURRENT MISCARRIAGE

Recurrent miscarriage can happen because of any of many possible reasons.

Lifestyle Factors

We've all heard about the dangers of tobacco, alcohol, and street drugs. They just aren't part of a healthy lifestyle. This is especially true as you try to conceive and also during your pregnancy. If you smoke during pregnancy, you are more likely to experience vaginal bleeding and miscarriage. Women who drink excessive alcohol or engage in illicit drug use have a definite increased risk of miscarriage.

If you participate in these activities, especially during pregnancy, stop doing so. It's not always easy to discontinue these activities on your own. Please speak with your doctor about a safe program that is tailor-made with your issues in mind.

Chromosomal Problems

Medical experts believe that the majority of all miscarriages are caused by chromosomal problems within the fetus. Chromosomes are tiny structures within the cells of the body that contain genes. These genes are what determine a person's characteristics, such as sex, hair color, eye color, blood type, and so on.

Both egg and sperm contain vast amounts of this genetic material. When the egg and sperm unite, a detailed series of intricate and complex steps must occur for them to form a fetus. When you stop to consider the elaborate series of events that must ensue with absolute perfection, it's not surprising that accidents and mistakes can happen and result in an abnormal fetus. In most cases, the abnormality is severe and not compatible with life. Therefore, when the miscarriage occurs, many people see it as nature's way of ending a pregnancy that would not have survived. Even so, it is still usually a very sad and emotional event.

One bright spot is that in most cases, chromosomal problems are usually an accident of that particular pregnancy and not likely to happen again in a later pregnancy. It should be noted, though, that the risk of such problems seems to increase with the woman's age.

In less than 5 percent of couples, the chromosome problem is inherited. This means that the problems passed on to the fetus come from an abnormality in either the mother's or father's chromosomes. If this is the situation, recurrent miscarriage will continue to take place until the parents have been appropriately diagnosed and treated.

The man or woman may not realize they have abnormal chromosomes because the individuals appear completely healthy and show no signs of physical or mental disabilities. Even so, the man or woman may possess abnormally arranged chromosomes that are balanced within them, so their outside physical bodies appear normal. To better understand this concept, imagine a couple in which one person has only 9 fingers and the other has 11. Together, they have the normal number of 20 fingers, but individually they possess a problem that could be passed on to their offspring. Abnormally arranged chromosomes can be passed along undetected in a similar way. These unbalanced forms of these chromosomal problems can result in miscarriage.

If your doctor suspects a chromosomal problem within you or your partner, genetic tests are available to diagnose this rare condition. That's why it's so important for you to receive genetic counseling following recurrent miscarriages.

Low Progesterone Level

The relationship between hormonal imbalance and miscarriages is uncertain. However, many medical experts believe that low progesterone levels during early pregnancy can lead to miscarriage.

To better understand this, you should know how progesterone works. When you ovulate, your ovary releases an egg. That egg was originally held within a follicle. The follicle becomes empty at the time of ovulation. The empty follicle is called your corpus luteum. Under normal circumstances, after ovulation, your corpus luteum begins to secrete progesterone. If no pregnancy occurs, the corpus luteum fades away and is absorbed by the body, and your menstrual period will come as usual. However, if a pregnancy happens, the corpus luteum serves as a temporary supplier of progesterone. That's important for the pregnancy because progesterone thickens the lining of the uterus to support and nourish the fertilized egg.

When progesterone levels are too low, the fertilized egg may have difficulty implanting itself within the uterine wall. In other cases, the fertilized egg may implant but the pregnancy cannot be properly supported because of low progesterone levels. In either case, bleeding and early miscarriage may result.

The causes of lowered progesterone level have not been identified. However, it is estimated that approximately 15 percent of women with fertility difficulties may experience this problem.

Your doctor can order a simple blood test that checks your progesterone level. If the blood test shows that your body is not making enough progesterone, you will likely be prescribed progesterone supplementation. This progesterone may be given to you in the form of suppositories or injections. Treatment with progesterone usually begins at the time of your positive pregnancy test and concludes at about the 13th week of pregnancy. By this time, the fetus and placenta are able to manufacture enough progesterone on their own to maintain the pregnancy.

Abnormalities of the Uterus

In some situations, you could be experiencing recurrent miscarriage because of abnormal anatomy within your own uterus or cervix. Medical research estimates that this occurs in approximately one in 700 women. If you do have an abnormally shaped uterus or cervix, chances are it happened during your own fetal development. Perhaps you were unaware of this condition until you tried to have a baby of your own. Having an abnormal uterus or cervix does not mean that you can't have children, but it may increase the odds of you having a miscarriage.

Several problems of the uterus have been linked to recurrent miscarriage, including the following:

- Septate uterus
- Uterine fibroids
- Incompetent cervix
- Endometrial polyps

A septate uterus is a rare abnormality that means your uterus is divided into two sections by a wall of tissue. This happened during your own fetal development. The two uterine cavities are abnormally shaped and smaller and are thus less capable of carrying a full-term pregnancy. Therefore, miscarriages and preterm birth are more likely with a septate uterus.

Fibroids are another potential structural problem of the uterus. Uterine fibroids are benign muscular bulges of tissue that grow within the uterine wall. It's certainly possible to have uterine fibroids and enjoy a completely normal pregnancy. However, sometimes these growths make it difficult for the egg to securely implant itself within the uterine lining. In such a case, an early miscarriage is likely. Uterine fibroids typically run in families.

An incompetent cervix is a condition where your cervix widens and opens too soon and loses the pregnancy. Incompetent cervix usually results in a somewhat later pregnancy loss, typically during your second trimester. That's when the pregnancy has grown a sufficient amount and the weight is too much for the weakened cervix to hold. Incompetent cervix could be a condition that you were born with, but most likely it is the consequence of a past surgery to your cervix.

Endometrial polyps are (usually benign) growths of fleshy tissue that protrude from the lining inside of your uterus. They may cause no symptoms. However, some women experience abnormal bleeding. If they become large or if multiple polyps exist, they may interfere with your ability to conceive or increase your risk of miscarriage. Abnormalities of the uterus and cervix are sometimes detected before your pregnancy. However, regrettably, they are usually discovered during an evaluation after you've already suffered recurrent miscarriages. If your doctor suspects abnormal anatomy of your uterus, you will most likely undergo a hysterosalpingogram (HSG) for diagnosis. This is an x-ray test that involves injecting a dye into the uterus through the vagina. Your reproductive tract will be highlighted on the x-ray, and a diagnosis can usually be made. The diagnosis for incompetent cervix is more difficult. Usually, a prior history of second-trimester pregnancy loss is required.

In many situations, these abnormalities can be treated with surgery. For septate uterus, many doctors recommend surgery to unite the two sections of the uterus. The result is a larger uterine cavity, which gives the upcoming pregnancy more room to grow. This is a complicated surgery; risks include hemorrhage and, in extreme cases, require a hysterectomy. Uterine fibroids that are bulging into the uterine cavity can often be removed during an outpatient surgery. This is typically a straightforward surgery, but as with all surgeries, the woman faces potential risk. If you have an incompetent cervix, your doctor may recommend a cerclage procedure to strengthen your cervix and prevent dilation. A cerclage is a tough band of suture sewn around the cervix, like a purse string, to hold the cervical tissue tightly together. This procedure is usually performed at about 12 weeks of pregnancy, after a live fetus has been confirmed on ultrasound.

If you are diagnosed with an abnormal structure of your uterus, your doctor will discuss with you the best options for your particular situation.

Medical Conditions

You may have a specific medical disease or ailment that makes miscarriage more likely. If any of these possible disorders are not adequately monitored and controlled with medication, they may increase your chance of early pregnancy loss. These medical conditions include:

- Pelvic infection
- Diabetes
- Insulin resistance syndrome

- Thyroid disease
- Thrombophilia
- Lupus
- Antiphospholipid syndrome

If you have one of these disorders, it's best to work with your doctor and ensure that your condition is under excellent control before even trying to become pregnant. Sometimes you may not be aware that you have a disease until you have already become pregnant. In this situation, work with disease specialists to improve your chances for a successful, healthy pregnancy.

Pelvic Infection. Certain bacteria and viruses may increase your risk of miscarriage. Infections such as rubella (German measles), herpes, chlamydia, and cytomegalovirus may adversely affect fetal development and lead to miscarriage.

At the beginning of your pregnancy, you will take a blood test to determine if you are immune to rubella. If you are not immune, you are at risk. Do not expose yourself to others with measles or known rubella virus. You cannot be treated during pregnancy, and you may only safely receive the vaccination when you are not pregnant. That's why you should know your rubella status prior to becoming pregnant. That way, you can receive the rubella vaccine prior to trying to conceive.

Vaginal infections are uncomfortable and may harm the fetus, especially if they spread upward into the uterus. Signs of vaginal infection include itching in the genital region, vaginal odor or discharge, and discomfort during urination. In more advanced cases as the infection spreads into the uterus, symptoms may also include fever and abdominal tenderness.

Treatments with antibiotics, vaginal creams, and suppositories are usually quite successful. Of course, you should be evaluated and treated for infection, whether you are pregnant or not. However, it's especially critical that you receive treatment promptly when you are pregnant. Hopefully, this will minimize the effects on the fetus and also help prevent miscarriage.

Diabetes. Diabetes is a serious medical condition in which your body is unable to produce proper amounts of insulin. Insulin is important because it helps your body break down glucose (sugar) to be used for energy. Some women acquire diabetes only during their pregnancy, known as gestational diabetes. However, in most cases, it's the women who already have diabetes before they become pregnant who are at the highest risk of miscarriage. About 4 percent of pregnant women are diabetic prior to becoming pregnant. The younger you are when you acquire the disease, the more severe and difficult it is to control.

Diabetes has been linked to many potential complications of pregnancy, including miscarriage, urinary tract infections, high blood pressure, fetal growth problems, and birth defects. Most of these complications occur because the sugar level is extremely high or not well controlled during the course of the pregnancy. It's certainly possible to enjoy a healthy successful pregnancy if you have diabetes. Check with your doctor to make sure that you receive proper treatment and careful monitoring of your sugar levels.

Diabetics are encouraged to follow a well-balanced and sensible diet authorized by the American Diabetes Association. In most cases, you will also need blood sugar reducing pills and/or insulin injections to treat your condition.

Insulin Resistance Syndrome. People sometimes refer to this condition as prediabetes because the two conditions are similar. You already know that insulin is a hormone that helps your body store sugar (glucose). That's important because your body uses this stored sugar for energy. With insulin resistance syndrome, your tissues no longer respond to insulin, and you are therefore not able to effectively store sugar. Your body takes action by producing more insulin, but alas, all this does is trigger other hormones and tissues to become out of balance. That's why insulin resistance syndrome is often associated with other health problems, such as high cholesterol, high blood pressure, heart disease, and polycystic ovary syndrome (PCOS).

We discussed PCOS in Chapter 1 as a potential cause of infertility. The resulting out-of-balance hormones can lead to male pattern hair growth, acne, and lack of ovulation. Women with PCOS may also have a higher miscarriage rate, but this has been a topic of controversy, according to Duke University School of Medicine.

No simple test exists to diagnose insulin resistance syndrome, so if you think you may have it, talk with your doctor. You are more likely to have it if one or more of the following is true for you:

- You have a family history of diabetes.
- You have a history of gestational diabetes.
- Your blood sugar levels are higher than normal but not quite high enough for diabetes.
- You are overweight or obese.
- You have more fat around your waist than around your hips.

The American Academy of Family Physicians recommends these steps to ward off insulin resistance syndrome:

- Maintain a healthy weight.
- Get 30 minutes of regular exercise each day.
- Eat foods high in dietary fiber, such as fruits, vegetables, and whole grains.

Treatment may also involve prescription medication and will vary depending on your particular situation.

Thyroid Disease. Your thyroid gland is located at the front of your neck. This important gland secretes hormones that are necessary for well-balanced metabolism. In some cases, your thyroid gland may become underactive (hypothyroidism). In other situations, your thyroid gland may become overactive (hyperthyroidism). In either case, you may experience potentially serious consequences if your thyroid isn't functioning properly.

Hypothyroidism is often associated with infertility. If you become pregnant and have untreated low thyroid function, a miscarriage may result. That's because the fetus depends on your normal thyroid activity for early development. Your thyroid hormones are very intertwined with your other reproductive hormones and impact your menstrual cycles, estrogen/progesterone levels, and risk of miscarriage. Hypothyroidism can be easily diagnosed with a sample of your blood. Treatment with thyroid replacement medication is recommended and considered safe for use during pregnancy.

Hyperthyroidism affects less than 1 percent of pregnant women. An overactive thyroid is not typically linked to miscarriage. However, women with an overactive thyroid function are at increased risk for delivering low birth weight babies. Hyperthyroidism can be easily diagnosed with a sample of your blood. Treatment usually consists of thyroid-lowering medication. In some circumstances, thyroid surgery may be necessary.

If you have under- or overactive thyroid function, your doctor will monitor you carefully during pregnancy.

Thrombophilia. Thrombophilia is a blood disorder that can cause your blood to clot more than normal. This medical condition is thought to be inherited, and it has been estimated that as many as one in five people have some sort of thrombophilia.

All pregnant women are more susceptible to blood clots than their nonpregnant counterparts. That's because normal pregnancy hormones change your body's blood-clotting properties. In most cases, your body is able to compensate for these changes. In fact, many women with a thrombophilia disorder are able to have a healthy pregnancy. However, in some situations, pregnancy complications such as miscarriage and stillbirths may occur.

Medical experts are still researching which thrombophilias lead to pregnancy difficulties. One specific thrombophilia, called Factor V Leiden mutation, has been linked to pregnancy complications. This inherited blood abnormality causes you to form blood clots within your blood vessels. A miscarriage is likely if a blood clot forms in your blood vessels that lead to the placenta.

Thrombophilias can be diagnosed through special blood testing. However, in some cases, certain thrombophilias may be too rare or unknown for sufficient diagnosis.

If you are diagnosed with a blood-clotting disorder, your doctor will prescribe medication. The usual first line of treatment is aspirin. Your doctor may decide that you could also benefit from a blood thinner medication, such as heparin. Heparin is given in low doses in the form of daily injections. It does not cross the placenta and is considered safe for the pregnancy. A relatively newer form of heparin, referred to as low molecular weight heparin, is often recommended because it lowers the risk of side effects such as bone loss and injection site bruising.

In addition to heparin, some doctors also prescribe folic acid supplements. Folic acid slows blood clotting when taken in high doses. Doctors always recommend that a woman considering pregnancy take a folic acid supplement. That's because it has been proven to reduce the risk of neural tube defects (such as spina bifida) in the unborn baby. However, if you have delivered a baby with a neural tube defect in the past, your doctor will likely prescribe folic acid in high dosage. This treatment will hopefully prevent miscarriage, blood clot problems, and neural tube defects.

Lupus. Lupus is an inflammatory disease of the body and primarily affects young women. You are probably already aware if you have lupus; most likely, you were diagnosed with lupus during your teens or early 20s.

Lupus occurs in about one in 700 women and is characterized by fever, sensitivity to light, joint pain, rash on the face, fatigue, and weight loss. Lupus is known to be a disease with flare-ups followed by periods of remission, and in most cases, these lupus symptoms begin abruptly, last for weeks, and then disappear for a while.

The rate of miscarriage for women with lupus is approximately 25 percent. The risk is greater if you experience a flare-up during your pregnancy. Lupus is classified as an autoimmune disease, which means your own body is trying to reject itself. Miscarriage rates are thought to be higher among lupus patients because their bodies consider the fetus to be a foreign object and try to reject it. If you have lupus and do not miscarry, your pregnancy may still be at risk. Babies born to mothers with lupus have an increased chance of heart abnormalities, usually heart block. Therefore, pregnant women with lupus require close medical supervision.

If you think you may have lupus and have not officially been diagnosed, be sure to discuss an evaluation with your doctor. Your doctor will perform a detailed physical examination and check specific blood tests to make the diagnosis.

If you have been diagnosed with lupus and desire pregnancy, be sure to talk with your doctor about your specific circumstances. In many cases, your doctor will recommend steroids and/or low-dose aspirin prior to your becoming pregnant. Many medical experts believe that such treatment may minimize the complications of lupus, because it works to reduce the inflammation that usually accompanies lupus. It's also best to not become pregnant until your lupus has been in remission for at least six months. Depending on your particular disease process, it may become necessary for you to take medication during pregnancy. If so, the usual prescriptions are steroids and Imuran (azathioprine). With optimal health care and close medical supervision, women with lupus have a greater chance of enjoying successful pregnancies and delivering healthy babies.

Antiphospholipid Syndrome (Hughes Syndrome). Antiphospholipid syndrome is a disease of your immune system. People with this disorder possess an increased tendency to form clots within their blood vessels, usually in the lower legs, heart, and brain. Pregnant women with antiphospholipid syndrome experience a higher rate of miscarriage.

This disorder is thought to be caused by antiphospholipid antibodies. Antibodies are made by your immune system for the purpose of fighting infection. However, in this case, as with other autoimmune diseases, the antibodies sometimes mistakenly attack your own body's tissues. Like lupus, this autoimmune disease is also more common in women.

If you have this syndrome and become pregnant, you are at increased risk of developing blood clots in the placenta, which may lead to miscarriage. According to the Hughes Syndrome Foundation, 15 percent of women with three or more consecutive miscarriages have positive antiphospholipid syndrome tests. If you are pregnant and do not miscarry, you are still at risk for other pregnancy complications, including preeclampsia, poor fetal growth, and premature delivery.

Your doctor can order specific blood tests to evaluate you for antiphospholipid syndrome. If you are diagnosed with antiphospholipid syndrome, your doctor will likely prescribe medication. The main purpose of treatment is to thin your blood and reduce the incidence of clotting. Most patients are prescribed low-dose aspirin and/or heparin injections. Some doctors also recommend steroids in an effort to reduce your body's inflammation within your tissues and bloodstream. When you become pregnant again, your health care professional should carefully monitor your pregnancy.

DIAGNOSING THE CAUSE OF RECURRENT MISCARRIAGE

Unfortunately, you may already have suffered one or more miscarriages before a thorough evaluation is performed. Work with your doctor to try to find the cause of your recurrent miscarriages. Talk with your doctor about your medical history, your experiences during past pregnancies, and any risk factors or medical conditions that you may have. Your doctor will want to perform a complete physical examination and will also likely order many diagnostic tests in an attempt to determine a cause for the miscarriages. Following is a checklist of possible tests and studies that you may be asked to undergo:

- **Blood tests:** Your blood will be checked for progesterone level, certain viruses, diabetes, thyroid function, blood-clotting disorders, other immune disorders.

- **Pelvic infection testing:** The vagina and uterus may be swabbed and the swabs sent to the laboratory to test for infection.

- **Genetic evaluation:** The miscarriage tissue, you, and your partner may be tested for the presence of abnormal chromosomes.

- **Ultrasound:** Ultrasonic sound waves are used to create an image of your pelvis on a monitor and your pelvic anatomy can be evaluated for possible problems.

- **Sonohysterogram:** In this specific type of ultrasound of the uterus, sterile water is first injected into the uterus for better viewing and evaluation of potential abnormalities.

- **Hysterosalpingography:** This is a special type of x-ray (called fluoroscopy) of the uterus and fallopian tubes performed after injection with dye. It helps detect some problems within the uterus and pelvic anatomy. However, HSG is best suited to determine the openness of the fallopian tubes.

- **Hysteroscopy:** A narrow telescope-like device is inserted into the uterus to view the inside of the uterus and check for abnormalities.

Remember that even if no underlying cause is found, many women go on to have future successful pregnancies. If you and your doctor do find an underlying cause, treatment options are available so that you can hopefully enjoy future successful pregnancies.

Ectopic Pregnancy

If you've endured an ectopic pregnancy, you know how difficult that experience can be. You are initially excited with your newly positive pregnancy test. Your emotions run high as you experience the excitement and joy associated with those early days of pregnancy. However, within a few weeks, you start to bleed or perhaps experience one-sided pelvic pain. An ultrasound shows that the pregnancy is not located within your uterus. Instead, the pregnancy is growing somewhere else, perhaps within your fallopian tube or another place in your pelvis. With tremendous sadness and concern, you must come face-to-face with your ectopic pregnancy.

WHAT IS AN ECTOPIC PREGNANCY? WHAT HAPPENS TO MY BODY?

An ectopic pregnancy is a pregnancy that implants and grows outside of the uterus. The most common site for this to occur is in the fallopian tube. However, ectopic pregnancy can also occur in the ovary, the cervix, or elsewhere within the pelvic cavity.

Actually, when you stop to think about it, it's a wonder that more pregnancies don't implant within the fallopian tube. That's because even under normal circumstances, fertilization (the union of the sperm and egg) occurs inside one of the fallopian tubes. Within a few days, as the fertilized egg continues to develop, it is supposed to move into the uterus to properly implant and grow. However, in the case of an ectopic pregnancy, the fertilized egg never makes it to the uterus. Instead, it tries to grow within the tube. Rarely, it may attach itself to an ovary or another pelvic organ.

The two primary symptoms of ectopic pregnancy are vaginal bleeding and one-sided pelvic pain. These may vary in intensity depending on how far the pregnancy has progressed. Ectopic pregnancies are dangerous because they may lead to rupture of the fallopian tube, along with severe hemorrhage. In extreme cases, the intra-abdominal bleeding can become catastrophic and even fatal to the woman. (See Figure 2.1.)

WHO IS AT RISK? WHAT CAUSES ECTOPIC PREGNANCY?

Ectopic pregnancy occurs at the rate of about one in 60 pregnancies. However, it has been reported with the incidence closer to approximately one in 30 pregnancies when IVF (in vitro fertilization) is used.

Sometimes ectopic pregnancy happens for no apparent reason. However, certain risk factors have been found to increase the chances for ectopic pregnancy. These risk factors are:

- History of severe pelvic infections
- Endometriosis
- Cigarette smoking
- Increasing maternal age

- History of infertility
- Prior surgery on the fallopian tubes
- Prior pelvic or abdominal surgery (scar tissue)
- Previous ectopic pregnancy

HOW IS ECTOPIC PREGNANCY DIAGNOSED?

If your doctor suspects that you have an ectopic pregnancy, he or she will perform certain tests. The doctor will likely perform a pelvic exam, check your blood pressure and pulse, perform an ultrasound, and draw your blood to check your pregnancy hormone levels. The diagnosis of ectopic pregnancy may not be apparent right away. Sometimes it takes a few days of observation and additional testing before the diagnosis is clear. The use of sophisticated ultrasound technology and accurate hormonal monitoring now makes it possible to detect most ectopic pregnancies when they are still in the very early stages. Early diagnosis helps to lessen your chance of tubal rupture and severe hemorrhage.

Figure 2.1.   Ectopic Pregnancy

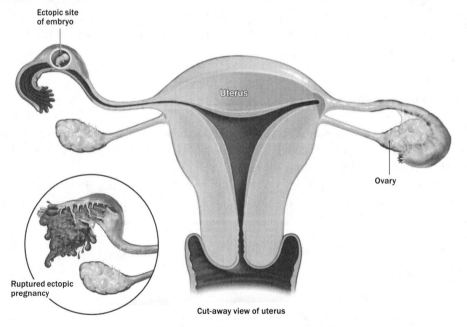

Illustration copyright © Nucleus Medical Art, all rights reserved, nucleusinc.com.

HOW IS ECTOPIC PREGNANCY TREATED?

Many people wonder if the developing ectopic pregnancy can be removed from the tube (or another pelvic location) and be transplanted properly into the uterus. Unfortunately, despite much emerging technology in the field of reproductive medicine, transplanting an ectopic pregnancy has not yet been accomplished. Therefore, all ectopic pregnancies must be ended.

Once the diagnosis of ectopic pregnancy has been made, treatment is largely based on how far along your pregnancy has progressed and what symptoms you are experiencing. Sometimes the medication methotrexate may be used to dissolve the pregnancy. (Methotrexate is best known as a chemotherapy medication to treat cancer patients.) If successful, this medication allows you to avoid surgery and keep your fallopian tube intact. If the medication does not work as intended, surgery may eventually be required.

If your pregnancy is further along or if the tube has already ruptured, surgery is often required. In most cases, the surgery can be performed through a small incision with the laparoscope. The laparoscope is a thin telescope-like device with light that is inserted through a small opening in your abdomen. Other times, especially if significant blood loss has occurred, a larger incision and hospital stay may be required. In either case, some or all of your fallopian tube may need to be removed. If your entire tube is removed, then you must rely on your remaining fallopian tube for future pregnancies, which is certainly possible.

Follow-up care after an ectopic pregnancy is very important. Your blood should be checked several times over the next two to three weeks to ensure that the pregnancy hormone continues to decrease and return to zero. When you become pregnant again, you should see your doctor immediately for an ultrasound and hormonal blood evaluation.

Molar Pregnancy

If you have undergone a molar pregnancy, you've likely experienced a whole array of emotions and concerns. Of course, you are initially excited when your pregnancy test turns positive. Perhaps you've even shared your good fortune with friends and family. Then, within a few weeks, you notice that something doesn't seem quite right with your pregnancy. Perhaps you begin to experience vaginal bleeding. Or maybe your uterus seems larger than you would have expected. You consult with your doctor, who draws your blood to check for hormones and also orders an ultrasound. Sadly, your hormonal blood levels are extremely high, and the ultrasound shows that your uterus is filled with abnormal tissue. The doctor explains molar pregnancy to you, and your dreams for a baby suffer a crashing blow.

WHAT IS A MOLAR PREGNANCY? WHAT HAPPENS TO MY BODY?

Molar pregnancy is a rare condition that results in growth of placenta-like abnormal tissue within the uterus. A molar pregnancy can also be called a hydatidiform mole or gestational trophoblastic disease.

Like a normal pregnancy, a molar pregnancy is also originally formed from a fertilized egg. Of course, in the case of a normal pregnancy, the fertilized egg grows and develops into a fetus and placenta. With a molar pregnancy, a genetic error occurs, and the fertilized egg grows abnormal cells and fills the uterus with a mass of placenta-like tissue.

The two different types of molar pregnancy are complete (the most common type) and partial. A complete molar pregnancy comprises entirely abnormal placenta-like cells; no fetus is present. Partial molar pregnancies have the same abnormal cells present in complete moles but also contain an extremely malformed fetus with fatal defects.

The main symptom of molar pregnancy is first-trimester vaginal bleeding. In addition, some women notice that their belly is growing faster and larger than they expected. The enlarged belly may be caused by the mass of placenta-like tissue within your uterus or sometimes by enlarged ovarian cysts. The ovarian cysts are large fluid-filled sacs within your ovaries and are caused by molar pregnancy hormones.

WHO IS AT RISK? WHAT CAUSES MOLAR PREGNANCY?

Molar pregnancies occur in about one in 1,000 pregnancies. Women younger than 20 or older than 40 appear to be at increased risk. The cause of molar pregnancy is not completely understood. Various theories point to a defective egg, abnormalities within the uterus, or nutritional deficiencies. Diets low in protein, folic acid, and carotene may be a risk factor. More research is needed to better identify the risk factors and causes of molar pregnancy.

HOW IS MOLAR PREGNANCY DIAGNOSED?

If your doctor suspects that you have a molar pregnancy, he or she will perform a pelvic exam to see if your uterus is larger than expected. The doctor will also order your blood to be drawn and checked for your level of pregnancy hormone, called human chorionic gonadotropin (hCG). It is normally produced by the placenta but is produced in massive quantities in the case of a molar pregnancy. Thus, if your hCG level is extremely elevated, a molar pregnancy may be more likely.

Your doctor will also order an ultrasound of your pelvis. Molar pregnancy has a very distinct look on ultrasound, so it is easy to diagnose.

If a molar pregnancy is diagnosed, you must be checked out thoroughly for other medical conditions. That's because molar pregnancy is sometimes associated with preeclampsia and hyperthyroidism. Your doctor will want to closely monitor your blood pressure and also check your blood for thyroid function. If these conditions are present, they will go away once the molar pregnancy has been terminated.

HOW IS MOLAR PREGNANCY TREATED?

Molar pregnancy is treated by removing the pregnancy with a D&C. For this procedure, you are first given anesthesia to ensure that you are comfortable. Then the doctor will open your cervix and remove the tissue from within the uterus. No further treatment is required in about 90 percent of women who undergo a D&C for molar pregnancy. However, you should know that follow-up care is very important. Your doctor will check your blood for hCG hormone levels for the next 6 to 12 months to make sure that the level returns to zero.

If your hCG hormone levels do not return to zero, your doctor may suspect that abnormal molar pregnancy cells are still present. Abnormal cells remain in about 10 percent of women who are treated with a D&C for molar pregnancy. In such cases, chemotherapy may be required to remove the remaining abnormal tissue. In extremely rare cases, hysterectomy is required. Cure rates for persistent molar pregnancy are almost 100 percent.

If you have experienced a molar pregnancy, your doctor will probably recommend waiting six months to a year before trying to conceive again. The reason is to ensure that your hCG hormone levels return to zero and also that your menstrual cycle and your general health get back to normal. Sometimes your doctor may recommend that you take birth control pills during this time to ensure that you don't become pregnant.

Once cleared to try again, you will hopefully conceive a perfectly normal pregnancy. The American College of Obstetricians and Gynecologists reports that the chances of having another molar pregnancy are only about 1 percent.

Coping Emotionally with Early Pregnancy Loss

Most women who experience early pregnancy loss go on to have a healthy pregnancy later. Even so, the loss of a pregnancy can be very difficult. Adjusting to the loss takes time and a great deal of emotional support.

You will probably go over and over the experience in your mind and try to understand what went wrong. You may even blame yourself for the loss, though it is rare that the woman is at fault.

The loss of a pregnancy can generate a wide range of emotions. Most women experience a great deal of sadness and grief. You may find yourself crying unexpectedly and breaking down, especially when you see someone else's baby. Anger, guilt, and disappointment are also emotions you can expect. You may wonder why you must endure this loss when pregnancy seems so easy for others. Some women even experience unexpected physical changes, such as headaches, reduced appetite, fatigue, and insomnia. Please know that these changes are all normal and part of a healthy healing progression.

As you begin your healing process, realize that it will take longer for your emotions than your physical pain to heal. Even a very strong person can experience the emotional impact very deeply. Be patient with yourself, and cry if you feel like crying.

Your emotional approach to this pregnancy loss may be different from your partner's. After all, you are the one who experienced the physical and hormonal changes of pregnancy. Your partner will have his own unique way of grieving. Some men feel that they must be strong for both of you and will not let his emotions get in the way. Unfortunately, this can create tension between the two of you. Communicate openly and honestly with your partner. Your feelings will improve when you are sensitive, accepting, and tolerant to each other's needs.

You may also find that it helps to share your thoughts with others. Start by talking with close family members and friends. They love you and want to share in both the ups and downs of your life. Their encouragement is crucial to helping you through this difficult and emotional time.

It may help you to speak with other women who have also experienced miscarriage. Many women state that they didn't realize how many other women had miscarriages until they started talking with others about it. You can probably find nearby support groups that are eager to help you.

If you continue to struggle with your feelings, be sure to talk with your doctor. In some cases, short-term medication may help reduce your depression and anxiety. You may also want to consider a professional counselor who can help you better cope with your emotions.

Deciding to become pregnant again is often a complex and worrisome decision. Some people believe that the appropriate time to become pregnant is when you and your partner feel physically and emotionally ready. When that time comes, hopefully you realize that the miscarriage was not your fault and you are ready to move forward.

Positive Actions You Can Take to Reduce the Chance of Early Pregnancy Loss

If you have experienced recurrent miscarriage or other pregnancy loss, you can still feel hopeful for your upcoming pregnancies. You may be able to improve your chances of having a successful pregnancy by taking certain positive actions, such as these:

- Undergo a complete medical workup before you try to get pregnant again. Work with your doctor to evaluate risk factors and causes of your past pregnancy loss.

- Take the prenatal vitamins and any other medication that have been prescribed by your doctor.

- Keep up a healthy lifestyle by eating sensible foods, exercising, and avoiding alcohol, tobacco, and illegal drugs.

- Plan your pregnancy, follow your menstrual cycle, and know when you are ovulating.

- If you think that you might be pregnant, see your doctor right away for an early diagnosis and evaluation.

- Remind your doctor of your past losses, and share your concerns and questions.

- Follow your doctor's orders, and be sure that he or she monitors your health and the pregnancy very closely.

Conclusion

Please remember that you will have a good chance for a successful pregnancy even if you have experienced pregnancy loss in the past. This is true even if the cause of the past loss cannot be found. Your future pregnancy will most likely demand special care, close monitoring, and sometimes medication. Most experts agree that if you successfully reach 13 weeks with a normal-appearing fetus and heartbeat on ultrasound, you will very likely go on to have a normal pregnancy.

Also, make sure that you feel comfortable with your physician during your upcoming pregnancy. When you've experienced pregnancy loss, it's even more important that you are under the care of a competent and compassionate physician.

Summary

Here is a summary of the important concepts discussed during this chapter.

Miscarriage

- This is the most common type of pregnancy loss and occurs in 15 to 20 percent of all pregnancies, usually during the first three months of pregnancy.
- Symptoms of miscarriage include vaginal bleeding and cramping in the lower abdomen or back.
- The cause of miscarriage is usually not known, but it is estimated that more than half are due to chromosome problems within the fetus and occur randomly.
- Miscarriage is not caused by work, exercise, sex, most falls, frights, stress, or morning sickness.
- Miscarriage is diagnosed based on a combination of your symptoms, pelvic examination, blood hormone levels, and pelvic ultrasound.

Recurrent Miscarriage

- If you have experienced two or more miscarriages in a row, you may need some special medical attention to investigate for potential underlying medical problems.
- Potential causes of recurrent miscarriage include the following:
  - Lifestyle factors (tobacco, alcohol, street drug use)
  - Chromosomal problems
  - Low progesterone level
  - Abnormalities of the uterus
  - Certain medical conditions
- In about one half of cases, no underlying cause can be found.

Ectopic Pregnancy

- An ectopic pregnancy is a pregnancy that implants and grows outside of the uterus, most commonly within your fallopian tube.
- Symptoms of ectopic pregnancy include vaginal bleeding and one-sided pelvic pain.

- The cause of ectopic pregnancy is sometimes not known; however, women with the following risk factors have a higher chance of developing an ectopic pregnancy:
  - History of severe pelvic infections
  - Endometriosis
  - Cigarette smoking
  - Increasing maternal age
  - History of infertility
  - Prior surgery on the fallopian tubes
  - Prior pelvic or abdominal surgery
  - Previous ectopic pregnancy
- Ectopic pregnancy is diagnosed based on a combination of your symptoms, pelvic examination, blood hormone levels, and pelvic ultrasound.
- Early diagnosis and treatment is important because it lessens your chance of tubal rupture and severe hemorrhage.

Molar Pregnancy

- A molar pregnancy is a rare condition where abnormal placenta-like tissue grows within the uterus. In most cases, no fetus is present.
- Symptoms of molar pregnancy include vaginal bleeding and the belly growing faster than expected.
- The cause of molar pregnancy is not completely understood; however, women younger than 20 or older than 40 appear to be at increased risk.
- Molar pregnancy is diagnosed based on a combination of your symptoms, pelvic examination, blood hormone levels, and pelvic ultrasound.

Coping Emotionally with Early Pregnancy Loss

- The loss of a pregnancy can be very difficult, both emotionally and physically. It usually takes longer for your emotions than your physical pain to heal.
- You can take positive actions to reduce your chances of another early pregnancy loss.
- Keep in mind that most women who experience early pregnancy loss go on to have a healthy pregnancy later.

CHAPTER 3

Basic Male and Female Anatomy and How Things Work

To fully understand fertility evaluation and treatment, you must have a good knowledge of basic male and female reproductive anatomy and their inner workings. With this increased knowledge, you'll be better equipped to communicate with your doctor and play a larger role in your own health care decision making.

Male Reproductive Anatomy

The male anatomy can be divided into external and internal reproductive organs.

EXTERNAL MALE REPRODUCTIVE ORGANS

The external male reproductive organs consist of the penis and two testicles. The two testicles are located in a sac called the scrotum. When a male baby is born, his penis is fully formed and his testicles have usually descended from his pelvis and into the scrotum.

Penis

The penis is located on the outside of the male pubic region. It comprises three muscular bundles. During sexual excitement, these tissues become engorged with blood and expand. This causes the penis to become erect and firm. At the peak of sexual excitement, the man usually ejaculates semen from the opening at the tip of his penis.

The penis serves two primary functions: to provide an outlet for urination and to provide an outlet for the release of sperm. By fortunate design, these two functions cannot happen at the same time because of specially designed valves.

Testicles

The two testicles are egg-shaped glands held within the scrotum. The scrotum is located underneath the penis and hangs outside of the body cavity. The testicles should hang outside of the body cavity to optimize sperm production because sperm production is most effective when performed at slightly below body temperature. Unfortunately, placement of the scrotum outside of the body cavity puts the testicles at greater risk for injury. Therefore, the testicles should be protected with a jockstrap or protective cup during sports or other strenuous activities.

The testicles serve two primary functions: the production of the hormone testosterone and the production of sperm. The testicles are sometimes referred to as counterparts to the woman's ovaries. That's because the testicles produce sperm, which is the sexual equivalent to the woman's ovaries containing eggs.

The production of sperm begins in the testicles. The early sperm cells are rather primitive and are not fully formed. They begin their maturing process within the testicles and continue to develop there for about two weeks. At that time, they move on to a nearby structure called the epididymis, where they develop further.

INTERNAL MALE REPRODUCTIVE ORGANS

The internal male reproductive organs consist of the epididymis, vas deferens, seminal vesicles, prostate gland, ejaculatory ducts, and urethra. (See Figure 3.1.)

Epididymis

The epididymis is a long, thin, hollow coiled tubular system within the scrotum. A man has two epididymides; each one sits on top of its corresponding testicle. Sperm that are still maturing leave the testicle, enter one end of the epididymis, and loop and coil along the path. The sperm's journey takes about 10 days, and by the end of this course, the sperm are completely mature. The tail end of the epididymis acts as a sort of holding and storage tank for the mature sperm. It is connected to a straighter, thicker tube called the vas deferens.

Figure 3.1. Male Reproductive System

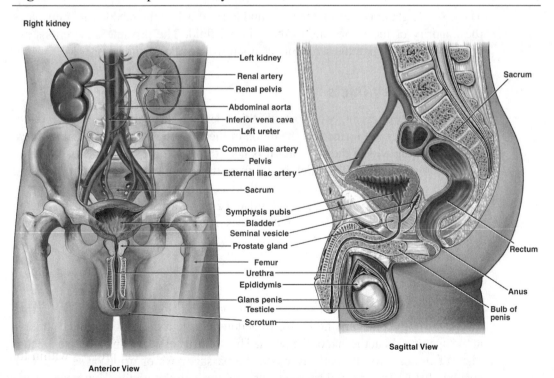

Illustration copyright © Nucleus Medical Art, all rights reserved, nucleusinc.com.

Vas Deferentia

The vas deferentia consist of two tubes that serve as sperm ducts. The vas deferentia actually look a lot like strands of spaghetti, but they serve as the pipes and plumbing works for sperm. They transport the mature sperm from the epididymis and into the pelvic cavity. Once inside the pelvic cavity, the vas deferentia pass over the bladder and eventually connects with the seminal vesicles to form the ejaculatory ducts. Just prior to ejaculation, the sperm are mixed with the seminal fluid. The seminal fluid is composed of secretions from the seminal vesicles and the prostate gland.

Seminal Vesicles

Seminal vesicles are two small glands located just behind the bladder. Their purpose is to secrete a thick liquid that accounts for about 30 percent of the semen fluid volume.

Prostate Gland

The prostate gland is a walnut-sized gland located below the bladder. It contributes the majority of the secretions to the seminal fluid. The prostate's secretions are opaque white and give the semen its characteristic milky white color.

Ejaculatory Ducts

The ejaculatory ducts are two short tubes that descend through the prostate and into the urethra. They are formed by the union of the vas deferens, the seminal vesicles, and an opening within the prostate. It is here that the three components of semen are combined together. The thick liquid from the seminal vesicles, the milky fluid from the prostate, and the sperm from the vas deferens all combine here to make semen. Semen is 98 percent seminal fluid and 2 percent sperm. It will eventually be ejaculated from the penis. (If ejaculation does not occur, then the sperm will merely be absorbed by the body.)

Urethra

The urethra is the major transporting tube for both urine and semen. The urethra originates in the bladder, and it also runs down through the prostate gland. It ends at the opening slit at the end of the penis. The urethra possesses an elaborate mechanism of muscles to alternatively block the passageways of urine or semen. This ensures that both urine and semen can travel through the urethra, but never at the same time.

How the Male Reproductive Process Works

Along with normal male reproductive anatomy, the proper levels of hormones and sperm production are required to achieve maximum fertility.

HORMONES

Hormones are produced by the body to transmit instruction from one area to another. The same hormones are produced in both men and women, but in different amounts. It helps to understand how the reproductive hormones react within the body. They play an important role in fertility.

A small area located within the midportion of the brain is known as the hypothalamus; nearby lies a grape-sized gland called the pituitary gland. Together these two structures control the production and release of the body's hormones.

The hypothalamus monitors the hormone levels in the bloodstream. Just like all of the hormones within the body, the reproductive hormones are constantly being monitored and adjusted depending on your physical and emotional demands. The hypothalamus sort of acts like the CEO of a corporation, just sitting by and monitoring what's going on and barking orders from time to time. The hypothalamus will send a message in the form of gonadotropin-releasing hormone (GnRH) to the pituitary gland. In this example, the pituitary gland is the worker. It must calculate which hormones are needed and the required amounts of each and release this message in the form of gonadotropins. The specific names of these gonadotropins are follicle-stimulating hormone (FSH) and luteinizing hormone (LH). As discussed in Chapter 1, in men, FSH stimulates sperm production and LH stimulates the testicles to release testosterone.

Unlike in the female, the production of these hormones does not fluctuate on a monthly cycle, and male hormone levels remain relatively constant. These hormones play a critical role in a man's fertility. Men need proper levels of FSH, LH, and testosterone for healthy sperm production.

SPERM

Sperm are the smallest cells in a man's body. They look like microscopic tadpoles. A sperm is made up of a head, a midsection, and a tail. The head of the sperm contains the genetic material. Each sperm, when fertilized with an egg, contains enough genetic material to form a human being. The midsection provides energy and nourishment for the sperm. The tail is used to propel the sperm along the reproductive tract. The head of the sperm is covered by a protective structure called an acrosome.

The acrosome contains essential enzymes that give the sperm their ability to penetrate the egg's surface and fertilize it.

Sperm Production

The early sperm cells that begin to develop within the testicles are primitive and do not yet have tails. These developing sperm remain within the testicles for a little more than two months. During that time, they grow and develop into more mature sperm. At the end of this time, the almost fully developed sperm move on to the epididymis. The still developing sperm will use the next several weeks within the epididymis to become fully formed and capable of fertilization. This entire sperm production cycle takes about 90 to 100 days. Thus every three months or so, a man produces an entirely fresh new quota of sperm. If a supply of old sperm was never ejaculated, it will simply be absorbed by the body.

Sperm Ejaculation

Approximately 100 million sperm are released during a normal ejaculation. Medical research indicates that about 90 percent of these sperm are killed by vaginal secretions. Even if sexual intercourse occurs under the best possible conditions, only a few hundred or a few thousand sperm actually make it through the cervix, into the uterus, and up one of the fallopian tubes. Of those sperm, about half will swim up the wrong fallopian tube. (That is, the egg is waiting in the other fallopian tube.) Therefore, of the millions of sperm ejaculated, there may be only 100 or so candidates available to fertilize the egg. If no egg is present, some sperm may stay in the fallopian tube and wait. In these conditions, some sperm may live for about 12 to 20 hours; some experts claim that the sperm may live up to 72 hours.

Female Reproductive Anatomy

Reproductive anatomy in the female can be divided into external and internal pelvic organs.

EXTERNAL FEMALE REPRODUCTIVE ORGANS

The external female reproductive organs are collectively called the vulva. The vulva comprises the labia majora and minora, clitoris, urethra opening, vaginal opening, and lubricating glands. (See Figure 3.2.)

Figure 3.2. Female Genitalia

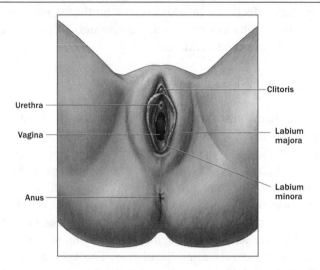

Illustration copyright © Nucleus Medical Art, all rights reserved, nucleusinc.com.

Labia Majora and Minora

These are two sets of skin folds that protect the vaginal opening. The labia majora are the outer folds and the labia minora are the inner folds.

The labia majora skin folds contain hair and sweat glands. The inner labia minora do not contain hair, but they produce a white lubricant called smegma. The labia minora are very sensitive to the touch and during sexual arousal may engorge and grip the penis. Both labia majora and minora fold over the vaginal opening and help to protect the vagina from infection and disease.

When the folds of the labia majora and minora are spread apart, the clitoris, urethra opening, vaginal opening, and two pairs of lubricating glands can be seen.

Clitoris

The clitoris is located at the upper portion of the vulva, where the labia minora folds meet. The clitoris is typically considered to be the most sensitive spot in a woman's genitalia. During sexual arousal, the clitoris may enlarge slightly.

Urethra Opening

The urethra is a short tube that transports urine from your bladder to the outside of your body. The urethra measures only about an inch and a half in length, which is much shorter than a man's urethra. This fact helps to explain why women are more prone to urinary tract infections. In addition, the urethra opens very close to the vaginal opening. This results in irritation and discomfort of the urinary tract after prolonged or vigorous sexual intercourse.

Vaginal Opening

The vagina is a flexible, muscular passageway lined with moist membranes. It extends from about four to five inches from the vulva and ends at the cervix. The vagina secretes an odorless watery discharge that keeps it moist and clean. The discharge maintains a slightly acid environment within the vagina, which helps prevent infection. Because of the influence of reproductive hormones, the vagina tends to become more lubricated during ovulation, pregnancy, and sexual excitement.

The vagina has numerous functions. It is the outward passageway for menstrual blood flow. It also serves as a guide for the penis during sexual intercourse and holds the semen near the cervix after ejaculation. The vagina is capable of great expansion and flexibility when it functions as the birth canal during childbirth.

Lubricating Glands

Two sets of lubricating glands are located within the vulva. The Skene's glands are located on either side of the urethra. These glands secrete a lubricating fluid during sexual arousal. The other set of glands is the Bartholin's glands. They are located under the two sides of the labia majora. The Bartholin's glands are especially susceptible to sexually transmitted disease infection. If these glands become infected, they may swell to the size of a golf ball.

INTERNAL FEMALE REPRODUCTIVE ORGANS

The internal female reproductive organs consist of the cervix and uterus, two fallopian tubes, and two ovaries. (See Figure 3.3.)

Cervix and Uterus

The cervix is a small rounded structure that is about an inch and a half across. It separates the vagina from the uterus. It juts out like a bottleneck into the upper part of the vagina. The cervix, which is actually the lower part of the uterus, opens into the uterus via a narrow cervical canal.

The cervical canal is lined with glands that produce cervical mucus. This cervical mucus plays an important role in fertility. Most of the time, the cervix is filled with a

Figure 3.3. Female Reproductive Organs

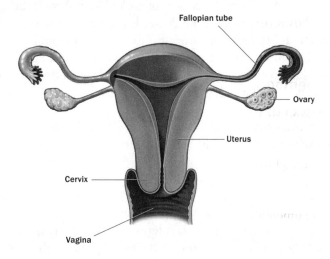

Illustration copyright © Nucleus Medical Art, all rights reserved, nucleusinc.com.

thick plug of mucus that acts as a barrier to foreign objects and infection. However, during ovulation, hormones transform the mucus to become thin and stretchy. Thin mucus provides a very hospitable environment for sperm. It allows sperm to pass through the female reproductive tract to reach and fertilize the egg. If the cervix is diseased or injured, the quality and quantity of cervical mucus may adversely affect your fertility.

The uterus is also sometimes referred to as the womb. It is a pear-shaped muscular organ that is supported within your pelvis by strong ligaments, and its primary purpose is to hold a pregnancy. When you are not pregnant, your uterus is about the size of your fist. However, with pregnancy, it has amazing capability to stretch to accommodate a full-term baby.

The lining of the uterus is called the endometrium (or endometrial lining); it is greatly influenced by your reproductive hormones. When you become pregnant, the lining thickens and becomes the implantation site for the developing fetus. If you are not pregnant, this endometrial lining is shed each month during your menstrual blood flow.

Fallopian Tubes

The fallopian tubes are two hollow spaghetti-like pipelines that originate on either side of the uterus and lead toward each of your ovaries. Each fallopian tube measures about four inches long.

The end of each fallopian tube has fingerlike projections called fimbriae, which hang over each ovary. A fallopian tube sort of looks like a flower; the long stem is the tube itself, and the open blossoming flower is the fimbriae at the end. The fimbriae are responsible for transporting the egg from the ovary and into the fallopian tube. During ovulation, the fimbriae grasp the newly released egg, much like an elephant uses its trunk to pick up a piece of fruit, and place it inside one of the fallopian tubes. Tiny fine hairlike projections line the inside of the fallopian tube and move the egg along the tube.

Fallopian tubes are extremely delicate and very fragile structures. That's why they must be in excellent condition to optimize fertility.

Ovaries

The ovaries are two almond-sized structures attached to either side of the pelvis. Each ovary is located on either side of the uterus, just below the corresponding fallopian tube. The ovaries have two main functions: to produce the female sex hormones (estrogen and progesterone) and to release the eggs. The process of releasing the egg or eggs is called ovulation.

When a baby girl is growing in the uterus, she has about 7 to 8 million immature eggs. That decreases to about 3 to 4 million immature eggs by the time she is born. By the time she reaches puberty, a woman's ovaries contain about 700,000 to 800,000 immature eggs. The typical woman will use about 300,000 of these eggs during the approximately 400 ovulations that occur during her reproductive life span.

The ovaries play a crucial role in fertility, and disorders of the ovaries can lead to infertility. However, if you lose an ovary for any reason, the remaining ovary will usually compensate and take over the entire workload of egg releasing and sexual hormone production.

How the Female Reproductive Cycle Works

In addition to normally functioning female anatomy, proper hormone levels and ovulation are important to achieve maximum fertility.

HORMONES

As previously discussed, the same reproductive hormones are produced in both men and women, but in varying amounts. They play an important role in fertility and preparing the body for pregnancy. It helps to understand how the reproductive hormones react within your body.

Just as with the case of the male, already discussed, the hypothalamus and nearby pituitary gland control the production and release of your body's hormones.

In a woman, FSH and LH stimulate the ovaries to produce estrogen and progesterone. These female hormones fluctuate throughout the monthly menstrual cycle and play a critical role in your menstrual cycle and ovulation.

MENSTRUAL CYCLE

Each month your reproductive hormones cause the uterine lining to thicken and prepare for possible pregnancy. The rising levels of hormones also cause the cervix to produce thinner cervical mucus, making it easier for sperm to successfully pass into the uterus.

About midway through your monthly cycle, an egg is released by one of your ovaries. This process is called ovulation. If the egg becomes fertilized by a sperm, it moves into the uterus, implants within the uterine lining, and develops into a fetus. If pregnancy does not occur, the hormones taper off, and the lining of the uterus (endometrium) is eventually shed as your monthly cycle bleeding.

Your monthly period is the shedding of the lining of the uterus; it usually lasts from five to seven days. The first day of bleeding is referred to as day 1 of your cycle. The average menstrual cycle lasts approximately 28 days but may vary from 23 to 35 days and still be considered normal. Here is a summary of important menstrual cycle events:

Day 1   The first day of your menstrual period is considered day 1 of your cycle.

Day 5   Hormones signal your endometrium to thicken and prepare for a possible pregnancy.

Day 14   Ovulation occurs. This means that an egg is released from an ovary and moves into a fallopian tube.

Day 28   If the egg was not fertilized, hormones have dropped and endometrium is shed.

OVULATION

Each month, under the influence of your reproductive hormones, one of your ovaries selects between 10 and 20 eggs to become possible candidates for release. The number of eggs decreases with age until menopause, when ovulation stops completely. The chosen eggs begin to mature within their own sacs, called follicles. In most cases, only one follicle matures and one egg is released each month. Some women feel a cramp on one side of their pelvic region during this time. Next, the egg moves into one of the fallopian tubes, where it can be fertilized by a man's sperm. The remaining partially developed eggs and follicles will disintegrate. That's why it's a myth that fertility treatments use up a woman's eggs more quickly than normal. In any given cycle, the same number of eggs are recruited and selected for possible ovulation. However, with fertility treatments, more of those chosen eggs are able to develop further and ovulate with the potential to become an embryo, whereas normally only one egg is released during ovulation.

In most cases, ovulation occurs about 14 days before the start of your next menstrual period. That means if you have an average 28-day menstrual cycle, ovulation will occur on about day 14. If you have a 30-day cycle, ovulation will probably occur on day 16, and so on. Timing is critical for pregnancy to occur. Pregnancy can only occur if you have sexual intercourse during or near the time of ovulation. Once the egg has been released, it is able to be fertilized during that specific 12-to-24-hour period. Given that sperm may live as long as 72 hours, you have approximately a three-day window each month to conceive.

Eggs

Many people are surprised to learn that the human eggs are the largest cells in the human body. The human egg is about the size of a grain of sand and can actually be seen by the human eye without a microscope. Eggs are also sometimes referred to as ova or oocytes.

The human egg has a very similar framework to that of the chicken egg. The center of the human egg holds the nucleus and all of the genetic material, which is comparable to the chicken egg's yellow yolk. The fluid that surrounds the center is called the ooplasm and contains tiny structures that provide energy and nourishment for the egg. This surrounding fluid can be compared to the egg white in the chicken egg. The human egg is surrounded by several protective layers. The innermost layer, called the perivitelline membrane, is similar to the membrane found just inside of the chicken egg shell. The middle layer, called the zona pellucida, is much like the shell of a chicken egg. The third and outer layer is called the cumulus granulose. This is a special thick and firm protective layer.

Fertilization

To summarize, fertilization occurs when the sperm and the egg finally get together. Of the 100 million sperm ejaculated into the woman's vagina during sex, only a few hundred to a few thousand successfully make it into the two fallopian tubes. Many sperm are killed along the way by the hostile acid environment in the vagina or cervix. Still other sperm are simply not able to survive the long swim.

It is estimated that sperm may be able to live within the woman's fallopian tubes for up to three days. But remember that a woman's egg can only be fertilized within a specific 12- to 24-hour period. Therefore, pregnancy may occur during a time period of just two or three days each month. If any one sperm joins with a woman's egg, the process is called fertilization. When fertilization occurs, it almost always happens within the fallopian tube. The fertilized egg then travels through the fallopian tube and enters the uterus for implantation. (See Figure 3.4.)

These events must all methodically take place for a viable pregnancy to result. For example, both the egg and the sperm must be healthy. The body's hormones must be in proper balance. The lining of the uterus must be healthy and ready for implantation. If the fertilized egg implants anywhere but in the uterus, it is referred to as an ectopic pregnancy and must be detached. If any problem or obstacle arises within this essential chain of events, infertility issues may result. The chain of events looks like this:

- As the sperm travels through the woman's reproductive tract, it slowly releases enzymes from the sperm's acrosome.

- The sperm is now able to attack the cumulus granulose (outermost protective layer) and the zona pellucida (the shell-like covering) of the egg.

Figure 3.4. Fertilization

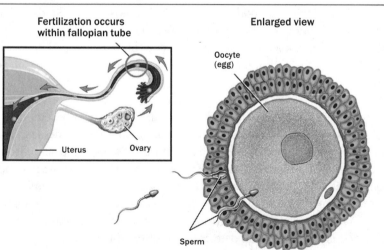

Illustration copyright © Nucleus Medical Art, all rights reserved, nucleusinc.com.

- Several sperm fuse with the zona pellucida, but only one sperm successfully penetrates the egg.

- The successful sperm sheds its body and tail so that only the head (containing the genetic material) actually enters the egg.

- When fertilization occurs, the newly fertilized egg starts to grow and develop into an embryo.

- The embryo is propelled by the fallopian tube and begins its three- to four-day journey into the uterus.

- Approximately two days after reaching the uterus, the developing embryo has about 100 cells. These cells then burrow their way and implant into the lining of the uterine wall.

- A portion of the developing embryo makes contact with the mother's circulatory system and becomes the beginning of the placenta. The placenta will provide the embryo with a source for growth and nourishment.

CHROMOSOMES AND THE GENETIC DESIGN

Both egg and sperm contain important genetic material. The reason that the egg is so much bigger than the sperm is because the egg contains both genetic material plus nourishment supplies to support the developing embryo. In contrast, sperm are almost entirely little bags of genetic material, propelled by a tail.

Chromosomes are the important genetic material that provides the personal traits and characteristics of every individual. With the exception of the egg and the sperm, every cell within the human body contains 46 chromosomes (23 pairs). The egg and the sperm each contain 23 chromosomes. When combined together, they form the required 46 chromosomes (23 pairs) for a new human being. The newly formed human being receives half of its genetic material from the mother and the other half from the father.

Of the 23 chromosomes within the egg and the sperm, 22 of the chromosomes determine various characteristics and traits of the individual (eye color, intelligence, hair color, and so on). The 23rd chromosome is considered the sex chromosome because it determines the sex of the baby. Within the egg, the sex chromosome is always an X chromosome. Within the sperm, the sex chromosome may be either an X chromosome or a Y chromosome. If the egg and sperm that combine each have an X chromosome, the baby will be a female, or XX. However, the baby will be a male, or XY, if the egg has an X chromosome and the sperm has a Y chromosome. This is why it is the sperm that determines the sex of the baby.

Conclusion

Hopefully, you now have a better understanding of male and female anatomy and how they work together to conceive a baby. Be sure to use this information to your advantage and maximize your own fertility. Armed with this knowledge, you'll be more confident and better equipped to ask questions and play an active role in your fertility decision-making treatments.

Summary

Here is a summary of key facts and important concepts discussed in this chapter.

Hormones

- Hormones are produced by the body to transmit instruction from one area to another. The same hormones are produced in both men and women, but in varying amounts.

- Hormone levels are monitored and controlled by areas of the brain called the hypothalamus and the pituitary gland.

- The gonadotropin hormones are FSH and LH. In men, FSH stimulates sperm production and LH stimulates the testicles to release testosterone. In women, they play a critical role in the monthly menstrual cycle and ovulation.

External Male Reproductive Organs

- The penis provides an outlet for urination and release of sperm.

- The testicles are responsible for production of testosterone hormone and the production of sperm.

Internal Male Reproductive Organs

- The epididymis acts as a holding and storage tank for mature sperm.

- The vas deferens serves as the plumbing to transport the mature sperm.

- The seminal vesicles are two small glands that secrete a liquid that accounts for 30 percent of the semen fluid volume.

- The prostate gland, located below the bladder, contributes the majority of the secretions to the seminal fluid.

- The ejaculatory ducts are two short tubes that are formed by the union of the vas deferens, the seminal vesicles, and the prostate gland. It is here that the components of semen are combined together and made ready for ejaculation.
- The urethra is the major transport tube for urine and semen.

Sperm

- Sperm develop and grow in the testicles and then move on to the epididymis until they are completely mature.
- It takes about 90 to 100 days to form an entirely fresh new supply of sperm.
- Sperm are the smallest cells in the human body; they resemble tiny tadpoles.
- Approximately 100 million sperm are released during a normal ejaculation. However, due to harsh conditions of vaginal secretions and a long difficult journey, only about 100 or so sperm make it into the fallopian tube and become candidates to fertilize the egg.
- Sperm typically live for about 12 to 20 hours; however, some experts claim that they may live as long as 72 hours.

External Female Reproductive Organs

- The labia majora and minora are two sets of skin folds that protect the vaginal opening.
- The clitoris, typically considered to be the most sensitive spot in a woman's genitalia, is located where the labia minora folds meet.
- The urethra opening is a short tube that transports urine from your bladder to the outside of your body.
- The vagina is a flexible, muscular passageway lined with moist membranes; it serves as the outward passageway for menstrual blood and as a guide for the penis during sex and functions as the birth canal during childbirth.
- The lubricating glands secrete lubricating fluid, especially in response to sexual arousal.

Internal Female Reproductive Organs

- The cervix is the opening of the uterus; it separates the vagina from the uterus.
- The uterus—also called the womb—is a pear-shaped organ that holds the pregnancy; when you are not pregnant, the lining of the uterus is what's shed each month during your menstrual blood flow.

- The fallopian tubes are two delicate hollow tubes that run from either side of the uterus and toward each of the ovaries; this is where conception occurs.

- The ovaries are two almond-sized glands on either side of the uterus; filled with eggs, they also produce estrogen and progesterone.

Menstrual Cycle

- Each month your reproductive hormones cause the uterine lining to thicken and prepare for a possible pregnancy.

- About midway through your monthly cycle, an egg is released by one of your ovaries; this is called ovulation.

- If this egg is fertilized, it moves into the uterus and develops into a fetus.

- If this egg is not fertilized, your hormones begin to taper, and the lining of your uterus is shed as your monthly cycle bleeding.

- Most women's menstrual periods last between five and seven days.

- The average menstrual cycle lasts about 28 days but may vary from 23 to 35 days and still be considered normal.

Ovulation

- Each month, your ovaries select between 10 and 20 eggs to become possible candidates for release, also known as ovulation.

- During ovulation, the sac holding the egg, called the follicle, bursts open and the egg is released. In most cases, only one egg is released each month.

- In most cases, ovulation occurs about 14 days before the start of your next menstrual bleeding.

- Pregnancy can only occur if you have sexual intercourse during or near the time of ovulation.

- In contrast to a man, who produces new batches of sperm every 100 days, a woman is born with her lifetime supply of eggs.

- The human egg is about the size of a grain of sand and is the largest cell in the human body.

Chromosomes and Genetic Design

- Chromosomes are the important genetic material that provides the personal traits and characteristics of every individual.

- Both the egg and sperm each contain 23 chromosomes. When combined together, they form the required 46 chromosomes (23 pairs) for a new human being.

- Of the 23 chromosomes within the egg and the sperm, 22 of them determine various physical and mental characteristics of the individual.

- The 23rd chromosome is considered the sex chromosome because it determines the sex of the individual. Within the egg, the sex chromosome is always an X. Within the sperm, the sex chromosome may be either an X or a Y.

- When the sperm and the egg combine, the sex chromosome will be either XX for a female child or XY for a male child.

CHAPTER 4

Testing for Infertility

Most medical experts agree that if you have been trying for more than a year to get pregnant, you should have your situation evaluated by your doctor. However, if you are older than 35, you should contact your doctor after just six months of trying to conceive. Your regular OB/GYN doctor may initiate some preliminary testing before referring you to an infertility specialist.

Types of Doctors: What's the Difference?

What does it really mean when a doctor refers to himself or herself as an infertility specialist? You should understand about your doctor's educational background and specialized training. That way you can be sure that you have the best doctor for your particular situation.

OBSTETRICIANS/GYNECOLOGISTS (OB/GYNS)

Obstetricians/gynecologists are doctors who graduated from medical school and then continued on to do a four-year residency specializing in women's health. In the United States, these doctors are tested and board certified by the American College of Obstetricians and Gynecologists (ACOG). Take a look at the ACOG website (acog.org) for additional information.

These health care providers are the ones that most women go to for basic female needs, such as Pap smears, birth control, female infections, and routine pregnancy and delivery. As far as fertility evaluation, the OB/GYN is capable of beginning some initial testing and treatment. For example, your OB/GYN doctor may order blood tests, perform a laparoscopy, or prescribe a trial of a low-dose fertility medication. The amount of fertility evaluation and treatment that your OB/GYN can provide is likely the result of the doctor's own training, interest, and comfort in the field of fertility. However, at some point, if you do not become pregnant from these preliminary methods, you will likely want to see a fertility specialist, the reproductive endocrinologist.

REPRODUCTIVE ENDOCRINOLOGISTS (FERTILITY SPECIALISTS)

The reproductive endocrinologist has even more training than the OB/GYN doctor. These doctors have completed all of the requirements of the OB/GYN physician just discussed plus two to three additional years of fertility and reproductive procedure training. They are members of the Society for Reproductive Endocrinology and Infertility (socrei.org). They may choose to become board certified by the American College of OB/GYN in Reproductive Endocrinology & Infertility (acog.org).

The primary role of the reproductive endocrinologist is to help you create your family. Most women use these doctors when they need additional assistance to become pregnant or avoid recurrent miscarriages. The reproductive endocrinologist is trained to diagnose and treat both female and male fertility issues. Of course, these doctors prescribe fertility medications and carry out advanced laparoscopy and hysteroscopic procedures. In addition, they can also boost your fertility with inseminations, in vitro fertilization (IVF), sperm injections, donor egg programs, and other advanced reproductive technologies.

Once you become pregnant, the reproductive endocrinologist usually cares for you and monitors your progress during your first couple of months. By the end of your first trimester, the doctor will refer you back to your OB/GYN physician for routine prenatal care.

WHAT ARE THE PROS AND CONS CONCERNING THE SELECTION OF A DOCTOR?

As with most things, you will have to evaluate benefits and drawbacks when selecting the best type of doctor to meet your needs. Here are some points for you to consider regarding OB/GYN physicians:

Pros

- Most of the tests and procedures done are covered by your health insurance.
- You may already know and feel comfortable with this doctor.

Cons

- These doctors are not specially trained or focused on fertility concerns.
- Being around lots of big, pregnant women in the waiting room might be depressing for you.
- Tests and procedures that you undergo with an OB/GYN may have to be repeated by the fertility specialist.

And here are some points for you to consider regarding reproductive endocrinologists (fertility specialists):

Pros

- These doctors are the genuine fertility specialists—their education, training, and practice are focused on fertility.
- These doctors are capable of performing advanced reproductive technologies.

Cons

- Some of these doctors' services may be covered by your health insurance, but most are not.
- You probably don't know this doctor yet and will need to spend time getting to know and becoming comfortable with him or her.

Finding a Fertility Specialist

Depending on your needs and particular situation, you'll probably go to your regular OB/GYN physician for your initial fertility workup. If you become pregnant, that's terrific! If you do not become pregnant under the care of your OB/GYN physician, ask him or her about a referral to a fertility specialist.

You will probably want to interview several fertility specialists before making your final choice. Feel free to ask your OB/GYN to give you several names and tell you a little about each one. Also, ask your friends and coworkers if they have experience with a particular physician. Try to find out what they liked or did not like about that doctor. If there is a medical school in your area, call and ask about recommendations for fertility specialists.

NARROWING YOUR SEARCH

As you compile your list of potential fertility specialists, you may want to make a list of questions to ask over the phone. This may be a time-saving measure to help you reach a decision, before you even schedule an office visit. Here are some points for you to consider:

- Does your health insurance cover fertility treatments?
- Is the doctor or clinic on your preferred health insurance list?
- Did the doctor do a fellowship in reproductive endocrinology and infertility?
- Is the doctor board certified in OB/GYN and also in reproductive endocrinology?
- Is the doctor a member of the American Society for Reproductive Medicine?
- Does the clinic have an IVF lab and is it accredited by the College of American Pathologists?
- What other specialists does the clinic have on staff? (In addition to the doctor, many clinics also have access to reproductive immunologists, embryologists, reproductive urologists, andrologists, and genetic counselors.)

QUESTIONS TO ASK THE FERTILITY SPECIALIST

Once you've narrowed down your choices of specialists, schedule an office visit with each one. Before you go in to meet with the doctor, spend some time thinking about what is important to you and your particular situation. Many women recommend writing down a list of questions ahead of time and bringing it with them to the office visit. That way you can make sure that you don't forget to bring up an important topic. Of course, you'll want to get information about the doctor and the clinic. You'll also want to know about the treatments available and their success rates. Another key purpose is for you to get an impression of the doctor and clinic to see if this is a place where you would feel comfortable.

Here are some questions you may want to ask during your first meeting with the specialist. Don't be embarrassed—they get asked these questions all the time!

- Where did you go to medical school and do your residency?
- How many years have you been in practice?
- Are you board certified?
- How many fertility specialists are on staff here?
- Will we work with only you or will other doctors participate in our care?
- Is there a physician on call after office hours and on weekends?
- Are you on the staff at a hospital? Which one(s)?
- What percentage of your patients have fertility problems?
- What percentage of your patients have been successfully treated?
- How do you plan to approach my case?
- Are both partners investigated at the same time?
- How long will our infertility evaluation take?
- What tests and procedures do you use to evaluate our fertility?
- What services and treatments do you offer?
- What happens if we require another treatment that you do not provide?
- How much will the proposed treatment cost?
- Do you accept medical insurance? How do you handle that?
- Do you offer any money back guarantee programs?
- What is your rate of live babies born per cycle? (That means the number of healthy babies born per fertility treatment cycle—it's intended as a measure of success rate for the patient.)
- What is your rate of take-home babies born per year?

You should be knowledgeable about the specialist's fertility success rate. However, keep in mind that some clinics may not have as high success rates as others because they might focus on high-risk or difficult-to-treat patients. The important thing is that you have a good understanding as to why that particular clinic's numbers are what they are.

Don't make a final decision about selecting your fertility specialist until you have had time to fully process your encounter. Be sure to evaluate what you experienced at the clinic with a critical eye.

GOOD VIBRATIONS: MAKING SURE THE SPECIALIST MEETS YOUR EMOTIONAL NEEDS

It is vitally important that you have a good feeling about the fertility specialist, the office staff, and the clinic itself. The process of fertility evaluation and treatment is stressful enough. That's why it's especially critical that you sense a good connection and feel comfortable around your fertility specialist.

If you find that the specialist or staff is not sensitive to your needs, talk with the doctor. It's far better to bring such topics out in the open, where they might be solved, than to become angry and dissatisfied. Hopefully, you can solve your concerns with an open and honest discussion. However, if you still feel dissatisfied or uncomfortable, change health care providers. After all, this is a very special time in your life. You deserve a competent and caring health care provider.

SECOND OPINIONS

Sometimes you don't really need to change physicians, but you'd like a second opinion. There's nothing wrong with that! In fact, most doctors are very supportive of you getting a second opinion. That's because the second opinion often reinforces their own decision making, and these conclusions make you feel more confident and comfortable.

Of course, sometimes you may get a second opinion that does not agree with your original doctor's recommendation. That's fine, too. Remember that differing opinions don't necessarily mean that one person is wrong and the other is right. Very often, the same problem may have several solutions. You may gain additional insight by speaking with another doctor, who can view your situation with fresh eyes.

If you decide to seek a second opinion, first check with your insurance company. Many health insurance companies will pay for you to receive a second opinion, especially if surgery or another invasive procedure is involved. Also, be sure to take copies of your medical records and test results with you.

You've Chosen Your Specialist—Now What?

If you are part of a couple, your partner should be with you during your first visit with the new doctor. In fact, it's best if your partner can accompany you to all of your appointments. That's because fertility is often a couple topic and both of you are involved in this experience.

If you are able, it's best to bring your medical records, test results, and report summaries with you for your new doctor's review. One of the doctor's first priorities will be to evaluate whether you have a fertility problem. The specialist will go over your complete medical history. You will be asked many questions about your medical conditions, gynecological issues, and the nature of your sexual relations. There will be considerable focus on your menstrual cycle, past pregnancies, sexually transmitted disease history, and birth control. You will also be asked about medications that you take, your family medical history, and your personal and lifestyle habits. Your partner may be asked many of these same questions. Just do your best to answer the questions and try to provide as many details as possible.

At the conclusion of your medical history interview, the doctor will perform a complete physical examination and may also order tests and schedule procedures. Be sure to ask if you don't understand or feel unsure about something.

Fertility Testing for Women

Most women will undergo several basic tests and procedures during a fertility evaluation. Depending on your particular medical history and situation, some of these examinations may play a more important role for you than others. In most cases, the fertility tests can be completed within a few menstrual cycles. Certain tests must be done during a specific time of your monthly cycle. Your fertility doctor will most likely ask you to prepare for a few of these tests beforehand. So beware, you may have to do a little preparation and homework!

Following are descriptions of a variety of tests and procedures that you may encounter during your fertility evaluation.

CHECKING FOR INFECTION

Most likely during your first pelvic examination, your specialist will check your cervix for the presence of viral or bacterial infection. This test is typically performed with a cotton swablike device and is not painful. Testing includes evaluation for chlamydia, gonorrhea, ureaplasm urealyticum, and other pathogens.

BLOOD TESTS

You can almost be sure that your fertility specialist will want to sample your blood and check it for various hormones and other factors. Your blood will typically be drawn on day 2, 3, or 4 of your menstrual cycle. Following are some of the more common blood tests that you may encounter:

Hormone Tests

- Follicle-stimulating hormone (FSH) and luteinizing hormone (LH)—provides information about your eggs and their fertility potential
- Progesterone—helps to determine whether ovulation is occurring
- Estradiol—assists in evaluating whether your ovaries will respond to certain fertility drugs
- Prolactin—may indicate presence of a pituitary brain tumor or could be a sign of abnormal thyroid function
- Thyroid testing—may provide information about your overall thyroid function

Infectious Disease Tests

- Human immunodeficiency virus (HIV)
- Hepatitis
- Syphilis
- Rubella (German measles) antibody

Immunologic Tests

- Antiphospholipid antibody (APA)—checks for certain clotting factors in the blood
- Antithyroid antibody (ATA)—if your thyroid levels are abnormal, tests for things that could interfere with thyroid function and normal metabolism
- Antisperm antibody (ASA)—if you've experienced failed fertilization attempts in the past or you're experiencing significant male factor fertility problems, evaluates if your body reacts against sperm

PELVIC ULTRASOUND EXAMINATION

A pelvic ultrasound exam will most likely be performed at some time during your fertility evaluation and treatment. This is an important procedure that uses ultrasonic sound waves to view your internal pelvic organs. It can provide a wealth of information about your uterus, tubes, and ovaries. The ultrasound exam is performed in your doctor's office or in a nearby hospital. The procedure is conducted either by your doctor or a specially trained ultrasound technician.

Ultrasound often plays an important role in both the diagnosis and treatment of infertility issues. For example, ultrasound can diagnose certain potential problems within your pelvis by identifying a mass or cyst. Ultrasound is also used in the treatment of infertility, such as retrieving eggs for in vitro fertilization (a process in which an egg is fertilized in a dish in a laboratory and then placed inside the woman to achieve pregnancy).

Your doctor may also want to get an estimate of how many eggs you have remaining. A good test for this is the antral follicle count (AFC). Antral follicles are tiny saclike structures that surround each egg. The doctor will visualize and measure these follicles within each ovary. For best results, this test must be performed early during your menstrual cycle, typically on day 3 of your cycle. The number of antral follicles found correlates well to the number of viable eggs that remain in your ovaries.

The pelvic ultrasound is almost always performed using a vaginal approach. That's because it allows the doctor to see your internal pelvic organs up close and with great detail and clarity. For this exam, you'll be asked to remove your underwear and recline on the exam table, much as you do for a pelvic or Pap test. You'll have a sheet draped over your lower body for privacy. The lights in the room will be dimmed and a specially shaped vaginal probe transducer will be inserted into your vagina. Prior to insertion, the probe will be covered with a lubricated condom for your safety and comfort. Because the transducer is inside of your vagina and close to your cervix, it is able to transmit clear and detailed images of your uterus, tubes, and ovaries, which are projected on the television-like monitor.

You will experience no pain or discomfort during the vaginal approach pelvic ultrasound. The ultrasound procedure takes between 15 and 30 minutes. Your doctor will have a conversation with you about the ultrasound examination's findings. You can then work together and plan your next step toward becoming pregnant.

BASAL BODY TEMPERATURE (BBT) TEST

Your doctor may request that you keep a basal body temperature (BBT) chart for a few months. The purpose of the BBT test is to determine whether you are ovulating. It's based on the knowledge that after you ovulate, progesterone hormone levels increase within your bloodstream. This increasing progesterone level causes your temperature to rise, at least a little bit.

This is a test that you will do in the privacy of your home. You'll need to buy a special BBT thermometer and chart paper. Your doctor will explain the details of how the test should be performed. After a few months, you'll bring your temperature charts with you to your doctor and together will discuss what they mean. See Chapter 5 for more details.

OVULATION PREDICTOR TEST

Sometimes, instead of the BBT just discussed, your doctor will recommend that you use a home ovulation predictor test. Like the BBT, the purpose of this test is to determine whether you are ovulating. It's based on the knowledge that luteinizing hormone (LH) reaches a high level in your urine about 24 to 36 hours prior to ovulation. This urine dipstick test picks up that increase in LH in your urine, as you are about to ovulate.

Like the BBT, this is a test that you'll do in the privacy of your home. Ovulation predictor kits may be easier and more accurate than the BBT, but they are also considerably more expensive. See Chapter 5 for more details.

ENDOMETRIAL BIOPSY

If your doctor recommends an endometrial biopsy, that means that he or she wants to obtain a small sample of lining (endometrium) inside your uterus. During a fertility evaluation, the purpose of this test is to determine if and when ovulation has occurred.

Typically, the endometrial biopsy is performed just a few days prior to the start of your next menstrual period. It is assumed that at that time, ovulation has already occurred and progesterone levels should be adequate within the uterus.

The endometrial biopsy is almost always performed in your doctor's office. For the procedure itself, you will be placed in a position very similar to when you are having a Pap test performed. The doctor then inserts a thin plastic strawlike tube through your cervix and into the uterus to obtain a piece of the uterine lining. You may experience some discomfort and cramping during the procedure. You may also have some slight spotting for a few days afterward.

The endometrial sample tissue is sent to the laboratory, where it is examined under the microscope. The examining pathologist will closely look at the tissue and see what progesterone effects it may or may not have. The examiner will be able to determine if ovulation occurred earlier that month. If adequate amounts of progesterone are present, then ovulation has likely occurred. It implies that your uterine lining should be capable of properly implanting a fertilized egg. However, if progesterone changes within the uterine lining are not adequate, it's concluded that your uterus cannot properly prepare for egg implantation. In many cases, the pathologist can even pinpoint the exact day that ovulation occurred just by examining progesterone's effects on the tissue.

Your endometrial biopsy results will provide information about your ovulation, progesterone levels within your uterus, and also the exact timing of your particular menstrual cycle.

HYSTEROSALPINGOGRAM (HSG)

The purpose of the HSG is to check for obstructions or growths within your uterus and fallopian tubes. Conditions such as blocked fallopian tubes, fibroids, and adhesions may be diagnosed during the HSG procedure. Your doctor may recommend that you undergo an HSG if he or she suspects that you have an abnormality within your uterus or fallopian tubes.

The HSG is performed shortly after you have completed your monthly period bleeding. The procedure is usually carried out in a hospital or an outpatient setting where x-ray equipment is available. Some large and well-equipped fertility offices may have this equipment on-site. For the procedure itself, you are placed in the same position as for a Pap test. The doctor places a thin tube into your vagina and threads it up into your cervix. A fluid dye is injected through the tubing while an x-ray of your pelvis is performed. X-ray images follow the contours of your pelvic organs as the dye fills your uterus and up into your fallopian tubes.

You may experience discomfort and cramping during the procedure, so you may wish to take pain medication in advance.

After the HSG, you may have minor cramps and discomfort for a few days. It is also normal to have slight vaginal discharge. Your doctor may recommend that you continue pain medication to minimize your discomfort. You may also be given a prescription for antibiotics, if your medical history indicates that you are at increased risk for infection. The antibiotics are a preventive measure to reduce the chance of developing a pelvic infection from the HSG procedure itself. Risks and complications with the HSG procedure are rare. However, be sure to call your doctor if you experience heavy bleeding or extreme discomfort or cramping pain.

Your doctor will discuss your HSG test results with you. If uterine fibroids are noted, they may or may not require treatment, depending on their size and position within your uterus. Blocked fallopian tubes are a fairly common finding among infertility patients. It has been estimated that almost 35 percent of infertility cases are due to blockage of one or both fallopian tubes. If this is your situation, your doctor will discuss treatment options. (See Chapter 1 for more information.)

A shortcoming of the HSG procedure is that it may not detect small lesions such as small polyps or fibroids within the uterus. It also does not provide any information whatsoever regarding the ovaries. On the positive side, a 2002 New Zealand study conducted at the University of Auckland showed an increase in conception rate in the months following the HSG procedure. This is thought to be due to the fluid dye pumped through the uterus and fallopian tubes during the HSG. This flushing of fluid may open and clear the passageway for the sperm and the egg to pass through and move about more easily.

HYSTEROSCOPY

Your doctor may recommend a hysteroscopy procedure to evaluate if you could have an abnormality within your uterus. The hysteroscope is a thin telescope-like instrument that is inserted through your vagina and cervix and then into your uterus.

This procedure provides the doctor with a way to view inside of your uterus and make a certain diagnosis. Sometimes, hysteroscopy is done in conjunction with a laparoscopy procedure (see below for discussion of laparoscopy).

The hysteroscopy procedure has many uses. When it comes to fertility evaluation, this procedure is often performed to evaluate a defect in the shape or size of the uterus. For example, if the patient has a septate uterus, the hysteroscopy may be able to diagnose this condition and also remove the membrane at the same time. The procedure may also be used to diagnose the presence of fibroids, polyps, or adhesions. These lesions might be missed during the HSG procedure (discussed previously); thus the hysteroscopy provides another way to detect uterine abnormalities. In some cases, these abnormalities can be surgically corrected during the same hysteroscopy procedure, if you are comfortable and under anesthesia.

Hysteroscopy may be performed in the doctor's office or in an operating room. For the procedure itself, your cervix will be dilated slightly to permit the hysteroscope to pass through. Then the thin hysteroscope will be inserted through your vagina and cervix and up inside of your uterus. A harmless liquid or gas may be passed through the hysteroscope to expand your uterus for optimal viewing. If surgery is required, small thin instruments are passed through the hysteroscope. You may experience some discomfort and cramping during the procedure. Depending on the situation, you and your doctor may decide that you will need anesthesia.

Hysteroscopy is considered a relatively safe procedure. There is a small chance of injury to the cervix or uterus, infection or bleeding, or side effects from anesthesia. However, overall these problems are quite rare.

After the hysteroscopy, you may feel some discomfort or cramping. You may also experience slight vaginal bleeding. Be sure to contact your doctor if you notice fever, severe abdominal pain, or heavy vaginal bleeding.

LAPAROSCOPY

At some point during your fertility evaluation, your doctor may recommend a laparoscopy. The laparoscope is a slender telescope-like device with a lens at one end and a fiber-optic light source at the other end. The laparoscope is inserted through a small incision in your abdomen and then into your abdominal/pelvic cavity. This surgical procedure is performed when the doctor needs to take a direct look into your abdomen and see your reproductive organs. Depending on the circumstance, your doctor may be able to treat the medical condition during the same procedure. Sometimes laparoscopy is done in conjunction with a hysteroscopy procedure.

The laparoscopy procedure has many uses. By viewing your organs directly, your fertility specialist may be able to diagnose such conditions as endometriosis, scarring and adhesions, fibroids, ovarian cysts, and blocked fallopian tubes.

For the laparoscopy itself, you will likely be scheduled at an outpatient surgical center. In most cases, you will be given general anesthesia so that you will be asleep during the procedure. Once you are asleep, the doctor will make a small incision inside or near your navel. Then a slender tubing will be placed and nontoxic gas will be advanced into your abdomen. The gas swells your abdomen so your internal organs can be seen clearly. The laparoscope is then placed through the incision for viewing of your organs. In most cases, several other small incisions are made within your lower abdomen. These small incisions are used for additional surgical instruments (such as scissors, laser, or clamps) during the procedure. The laparoscopic images are projected onto a television-like monitor. This allows for easier viewing by the surgeon. Also, these images may be photographed so that you can see them later. At the conclusion of the laparoscopic procedure, the instruments are removed and the gas is released from your abdomen. The small incisions are closed with sutures. You wake up shortly thereafter in the recovery room. In most cases, you can go home in a few hours.

Risks associated with laparoscopy are few, but it's wise to remember that it is a surgical procedure. There is some chance of bleeding, general anesthesia reaction, or injury to your internal organs. The most common internal organs that might be injured during a laparoscopy would be your bowels or bladder. Such injuries are rare but may be serious and could involve additional surgical repair and hospitalization.

After your laparoscopy, you may experience a mild amount of nausea, scant vaginal bleeding, and abdominal discomfort. These are all fairly common and normal symptoms following a laparoscopy. However, be sure to call your doctor if you experience fever, extreme discomfort, or inability to urinate.

Fertility Testing for Men

Fertility specialists usually prefer to work with both partners. Therefore, no matter what your female fertility testing indicates, most men will also be evaluated for their own fertility. A key difference, however, is that if the male partner requires surgical treatment, he will probably be referred to a urologist (a doctor who specializes in the urinary tract).

It's not surprising to discover that male fertility testing is typically much simpler and straightforward than a woman's. Part of that is because most of the male reproductive organs are located outside of the body. Another component is that male hormones are usually steadier and not subject to the monthly cyclic changes that women undergo.

During your first appointment, the fertility specialist will ask you and your partner about your medical conditions, medications, lifestyle choices, and family history. Focus may be placed on identifying certain fertility risk factors, such as a history of mumps, undescended testicles, STD infections, urological surgery, or exposure to toxins.

Additionally, most men will undergo several basic tests and procedures during a fertility evaluation. Some of these tests and procedures may not be indicated for your situation at all.

Following are descriptions of a variety of tests and procedures that you may encounter during your fertility evaluation.

BLOOD TESTS

Some of the more common factors that may be evaluated with your blood sample are:

Hormone Tests

- Testosterone—primary male hormone, directly linked to sex drive and function
- Follicle-stimulating hormone (FSH) and luteinizing hormone (LH)—both play a key role in sperm production
- Prolactin—may indicate presence of a pituitary brain tumor or could be a sign of abnormal thyroid function

Infectious Disease Tests

- Human immunodeficiency virus (HIV)
- Hepatitis
- Syphilis

INFECTION TESTS ON SEMEN

Certain viruses and bacteria can lead to infertility. Therefore, doctors will check for their presence in both partners. Some of the infection testing is done by evaluating a blood sample (see preceding). Other testing involves evaluating a semen sample.

The semen will be checked for the presence of white blood cells. If a large number of white blood cells are present, this may indicate an infection. The semen may also be tested for specific bacteria and viruses. Following are the key infections typically checked during a basic fertility evaluation of semen:

- Chlamydia
- Gonorrhea
- Ureaplasm urealyticum

URINE ANALYSIS

A urine sample and analysis can provide the fertility specialist with additional information. The urine is checked for the presence of bacteria and also for the presence of white blood cells. White blood cells may indicate an infection either within the urinary tract or the prostate gland. If infection is suspected, more tests will be performed and treatment given.

The urine is also checked for the presence of sperm. A high concentration of sperm in the urine may indicate retrograde ejaculation. Retrograde ejaculation, where sperm go backward into the bladder instead of moving forward into the penis, is a fairly common condition. If retrograde ejaculation is found, treatment is available.

SEMEN ANALYSIS

Performing a complete analysis of the semen is a major part of the male fertility assessment. This test checks for both the quality and quantity of sperm. The semen sample is obtained by the male partner performing masturbation. In some cases, the sample may be obtained at home. In other situations, the semen sample must be obtained at the clinic or laboratory.

Many fertility specialists recommend that the male partner refrain from sexual activity for at least three days prior to this test. That's because this is a reasonable amount of time to accurately evaluate an average sperm sample. However, because sperm counts and quality can vary, this test will likely be performed on several different occasions over the next few months.

Once the semen sample is obtained, it is analyzed in the laboratory. The semen sample is typically evaluated under a microscope and/or by computerized evaluation. The key features studied are:

- Volume—the amount of semen per ejaculation
- Thickness (viscosity)—the consistency of the semen

- Quantity (concentration)—the number of sperm present in the semen
- Shape (morphology)—the percentage of normally shaped sperm
- Movement (motility)—the ability of the sperm to travel and move forward properly

Volume

The total volume of semen per ejaculation is normally about one-half to one teaspoon. In scientific terms, that translates to about two milliliters. However, normal volume is considered one to six and a half milliliters per ejaculation. Higher or lower volumes may be associated with fertility problems.

However, the actual volume of semen does not necessarily correlate with the quantity of the sperm. Some men have low ejaculate volumes but high sperm count. Others may have high ejaculate volumes and low sperm count.

A low volume may mean that the semen does not contain all of the normal components of normal semen or may indicate a low testosterone level. A very high volume of semen may indicate an infection.

Some men do not have any semen at all. This may be due to retrograde ejaculation, where the sperm go backward into the bladder. It may also be related to a medical condition such as diabetes, prior surgery, or certain medications.

Thickness

The semen analysis takes a look at the thickness of the semen and the time it takes to liquefy. At the time of ejaculation, normal semen is a thick gel. Semen typically becomes a liquid within 20 minutes after ejaculation. This test measures the time for the semen sample to liquefy. If it takes longer than 60 minutes, this is abnormal and may be a sign of infection or other problems.

If the semen appears clumpy, this may indicate that a problem exists in the prostate gland. That's because the prostate gland is supposed to provide enzymes that cause the ejaculate to liquefy. On the other hand, if the semen appears runny, a problem may exist in the seminal vesicles. The seminal vesicles contribute proteins that cause the ejaculate to coagulate.

Quantity

One of the main components of a semen analysis is to count the number of sperm produced in the sample. The sperm count is estimated by careful analysis under a laboratory microscope. Normally, a fertile male ejaculates about 60 million or more sperm per milliliter. Although laboratory values may vary, most labs consider 20 to 150 million sperm per milliliter to be within the normal range.

There can be variations among sperm count even for the same person. Outside factors, such as a cold or flu, extreme stress, or another medical condition, may adversely affect a man's sperm count.

Upon occasion, some men may register a zero for sperm count. If this occurs, further testing is needed. Typically, the next test is checking the semen for the presence of a sugar called fructose. During normal sperm production, fructose is added to the semen by the epididymis. Therefore, if fructose is not present, there may be a blockage along the male's reproductive tract that is preventing the sperm from getting into the ejaculate. If fructose is present in the semen, this suggests that there may be a problem in the testicles' ability to manufacture sperm.

Even if the sperm count is normal, the sperm is not necessarily of good quality. For that, the semen analysis evaluates the shape and movement of the sperm.

Shape

A sperm that is shaped normally is more likely to fertilize the egg than one with a structural abnormality. It is considered a good sign of fertility to have at least 60 percent normally shaped sperm in a semen sample.

It's perfectly normal to have some abnormally shaped sperm in every semen sample. Sperm can be abnormally shaped in several ways, such as having two heads, two tails, a short tail, a tiny head (pinhead), or a round (instead of oval) shaped head. Abnormal sperm typically cannot move normally or penetrate an egg.

Movement

Another important component of the semen analysis is the study of how sperm move. The speed and direction of the sperm affect its ability to reach and then penetrate an egg. Under normal circumstances, sperm that have good motility can move through a woman's reproductive tract at the rate of two inches per hour. It is considered normal for at least 50 percent of the ejaculated sperm to demonstrate normal forward movement.

If a high percentage of sperm cannot "swim," or move forward, through the cervical mucus and female reproductive tract to reach an egg, then the man's fertility is likely impaired.

OTHER TESTS FOR SPERM

In addition to the basic semen analysis just discussed, sometimes additional tests for sperm are conducted. Depending on your circumstances, some of these tests may be performed on a sperm sample.

Sperm Chromatin Structure Assay

In recent years, medical research has shown that certain abnormalities found within the sperm's DNA can lead to infertility. In such cases, even a man with completely normal standard semen analysis may not be able to bring about pregnancy. That's because the sperm with the abnormal DNA is not able to fertilize the egg.

DNA damage may be found in sperm from both fertile and infertile men. Therefore, further investigation is required if this test is abnormal. Some causes of abnormal sperm DNA may be cancer treatments (radiation or chemotherapy) or varicocele (a group of dilated veins in the scrotum). Although rare, the sperm DNA may spontaneously revert back to normal. Other times, surgical or medical treatment is effective in returning the sperm DNA to normal.

Computerized Analysis of Sperm Motion

The computerized assisted analysis of sperm motion helps the fertility specialist show a relationship between sperm motility and fertility. This method of measuring sperm movement and speed is more precise than the basic evaluation done during a semen analysis.

This test is performed with a video camera connected to a microscope. The data is projected onto a TV-like monitor screen and then transferred to a computer especially programmed to analyze sperm motion. The computer indicates the sperm speed and also how straight the sperm move.

The sperm are rated on a grading system ranging from 1 to 4. Grade 1 sperm tend to wiggle in place without making forward progression. These are unlikely to have the capability to fertilize an egg. Grade 4 sperm tend to move quickly and in a very straight line. They are much more likely to successfully fertilize an egg. Many labs state that the sperm motion must average about 2+ to possess good fertility potential.

Hamster Test

The hamster test is a test of the sperm's ability to penetrate hamster eggs. This test may be recommended when the male partner has a normal semen analysis and the woman has no obvious fertility problem, but pregnancy is still not occurring.

Using special enzymes, the laboratory technician must first remove the special outer coating on the hamster eggs. The special coating is present to prevent animals other than hamsters from fertilizing the hamster egg. After the coating is removed, the sperm are mixed with the hamster eggs. The eggs are then examined to see how many of them have been penetrated by the sperm. Failure to penetrate a certain percentage of eggs may indicate male infertility and require other testing.

This test may be performed prior to IVF to see if that technology will be successful for the couple. Essentially, the hamster test is a trial run of IVF but uses hamster eggs instead of a woman's.

The hamster test has about a 90 percent accuracy rate. However, a potential drawback is that it may have to be performed several times to give the most accurate results. In addition, this test is quite expensive.

Antisperm Antibody (ASA)

For various reasons, a man may develop antibodies against his own sperm. If this occurs, antisperm antibodies attach themselves to the sperm's surface. This condition can adversely affect the sperm's movement and ability to fertilize an egg.

There are theories as to why sperm antibodies occur. It is believed that men can only produce antibodies against sperm when their sperm come into contact with their own blood. This may happen with an injury or during a surgery, such as a vasectomy.

Sperm antibodies can be measured either in the man's semen or from a blood sample.

TESTICULAR SPERM EXTRACTION (TESE) AND TESTICULAR SPERM ASPIRATION (TESA)

Sometimes your fertility specialist may recommend a special type of testicular biopsy. This procedure may be advised when the male partner has a completely normal physical examination but is not producing sperm.

For this test, tiny pieces of each testicle are surgically removed and evaluated. The scrotal area is numbed with local anesthesia. Then hair-thin samples of testicular tissue are removed with a needle. Using a microscope, the pathologist is able to identify sperm in various stages of development. Sperm are removed from the tissue for further evaluation.

Following are two similar but slightly different variations of this test:

- Testicular sperm extraction (TESE)—sperm is extracted from the tissue
- Testicular sperm aspiration (TESA)—sperm is aspirated from the sperm duct

TESE/TESA can be used to provide viable sperm for use during IVF. Sperm from men who have suffered past injury or sperm duct blockage can be obtained and used to father a child through IVF. Viable sperm can also be obtained from men who have undergone prior vasectomies, without reversing the vasectomy itself.

This procedure is typically performed on an outpatient basis. The entire procedure takes less than 30 minutes. No stitches are required. The procedure is considered safe and almost pain free. The man is usually able to return to work and his regular routine within a day or so.

VASOGRAM

A vasogram is a special x-ray study of the vas deferens. Recall that the vas deferentia are sperm ducts. They transport the mature sperm from the epididymis to the pelvic cavity and eventually into the ejaculatory ducts.

Your fertility specialist may recommend a vasogram if a blockage along the male reproductive tract is suspected. Even if an obstruction has already been diagnosed by another method, a vasogram can still be useful. That's because a vasogram can pinpoint the exact location of the blockage and assist in corrective surgery.

For the procedure itself, the doctor cuts a small incision into the scrotum and exposes the vas deferens. A special contrast dye is then injected into the vas deferens and x-rays are taken. The procedure is considered safe, quick, and relatively pain free. It is performed in the x-ray department of a clinic or hospital. In almost all cases, you can go home immediately following the procedure.

Conclusion

Getting tested for fertility problems is difficult enough. It's tough from an emotional point of view and certainly uncomfortable from a physical standpoint. And heaven knows, it's no treat from a financial perspective. That's why this chapter is dedicated to helping you understand the various fertility tests that may be offered to you. You'll be able to play a more informed and active role in your own health care decision making if you understand how a test works and what the test results mean.

It's also important for you to understand how to go about selecting your fertility specialist. Sometimes the world of medicine seems shrouded in secrecy. This chapter aims to open those doors and provide you with guidelines for finding the best fertility specialist for your situation. This is a very special yet complicated time in your life, and you deserve the very best doctor to help you through it.

Summary

Here is a summary of the important concepts discussed during this chapter.

Selecting Your Doctor

- OB/GYN doctors are physicians who graduated from medical school and then did a four-year residency specializing in women's health.
- A fertility specialist is a reproductive endocrinologist—they have the same training as the OB/GYN doctor plus an additional two to three years of fertility and reproductive fellowship training.

Fertility Testing for Women

- Most women will undergo various basic tests and procedures during a fertility evaluation. Your fertility specialist will work with you and decide which ones are appropriate for you.
- Tests for women:
  - Checking for infection
  - Blood tests—hormones, infection, immunologic
  - Pelvic ultrasound examination
  - Basal body temperature (BBT)
  - Ovulation predictor test
  - Endometrial biopsy
  - Hysterosalpingogram (HSG)
  - Hysteroscopy
  - Laparoscopy

Fertility Testing for Men

- Fertility specialists usually prefer to work with both of you as a couple. Therefore, no matter what your female fertility testing indicates, most men will also be evaluated for their own fertility.
- If the male partner is found to require a surgical procedure, he will most likely be referred to a urologist for treatment.
- Tests for men:
  - Blood tests—hormones, infection
  - Infection tests on semen

- Urine analysis
- Semen analysis—volume, thickness, quantity, shape, movement
- Other specialized testing for sperm
- Testicular sperm extraction (TESE) or testicular sperm aspiration (TESA)
- Vasogram

CHAPTER 5

Natural Ways to Become Pregnant

If you are like most people reading this book, you really want to have a baby. And at some point, you feel like you might try almost anything to become pregnant and bring home a healthy baby. That's perfectly normal. But before embarking on lots of uncomfortable and expensive procedures, doesn't it make sense to first try to maximize your fertility naturally? This situation doesn't apply to all women, for various personal reasons. However, most women prefer to try a natural approach to fertility, at least initially. This chapter discusses multiple ways to boost your fertility and maximize your chances to conceive naturally.

This natural approach to fertility has been very successful. It is particularly useful among women and men who have been diagnosed with unexplained fertility concerns. A British study conducted by the University of Surrey examined a group of couples with a prior history of infertility. These men and women made healthful changes in lifestyle and diet and took nutritional supplements and ended up achieving an 80 percent fertility success rate.

You and your partner should consult with your doctor several months before conceiving. Discuss any habits or lifestyle issues that may adversely affect your fertility. Also, if you have any type of medical condition, assure that is properly treated and that you are on pregnancy-safe medications.

Another consideration is prepregnancy vaccinations. Women who are not immune to chicken pox or rubella should receive vaccination for these ailments prior to becoming pregnant. By following these important steps several months prior to becoming pregnant, you'll rest assured that you have done the most to boost your natural fertility and increase your chances for a normal, healthy pregnancy.

Diet and Nutrition

Just about everyone has heard that a well-balanced nutritional diet is important as you prepare for pregnancy. Good nutrition adds to your overall health and may also help you to conceive. A well-balanced diet helps to regulate your hormones and nourish your reproductive system. Nobody expects you to eat perfectly all of the time; just do your best to optimize your fertility.

How many calories a woman needs depends on several factors, such as your body type, general health, and level of physical activity. According to the American College of Obstetricians and Gynecologists (ACOG), the average woman needs about 2,200 calories per day. Once you become pregnant, you need approximately 300 more calories each day to stay healthy and help the fetus grow.

Choose your foods wisely to ensure that you receive the best possible vitamins and minerals from natural whole foods. The food guide pyramid shown here is a guide provided by the U.S. Department of Agriculture and the U.S. Department of Health and Human Services. It has been designed to help nonpregnant women and men make nutritional food choices.

The Food Guide Pyramid

Fats, oils, and sweets—use sparingly

Milk, yogurt, and cheese group—2–3 servings daily (1 serving is 1 cup [236 ml] of milk or yogurt; 1 ½ ounces [43 gm] of natural cheese; or 2 ounces [57 gm] of processed cheese.)

Meat, poultry, fish, dried beans, eggs, and nuts group—2–3 servings daily (1 serving is 2–3 ounces [57–85 gm] of cooked lean meat, poultry, or fish; for other foods in this group, 1 ounce [28 gm] of meat = ½ cup [118 ml] of cooked dried beans = 1 egg = 2 tablespoons [30 ml] of peanut butter.)

Vegetable group—3–5 servings daily (1 serving is 1 cup [236 ml] raw, leafy vegetables; ½ cup [118 ml] of other cooked or raw vegetables; or ¾ cup [177 ml] of vegetable juice.)

Fruit group—2–4 servings daily (1 serving is 1 medium apple, banana, or orange; ½ cup [118 ml] of cooked or canned fruit; or ¾ cup [177 ml] of fruit juice.)

Bread, cereal, rice, and pasta group—6–11 servings daily (1 serving is 1 slice of bread; 1 ounce [28 gm] of cereal; or ½ cup [118 ml] of cooked cereal, rice, or pasta.)

[Note: metric conversions are estimates.]

There are additional tips you may wish to try in your diet to increase your reproductive health and your chances of conceiving. Some naturopathic practitioners recommend alkaline foods such as bean sprouts, peas, and milk. They also say to avoid acidic foods such as red meat and tea because they may further increase the acidity found in your cervical mucus, which could inhibit sperm. Proper hydration is also important. Try to drink at least 48 ounces of water each day.

Many practitioners recommend that you increase your intake of foods containing essential fatty acids. Examples are seeds, beans, nuts, and oily fish. Medical research has shown that essential fatty acids stimulate the production of reproductive hormones in both men and women.

Pumpkin seeds have been shown to benefit the reproductive health of both men and women. That's because they contain high levels of zinc, which is important for healthy reproductive organs.

You should avoid a few things when trying to become pregnant and also after you have become pregnant. A major concern is raw or undercooked fish, meat, and poultry, because of their potential to cause bacterial infection. It's also best to avoid fruits and vegetables that have been treated with potentially toxic chemical pesticides. Therefore, organically grown produce is usually considered a better choice.

Remember that a well-balanced and nutritional diet will help maximize your fertility. Does that mean you can't enjoy an occasional pizza or little piece of chocolate? Of course not! Just be sensible and do your best. If you have questions or concerns about calorie needs and specific diet recommendations, be sure to talk with your doctor.

Healthy Weight

Don't you just hate to get weighed at the doctor's office? It can be a humiliating and embarrassing experience for many women, me included. The truth is that most doctors don't really care about your exact weight. No one expects you to look like a skinny super model or movie star. However, your health care provider does want you to be at a reasonable and healthy weight. Before you become pregnant, you should try to be at a healthy weight. Being at a healthy weight makes it easier for you to conceive, because your metabolism and hormones are more likely to be in the proper balance.

So what defines a healthy weight? Most health care professionals use the body mass index (BMI) as a reliable indicator of body fat. The BMI is a way of correlating your body weight to your height. (A mathematical formula divides your weight in kilograms by your height in meters squared.) Table 5.1 summarizes what you need to know about BMI. Find your height along the left column, and then find your current weight in that same row. Then look up at the top of Table 5.1 to determine your BMI category.

Table 5.1. Body Mass Index Table

Height	Below 18.5: Underweight	18.5 to 24.9: Normal Weight Range	25 to 29.9: Overweight	30 or Higher: Obese
5' 2"	100 lb or less	101 to 135 lb	136 to 163 lb	164 lb or more
157.5 cm	45 kg or less	46 to 61 kg	62 to 73 kg	74 kg or more
5' 3"	104 lb or less	105 to 140 lb	141 to 168 lb	169 lb or more
160 cm	47 kg or less	48 kg to 63 kg	64 kg to 76 kg	77 kg or more
5' 4"	107 lb or less	108 to 144 lb	145 to 173 lb	174 lb or more
162.6 cm	48 kg or less	49 kg to 65 kg	66 kg to 78 kg	79 kg or more
5' 5"	110 lb or less	111 to 149 lb	150 to 179 lb	180 lb or more
165.1 cm	50 kg or less	51 kg to 67 kg	68 kg to 81 kg	82 kg or more
5' 6"	114 lb or less	115 to 154 lb	155 to 185 lb	186 lb or more
167.6 cm	51 kg or less	52 kg to 70 kg	71 kg to 83 kg	84 kg or more
5' 7"	117 lb or less	118 to 158 lb	159 to 190 lb	191 lb or more
170.2 cm	53 kg or less	54 kg to 71 kg	72 kg to 86 kg	87 kg or more
5' 8"	121 lb or less	122 to 163 lb	164 to 196 lb	197 lb or more
172.7 cm	55 kg or less	55 kg to 74 kg	74 kg to 89 kg	89 kg or more
5' 9"	124 lb or less	125 to 168 lb	169 to 202 lb	203 lb or more
175.3 cm	56 kg or less	57 kg to 76 kg	77 kg to 91 kg	92 kg or more
5' 10"	128 lb or less	129 to 173 lb	174 to 208 lb	209 lb or more
177.8 cm	58 kg or less	59 kg to 78 kg	79 kg to 94 kg	95 kg or more

[Note: metric conversions are estimates.]

According to the American Society for Reproductive Medicine, your best chance of conceiving is when your BMI is in the normal category. Women who are below or above their ideal healthy weight are more likely to encounter difficulties becoming pregnant. That's because your reproductive hormones levels are affected by your amount of body fat.

You've probably heard of women that are extremely thin and perhaps marathon runners or ballet dancers who do not have menstrual periods. That's because their level of body fat is so low, their reproductive hormones cannot function well enough to ovulate. According to a 2002 report by Dr. Rose Frisch published by the University of Chicago Press, a woman needs a minimum BMI of 18 to ovulate and increases her chances of becoming pregnant if she adds a few pounds and boosts her BMI to 19.

On the other end of the spectrum, women with too much body fat may also experience fertility problems. Excess body fat increases the production of estrogen, an important reproductive hormone. Too much estrogen can throw the menstrual cycle out of balance and may stop ovulation. The same report just mentioned concluded that a BMI higher than 25 is associated with slightly reduced fertility and a BMI higher than 27 puts the woman at risk of significantly reduced fertility. The conclusion coincides with what most fertility specialists already say—and that's to keep your BMI in the healthy midrange of about 19 to 25 to have the best chance of becoming pregnant.

If your BMI indicates that you are in the underweight, overweight, or obese category, talk with your doctor about a healthy program to get you within the normal range. Being at a healthy weight not only makes conceiving easier, it also makes for a healthier pregnancy.

Keeping Fit

Moderate exercise is an important component of your general good health. Along with a well-balanced diet, a reasonable exercise program may increase your chances of conceiving. It may also allow you to enjoy a more comfortable and healthful pregnancy.

It's always advisable to discuss your plans with your doctor before beginning any exercise program. That's because your current physical conditioning and activity level will play a role in your choice of exercise and the intensity of your exercise program. In most situations, even the most out-of-shape woman can begin a light, sensible exercise plan during the preconception period. In most cases, you can continue the exercise regimen once you become pregnant.

Exercises that are considered ideal for pregnancy include walking, swimming, and pregnancy yoga. Certainly, pregnancy is not the time to partake in rigorous sports, such as skiing, skating, or horseback riding. That's because you'll want to avoid potential injuries that could result from high-impact, jumpy, jarring motions.

Moderate exercise is a good way to naturally boost your fertility. Exercise helps to burn off excess body fat and allows hormones to reach a proper hormonal balance. When done just a few times per week, pregnancy-friendly exercises can help you better control your weight and prepare for the physical demands of childbirth. But be careful and don't overdo it! Too much exercising may reduce your body fat, cause your hormones to get out of whack, and actually impair your fertility.

Reduce Your Stress

De-stressing your life is easier said than done. The emotional stress of family, work, and daily chores can be taxing on anyone. When you add fertility issues into the mix, your stress levels may go off the charts.

Stress may be the cause of migraine headaches, backaches, ulcers, and a host of other common physical ailments. Is it any wonder that stress might also interfere with the reproductive process? Stress can cause you to stop ovulating and your menstrual periods to become irregular.

Recognize stress for what it is. One of the best things that you can do for yourself is to release that burden. Reducing the stress in your life can improve your overall general health and well-being. De-stressing can even greatly boost your fertility.

Hard scientific data is lacking, but some clinics in the United States claim to have increased fertility rates with meditation, yoga, visualization, and relaxation techniques. We may not completely understand how it works, but many health care providers believe that an important mind and body connection exists. Why not try it out and reap the benefits? You may want to enroll in a yoga or meditation class. Perhaps you could try something as simple as a deep breathing relaxation exercise each day. Some women find comfort in quiet time and prayer. Other women enjoy the interaction of a support group or learn stress-management techniques from a trained counselor.

Whatever you choose, reducing the stress in your life will undoubtedly improve your quality of life. And it just may boost your fertility as well.

Vitamins and Nutrients

Just about everyone knows about the importance of taking a daily prenatal vitamin. But did you know it's best to begin taking them even before you become pregnant? A good prenatal vitamin can supply you with important nutrients and increase your chance of conceiving. Even the best and most well-balanced diet in the world cannot contain all of the essential nutrients. That's why you should take a good prenatal vitamin, even when you are just starting to consider becoming pregnant. For those of you who have difficulty swallowing pills, chewable and liquid forms of prenatal vitamins are available. Talk with your pharmacist or doctor.

Men, too, should practice good nutrition with important vitamins and minerals. If your partner is agreeable, he can take a prenatal vitamin each day also. Contrary to old wives' tales, prenatal vitamins do not contain any type of hormone and will not cause your male partner to become feminine-like. If he prefers, he may want to try one of the many general multivitamins available as a supplement to a well-balanced diet.

Nutritionists have concluded that even slight vitamin and mineral deficiencies may interfere with egg and sperm production or lead to miscarriage. Therefore, both women and men should supplement their diets with these important nutrients.

It may take several months of vitamin supplementation before you notice a change in your general health or boost in your fertility. A woman should continue on her healthy diet and vitamins even after becoming pregnant. Men with fertility issues should have their sperm count rechecked about three to six months after beginning a well-balanced diet and vitamin program.

VITAMIN A

Prenatal vitamins typically contain vitamin A because it offers important health benefits for you and also your developing fetus. Vitamin A contains important anti-oxidants to fight toxins. It's also important in the development and maintenance of healthy eyes and vision. You probably remember your mother telling you to eat carrots so you would have good eyesight. That's because of vitamin A. In fact, prenatal vitamins contain the vegetable form of vitamin A, called beta-carotene. This is a healthy form of vitamin A and does not carry any known risks.

That's not the case for the animal form of vitamin A, known as retinol. It has been found that retinol can cause birth defects if taken in excessive amounts, more than 10,000 IU a day. Certainly, retinol is not recommended for use by pregnant women or those soon to become pregnant, and it is not typically used in prenatal vitamins.

It's easy to see the controversy and confusion surrounding the vitamin A issue. In fact, some health care providers have even gone so far as to advise against any vitamin A for pregnant women or those wishing to become pregnant. That is simply not good advice. Just remember that the vegetable form (beta-carotene) is healthy and useful to you and baby. But be sure to avoid the animal form of vitamin A, retinol.

VITAMIN B

The B vitamins are actually a group of eight separate vitamins that have been grouped together and called vitamin B-complex. Here is a list of the individual vitamins that form vitamin B-complex:

- B_1 (thiamine)
- B_2 (riboflavin)
- B_3 (niacin)
- B_6 (pyridoxine)
- B_9 (folic acid)
- B_{12} (cyanocobalamin)
- Pantothenic acid
- Biotin

The B vitamins are important for maintaining a healthy central nervous system and producing the genetic material DNA. The B vitamins also help in the movement and general function of your digestive tract. Numerous studies were conducted during the late 1980s examining the role of the B vitamins and proper hormone balance, especially progesterone levels. Most of these studies focused upon premenstrual syndrome (PMS) symptoms. The studies resulted in mixed results with some concluding that the B vitamins raised progesterone levels and helped PMS symptoms, whereas other studies found no effect. Even so, some health care providers today believe that vitamin B_6 may raise progesterone levels in women with irregular or absent menstrual periods and thereby increase their fertility. B_6 may also play a role in men's hormonal functioning. Additionally, vitamin B_{12} has been found to improve some men's low sperm counts.

Of all the members of the B-complex vitamins, folic acid receives most of the attention when it comes to pregnancy. That's because folic acid has been shown to reduce the risk of spina bifida and other neural tube birth defects in your baby. However, for folic acid to be most effective, you must be taking it before you become pregnant and continue during pregnancy. Because of this, the U.S. Public Health Service suggests that all women of child-bearing age take 400 mcg of folic acid each day. Folic acid is almost always included in your prenatal vitamins and is typically in 1 mg (1,000 mcg) dosage.

VITAMIN C

Vitamin C is important for both men and women. Many fertility specialists believe that your fertility may be decreased if you are deficient in vitamin C. This may be especially the case for people who smoke.

For women, vitamin C supplementation seems to play a role in the ovulation process. However, women should avoid extremely large doses of vitamin C because it has been shown to dry up cervical mucus and thereby prevent sperm from reaching the egg. Therefore, the recommended dose of vitamin C for women is limited to that in your prenatal vitamin and your well-balanced diet.

In men, vitamin C has been shown to help prevent abnormal sperm and also boost sperm mobility. A 2006 clinical Dubai study published in the *Journal of Medicinal Food* followed men who took 1,000 mg of vitamin C twice daily for two months. Results showed that they experienced significant increases in sperm count, sperm motility, and sperm shape. Although more research is needed to be conclusively proven, vitamin C supplementation may be beneficial for a man with fertility issues.

VITAMIN E

The benefits of vitamin E extend to both women and men. In fact, vitamin E is sometimes referred to as the antisterility vitamin because it has been linked to increased fertility in both sexes. Vitamin E appears to play an important role in reproductive function and helps to stabilize hormone production.

Increased production of cervical mucus in women can also be a benefit of taking vitamin E.

Among men, vitamin E may boost sperm quality. In one Israeli study published by Fertility Sterility in 1996, men who took 200 mg of vitamin E daily were able to dramatically increase their fertility rates after just one month.

ZINC

Zinc has been widely studied as an important nutrient for both female and male fertility. It plays an important role in the proper functioning of the reproductive organs. Zinc is also a key component of genetic material such as DNA and chromosomes. A zinc deficiency in either you or your partner could lead to chromosomal changes in egg or sperm cells, leading to fertility problems or miscarriage.

In women, zinc is a required nutrient for proper functioning of the hormones estrogen and progesterone.

For men, zinc plays a major role in sperm production and is required to form the outer layer and tail of the sperm. Several research studies from University Hospital Nijmegen, The Netherlands (one of which was published by Fertility Sterility in 2000), stated that a zinc deficiency in a man's diet is linked with lowered testosterone and lower sperm counts. A man's sperm count may be increased by adding 30 to 60 mg of zinc daily to a man's diet.

SELENIUM

Selenium is important for both female and male fertility. As an antioxidant, selenium works to prevent chromosome breakage, which has been correlated to birth defects and miscarriages.

In women, selenium works closely with vitamin E to assure elasticity of the tissues and organs. Women with selenium deficiencies are more likely to experience fertility problems.

Proper levels of selenium are important in men because it works to maximize sperm production. Men with low sperm counts are sometimes found to also have lower levels of selenium in their bloodstream.

ESSENTIAL FATTY ACIDS (EFAS)

Essential fatty acids (EFAs) are required in the functioning of hormones and the reproductive system.

EFAs are especially critical for women with minimal body fat, such as those who are very athletic or have a low BMI. Women who are very strict about following a low-fat diet should be sure to take a supplemental form of EFAs.

For men, EFAs play an important role in the production of semen. Men who are deficient in EFAs are more likely to experience low sperm count, poor sperm mobility, and inadequate sperm quality.

L-ARGININE

L-arginine is a type of protein called an amino acid. It appears to play an important role in sperm production. In fact, the head of sperm contains a large amount of L-arginine. Research has shown that men who supplement with L-arginine may increase both their sperm count and their sperm quality.

L-CARNITINE

Like L-arginine, L-carnitine is an amino acid. It also is required for the normal functioning of sperm cells. The Office of Dietary Supplements at the National Institutes of Health reports that the higher the L-carnitine level within the sperm cells, the better the sperm count and sperm quality. The ODS further states that larger and more carefully designed studies are needed to evaluate L-carnitine's potential value as an infertility treatment therapy.

The following list summarizes the important vitamins and minerals for you and your partner. Many of these nutrients will be found in your prenatal vitamin. You may also obtain some of these from a well-balanced diet. Exact dosages are not shown because they will vary depending on your particular body size, general health, and medical condition. Be sure to talk with your health care professional about how these nutrients will best maximize you and your partner's fertility.

Nutrients	Women	Men
Vitamin A (100% as beta-carotene)	√	-
Vitamin B$_1$ (thiamine)	√	-
Vitamin B$_2$ (riboflavin)	√	-
Vitamin B$_3$ (niacin)	√	-
Vitamin B$_6$ (pyroxidine)	√	√
Vitamin B$_9$ (folic acid)	√	-
Vitamin B$_{12}$ (cyanocobalamin)	√	√
Vitamin C	√	√
Vitamin E	√	√
Zinc	√	√
Selenium	√	√
Essential fatty acids (EFAs)	√	√
L-arginine	-	√
L-carnitine	-	√

Lifestyle: Things to Avoid

To boost your fertility, you will want to avoid certain things. This is a good time for you and your partner to take a look at your lifestyle, workplace, hobbies, and habits. It may be that some of your behaviors and exposures are unknowingly placing you at increased risk for fertility problems.

CAFFEINE

Plenty of evidence shows that caffeine decreases fertility. This seems to be particularly true in the case of coffee. And this applies to both women and men.

For women, caffeine is thought to interfere with the natural ovulation process. A National Institute of Environmental Health Sciences study published in *Lancet* in

1988 showed that as little as one cup of coffee per day can reduce your chances of conceiving by half. A different study, conducted by Yale University School of Medicine and published in the *American Journal of Epidemiology* in 1993, found that women who consumed more than 300 mg (equivalent to about three cups of coffee) daily had a 27 percent lower chance of conceiving per cycle compared to women with no caffeine intake. Also, women with modest caffeine intake—one or two cups of coffee daily—lowered their chances of conceiving by 10 percent.

In men, a study conducted in Milan, Italy, and published in 1993 in the *Archives Andrology* showed that sperm count and mobility decreased as the number of cups of coffee consumed increased.

To maximize your fertility, eliminate all caffeine-containing food and drinks for at least three months before trying to conceive. In addition to coffee, other items to avoid include colas, chocolate, and black teas. If you find that it is too difficult to do without these things, try substituting them with healthier alternatives such as herbal tea or decaffeinated coffee.

XENOESTROGENS

Xenoestrogens are estrogens that are found in the environment, usually from chemicals and pesticides. Fruits and vegetables may contain high levels of xenoestrogens.

If you ingest foods with high levels of xenoestrogens, your own hormones may become out of balance. Imbalanced hormones are sometimes the cause of fertility problems. Obviously, when you are trying to conceive, you want to have your hormones in excellent balance and working properly.

Some experts recommend that you eliminate your risk of excessive xenoestrogens by consuming only organically grown produce during your preconception time period and pregnancy.

SMOKING

Cigarette smoking has definitely been linked with fertility problems in women. According to the American Society for Reproductive Medicine (ASRM), virtually all scientific studies support the conclusion that smoking has an adverse impact on fertility. The ASRM patient fact sheet on smoking and infertility points out that smoking

- "is harmful to a woman's ovaries"
- "appears to accelerate the loss of eggs and reproductive function"

- "[interferes] with the ability of cells in the ovary to make estrogen"
- "causes a woman's eggs (oocytes) to be more prone to genetic abnormalities"
- "is associated with an increased risk of spontaneous miscarriage"

Smoking has also been linked to fertility problems in men. According to ASRM, it has been linked to decreased sperm count, reduced sperm mobility, and an increase in the number of abnormal sperm and function.

Smoking that takes place when a woman is pregnant has been associated with premature birth, low birth weight, and problems with the placenta. A baby that has been exposed to tobacco smoke also has a higher incidence of dying from sudden infant death syndrome (SIDS).

For your own health and the health of your future baby, now is a good time to quit smoking. If it's too difficult to stop cold turkey, at least cut down your use. Talk with your doctor about a safe program to help you quit smoking. Your doctor may be able to prescribe medication or refer you for counseling or treatment.

This is a good time for your partner to stop smoking, too. Secondhand smoke is not good for you or your baby. If you and your partner both smoke, get together and make an agreement to quit. You can make it a team approach as you work together to stop smoking and improve your overall health.

ALCOHOL

As you try to conceive, one of the best things you can do for yourself is to avoid alcohol. Your male partner should stop drinking, too.

A Harvard study published in 1994 by the *American Journal of Public Health* indicated that women who have even one alcoholic drink per day may reduce their chances of conceiving by up to 50 percent. Essentially, the more you drink, the less likely you are to conceive. Alcohol appears to increase your production of the hormone prolactin, which may cause your menstrual cycle to become irregular. To give both sides of the story, you should know that some other studies seem to suggest that light to moderate alcohol consumption may not have a direct correlation on fertility. However, those studies have not received much favor among U.S. medical practitioners. Even so, within the scientific world, this area remains somewhat controversial. To err on the side of caution, if you are having problems conceiving, it would seem wise to follow the healthiest program possible. Thus it seems reasonable to greatly minimize or completely abolish alcohol during this time in your life.

If you are having difficulty conceiving, your male partner shouldn't drink either. Alcohol has been shown to decrease a man's sperm count, reduce sperm mobility, and increase his production of abnormal sperm. Excessive alcohol consumption can also interfere with the body's absorption of important nutrients, such as zinc, which is essential for male fertility.

If you become pregnant and continue to use alcohol, the potential damage to the baby can last a lifetime. Alcohol has been linked to problems in the baby such as mental retardation and birth defects.

Because of these important factors, most health care providers recommend that you eliminate alcohol from your diet for at least three months before you try to become pregnant. This gives you the best possible chance of conceiving and increases your chances of a healthy pregnancy.

STREET DRUGS

Of course, you know that illicit drugs are not ever part of a healthy lifestyle. But as you try to become pregnant, you have even more reasons not to use street drugs.

For women, marijuana and other illicit drugs have been known to disrupt the menstrual cycle and the ovulation process. Cocaine and crystal meth can cause your blood pressure to rise dramatically and lead to serious medical conditions and malnutrition.

Marijuana is known to decrease fertility in men because it reduces sperm production. It also seems to play a role in decreasing sperm mobility and even reduces the enzymes that allow the sperm to penetrate the egg.

If you or your partner uses illegal drugs, please stop. Share your concerns with your doctor and work together to stop this unsafe practice. If you become pregnant while taking illicit drugs, these substances can permanently harm your baby. Drugs have been linked to mental retardation and birth defects among babies whose mothers used drugs during pregnancy.

CERTAIN PRESCRIPTION MEDICATIONS

Before you try to conceive, have a complete physical examination and medical checkup. One reason is to detect any new medical conditions that may require treatment. Another reason is to review your medications and make sure it is safe to continue taking them as you try to become pregnant.

Your doctor will want to review your list of current prescription medications. Although many medications can be safely taken during pregnancy, some may increase your chance of miscarriage or cause potential harm to the fetus. Be sure to talk with your doctor about how prescription medications affect your particular medical situation.

CHEMICAL TOXINS AND RADIATION

Some substances found at home or in your workplace could potentially reduce your fertility and harm your fetus once you become pregnant. These environmental toxins can prevent normal growth of the fetus and even cause physical or mental defects.

If you or your partner might be exposed to a potentially harmful substance, take steps to avoid it. Think about your home and workplace. Jobs involving heavy metals such as lead or mercury, chemicals in pesticides, or chemicals used in certain manufacturing (such as painting or printing) processes may be harmful to your fertility. Some of these toxins have been shown to damage sperm. These environmental toxins may also cause problems with the development of your unborn baby's central nervous system.

Jobs that involve a high level of radiation can adversely affect the fertility of men and women. It can also hurt the developing fetus. Try to avoid contact with radiation as you try to conceive and once you become pregnant.

The American College of OB/GYN states that the small amount of radiation that a person receives during a routine chest x-ray will not hurt your fertility or damage the fetus. If you need x-rays for a medical or dental condition, be sure to tell your doctor that you are trying to become pregnant or may already be pregnant. He or she can almost always take precautionary steps to reduce your risk of radiation, such as placing a shield over your abdomen or postponing the x-ray test itself.

Natural Ways to Monitor Your Own Fertility

One of the best ways of naturally boosting your fertility is to pinpoint exactly when you are ovulating. That's the time period when you are the most fertile. You maximize your chances of becoming pregnant if you have sexual intercourse just before your egg is released.

Several natural family-planning methods can help you figure out when you are ovulating. The most popular techniques are the rhythm (calendar) method, the basal body temperature method, and the cervical mucus method. Each of these techniques is discussed in detail next. Many women perform all three systems because when combined together, these methods will increase your chances of conceiving. That's because they are a very effective way to track your menstrual cycle and let you determine exactly when you are ovulating.

RHYTHM METHOD

This technique is also sometimes called the calendar method. To perform this method, you keep a calendar and record every day of your menstrual cycle for at least six months. From that information, you can calculate when you are ovulating and thus when you are most fertile.

As discussed in Chapter 3, your menstrual cycle is counted from the first day of bleeding (this is considered day 1 of your cycle) to the first day of the next menstrual cycle. For most women, this is typically about 28 days. However, it is not unusual for the number of days to range from 23 to 35.

Most women ovulate approximately 14 days before their next period. Therefore, if your cycle is 28 days long, you probably ovulate on day 14 (28 − 14 = 14). If your cycle is 35 days long, you probably ovulate on day 21 (35 − 14 = 21). If you have a shortened cycle of, say, 23 days, then you likely ovulate on about day 9 (23 − 14 = 9).

Once you determine the approximate date that you ovulate each month, you should have sexual intercourse surrounding that day. For example, if you seem to ovulate on day 14 of your cycle, you should have sex from about day 12 through day 16, so your timing will coincide with your most fertile phase.

The rhythm method is considered fairly easy to perform and has no side effects. However, this method has been criticized because it does not take into account your daily habits, sleep patterns, illnesses, stress, and so on. Therefore, this technique is useful but is not considered as reliable as other natural family-planning methods.

BASAL BODY TEMPERATURE (BBT) METHOD

The BBT method is based on the knowledge that most women have a slight increase in their normal body temperature just after ovulation. That's because your progesterone hormone levels increase with ovulation. This increasing progesterone level causes your temperature to rise, a least a little bit.

Here's how the BBT technique works. Every morning, first thing before you even get out of bed, you take your temperature and record it on a sheet of paper. Purchase a special thermometer (a BBT thermometer) at your local drugstore. A BBT thermometer is easier to use than a conventional thermometer because it has expanded and easy-to-read scale markings. BBT thermometers only register from 96 to 100 degrees F. These thermometers typically come with graph paper. If not, your doctor can provide you with blank BBT chart graph paper. Keep your BBT thermometer, your graph paper chart, and a pencil at your bedside. Take your temperature every single day, as soon as you awake, before getting out of bed or drinking or eating, and so on.

After two or three months, you'll likely be able to detect a pattern in your recorded temperatures. Hopefully, you'll notice that your temperature rises slightly after ovulation. Many women find that their temperature is somewhat lower during the first part of their cycle. Then it will typically rise slightly (between 0.4 and 0.8 degrees F) on the day of ovulation. Your temperature may stay elevated until just before the start of your next period. If you become pregnant, the temperatures typically continue to be elevated.

Figure 5.1 shows a sample of what a typical BBT chart might look like.

In this example, the woman probably ovulated on day 14. Notice that her temperature is approximately 0.5 to 1 degree higher during the last two weeks of her monthly cycle, after day 14. That's most likely because of the increased progesterone level after ovulation.

Your doctor will ask you to bring in a couple of months of your BBT charts for review. You and the doctor can discuss them and perhaps determine whether you are ovulating regularly. If you are ovulating regularly, it's essential that you have sexual intercourse on the days surrounding your most fertile time period.

Many women use this BBT method and find that it is fairly easy to perform. However, remember to do it exactly the same way every day, upon waking and before performing any activities. This is not always practical for all women. This

Figure 5.1. Basal Body Temperature Chart

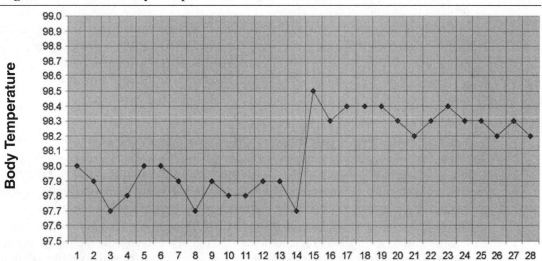

method is sometimes criticized because the temperature readings may be influenced by an illness, restless sleep, or varying work schedules.

CERVICAL MUCUS METHOD

The cervical mucus method involves changes in your cervical mucus as you near ovulation time. Keeping track of your cervical mucus and how it changes during the month will help you recognize the changes that occur with ovulation and be more aware of your body's natural cycle. To accomplish this technique, you need to examine your cervical mucus and notice the changes.

Most women notice that their vaginal area is fairly dry just after menstruation. A few days later, a thick, cloudy, and sticky mucus usually appears. Just before ovulation time, the mucus in that region typically becomes clear, wet, and slippery; resembles egg whites; and can be stretched easily between your fingers. The mucus stays this way for several days, and ovulation occurs near the end of this time. Be sure to have sexual intercourse during these critical few days. On the day following ovulation, the mucus usually become thick, cloudy, and sticky again or may even go away entirely and the vaginal area will become dryer.

You can check your cervical mucus in a number of ways, depending on which technique is the most comfortable for you. Many women merely wipe the vaginal opening with toilet paper before urination and observe the discharge on the tissue. Some women observe any discharge present on the underwear. Others are comfortable with obtaining mucus by placing a clean finger into the vaginal opening. Any of these techniques is acceptable.

Critics of the cervical mucus method note that some women may have difficulty assessing their own discharge. It does take practice, and this is something that you might want to discuss with your doctor. Also, your cervical mucus may change if you have a vaginal infection or medical illness or if you are taking certain medications.

COMBINING ALL THREE NATURAL METHODS

Many women keep a daily chart of all three methods: rhythm, BBT, and cervical mucus. Over a period of several months, these charts will help you keep track of your cycles and determine when you are ovulating. When used together, these three methods are fairly accurate at tracking fertility for most women.

Sometimes, for various reasons, these techniques don't work. Despite accurate record keeping, you and your doctor may not be able to determine whether ovulation is occurring. In such a case, the doctor may recommend that you try a slightly more sophisticated test called the ovulation predictor test.

OVULATION PREDICTOR TEST

Home testing kits are available from your drugstore to help detect ovulation, just before it occurs. The test is based on the amount of luteinizing hormone (LH) found in your urine. The LH reaches a high level in your bloodstream and urine about 24 to 36 hours prior to ovulation, which is often referred to as the LH surge.

If you check your urine with the test dipstick each morning, the test will likely be negative until the day of your LH surge. When your LH surge occurs, the test will be positive. This indicates that you should ovulate within the next 24 to 36 hours. Once you learn to pinpoint the day before ovulation, you can use this knowledge to boost your fertility.

This method seems so much easier than the time-consuming BBT method discussed earlier. Well, it is, and it's probably more accurate also. The downside is that these kits can be expensive, especially when you end up buying many of them in an effort to pinpoint your exact time of ovulation.

Here are some tips to keep in mind when using an ovulation predictor kit:

- Gather all of the materials you need prior to beginning the test.
- Follow the directions on the package exactly as they are written.
- Perform the test at the same time each day.
- Don't drink lots of water or fluids before the test (doing so could dilute urine and alter results).
- Talk with your doctor about medications that you are taking (some could alter results).
- Don't do this test if you are taking contraceptives or hormones.
- Try not to stress out—not every woman ovulates every month.
- For questions about your testing kit, ask your pharmacist or call the phone number included with your kit.

Other Natural Ways to Maximize Your Fertility

Here are some additional ways to boost your fertility.

AVOID ARTIFICIAL LUBRICANTS

To boost your fertility, avoid the use of artificial lubricants. These lubricants often contain chemicals that can damage or kill sperm. Clinical studies show that sperm mobility is reduced by 60 to 100 percent after one hour of contact with commercial lubricants. This applies to regular over-the-counter lubricants, petroleum jelly, plain glycerin, and even saliva.

Instead of using a lubricant, try to lengthen the amount of time you and your partner spend on sexual foreplay. For most women, more foreplay ensures arousal and increases their own natural vaginal secretions. If you still feel that you need an additional lubricant, try egg whites. Strange as it sounds, egg whites closely mimic your own fertile phase cervical mucus and have been shown to encourage sperm mobility.

DON'T DOUCHE

Douching seems to have fallen out of popularity in recent decades, and it's just as well. Douching with homemade mixtures such as vinegar or baking soda and water can change the pH balance inside your vagina. The same is true for commercially prepared over-the-counter douches. Because of the change in your vagina's pH balance, any sperm that is present may be damaged or killed. Douching can also wash away your natural cervical mucus, which is present to help sperm through the cervix on their way to the egg.

Douching after sex is not a good idea either because it may flush out any living sperm that is trying to make its way through your cervix and up to the egg.

ASSUME THE POSITION

Certain sexual positions may make it more likely that you will become pregnant. The missionary position is sexual intercourse with the man on top. This position is probably the best to boost fertility because it allows deep penetration and sperm is deposited closest to the cervix.

A good alternate position is the rear entry approach. With the man behind you, this position allows for deep penetration with semen depositing close to your cervix.

When sex is over and ejaculation has occurred, try to keep any semen from leaking out of your vagina for a while. Many women say that reclining on their back with hips elevated for about 15 minutes is an effective technique.

TIMING IS EVERYTHING

Of course, you already know that you should have sexual intercourse during your most fertile time of the month—that is, around the time of your ovulation. But did you also know that some holistic practitioners suggest that a couple's most fertile time of day is between 3 P.M. and 7 P.M.?

Medical research shows that the number and quality of sperm seem to peak in the late afternoon. In fact, some studies indicate that a man's sperm count may be up to 35 percent higher in the late afternoon when compared to the morning. Similar research concludes that women are most likely to ovulate between 3 P.M. and 7 P.M.

Some people jokingly refer to this time as happy hour and recommend that couples leave work a little early to enjoy a baby-making tryst.

KEEP THE BOYS COOL

You've probably already heard that boxers are better than briefs when it comes to fertility concerns regarding men's underwear. That's because the testicles need to be at a slightly lower temperature than the rest of the body to maximize sperm production. It stands to reason that testicles will enjoy slightly cooler temperature conditions when positioned in boxers as compared to the tight confines of briefs.

With the same cooler temperatures in mind, men with lower sperm counts should also not take extremely hot showers, baths, or Jacuzzi hot tubs.

TIPS TO BOOST YOUR FERTILITY—NATURALLY

So by now you have an even better understanding of how your body is influenced by outside factors such as nutrition, exercise, stress, and lifestyle habits. You also know how to calculate your most fertile time of the month. Use this knowledge to boost your fertility. In addition, following are some more tips that you can try in hopes of becoming pregnant the old-fashioned way.

- **Timing is critical.** Be sure to have sexual intercourse with your partner every day during your fertile time (the day of ovulation and the few days before and after).

- **Use gravity to your advantage.** Elevate your hips on a pillow and bend your knees during sexual intercourse.

- **Enjoy some quality snuggle time.** Have your partner remain inside your vagina for several minutes following ejaculation to maximize semen placement.

- **Relax and chill.** Be sure to remain lying in bed for at least 30 minutes following intercourse.

- **Keep it natural.** Avoid the use of lubricants or other products that might interfere with the natural pH balance and environment of your vulva and vagina during intercourse. Also, do not douche, but if you must, wait for at least one hour after intercourse.

Alternative Medicine: Exploring Nonconventional Treatments

In the United States, alternative medicine is defined as a system of treatments that are not typically recognized by the traditional medical community. Examples include aromatherapy, massage, acupuncture, and herbal remedies.

Many consider the United States to be the stronghold of high technology and scientific medicine. Nonetheless, surveys show that more than 20 percent of infertile couples have consulted an alternative medicine practitioner, primarily because they were unhappy and dissatisfied with conventional medical treatments.

A criticism of alternative medical techniques is that they lack scientific basis. This makes them difficult to analyze and, therefore, some of their claims difficult to confirm or deny. As a result, many conventional medical providers tend to dismiss the idea that any benefit comes as a result of alternative medicine practices.

As a patient, you will help yourself the most by becoming educated about all of your treatment options. Choose a competent, well-trained health care provider, no matter what form of treatment you choose. Also, understand the limitations of the various treatments. You may find that alternative medicine practices may benefit you and boost your fertility.

AROMATHERAPY

Unfortunately, no scientific evidence shows that aromatherapy can directly boost your fertility. However, clinical research has shown that aromatherapy can help reduce emotional stress. That can come in handy when you are experiencing the emotional tension often associated with fertility concerns. A study carried out by Dr. Gary Schwartz at Yale University found that aroma of various oils can favorably affect the nervous system and even reduce blood pressure. Examples of beneficial aromatherapy oils are spiced apple, clary sage, rosemary, tea tree, and lavender.

Some natural practitioners recommend aromatherapy in combination with massage. Massage improves your circulation of blood and also helps to relax muscle tension. When combined together, aromatic oils and healing touch are often able to relieve your anxiety and bring you to a peaceful state of relaxation.

ACUPUNCTURE

Acupuncture is the insertion of small needles along various parts of your body. The theory behind acupuncture involves rebalancing your body's power as it runs through energy fields called meridians.

Though still not completely accepted by traditional Western medicine, acupuncture has been shown in various clinical trials to benefit both female and male fertility problems.

One such study was conducted by the University of Heidelberg in Germany and published in 1992 by *Gynecological Endocrinology*. The study involved 90 women with irregular menstrual cycles. Half of these women were given acupuncture at treatment points on their ears. The remaining women were treated with hormones. The study found that women treated with acupuncture had 22 pregnancies. Women treated with hormones had 20 pregnancies. It was also noted that several undesirable side effects were seen among the women in the hormone group, but no side effects occurred in the acupuncture group. The study concluded that acupuncture may provide a valuable alternative for women with irregular menstrual cycles.

Another German study, conducted in 1984 by Fischl, Riegler, Bieglmayer, et al., showed that acupuncture may be beneficial in increasing sperm quality. Acupuncture was performed on 28 men with known sperm fertility problems. The men received multiple acupuncture treatments over a period of one month. The results showed a statistically significant improvement in sperm quality.

Acupuncture is gaining in popularity but is still not practiced among conventional health care practitioners in the United States. It is commonly performed in other parts of the world and also by trained alternative medicine professionals within the United States. If you decide to try acupuncture, be certain to select a well-trained and competent health care provider.

HERBAL REMEDIES

Herbs have been used for thousands of years in various parts of the world as treatment for medical ailments. Certain herbal remedies have been used to promote and boost fertility in both men and women.

Herbs are not regulated by a governmental agency, as the Food and Drug Administration does for prescription and some over-the-counter medication. Consequently, herbs that you may use could be contaminated or not contain the exact ingredients that are listed on the label. Because herbal medicine has not been widely studied and researched, we still do not know all of the potential associated side effects.

That said, herbal medicine may still offer benefits to you as you work to maximize your fertility. If you would like to try herbal medicine, you should do so only while under the care of a qualified practitioner, such as a naturopathic physician.

The following list itemizes herbs that may be useful to boost your fertility and promote healthy reproductive organ systems.

Herb	What It Does
Black cohosh	Relieves menstrual discomfort, may reduce hot flashes, acts as relaxant and sedative
Chaste berry (aka Vitex)	Promotes ovulation, regulates menstrual cycle, improves hormonal balance
Dong quai	Regulates menstrual cycle, improves hormonal balance, increases chance of implantation
False unicorn	Regulates menstrual cycle, restores male hormonal balance
Ginseng	Relieves stress, regulates hormones, is considered a reproductive tonic
Red clover	Provides estrogen-like compounds and may be useful in women who have low estrogen, improves hormone balance
Red raspberry	Eases menstrual discomfort, relieves nausea, is useful as a pregnancy herb
Saw palmetto	Strengthens male reproductive system, reduces enlarged male prostate
Wild yam	Relieves menstrual discomfort, provides estrogen-like compounds and may be useful in women who have low estrogen, improves hormone balance

In addition to working with your naturopathic physician, be sure to tell your other health care providers (family doctor, OB/GYN physician, fertility specialist, and so on) that you are taking herbal supplements.

Conclusion

Doesn't it make sense for us to combine the best of both worlds—the high technology of conventional medicine with the high touch associated with alternative medicine? This approach is called integrative medicine and continues to be pioneered by (my former medical school professor) Dr. Andrew Weil. Dr. Weil is a Harvard-trained physician but also heads a Tucson clinic that incorporates alternative medicine practices. The practice of integrative medicine says that you should feel free to explore all possible treatment options. Various forms of treatment are seen as complementary to one another. For example, you may choose to combine acupuncture therapy with in vitro fertilization. After all, both have the same goal, which is to boost your fertility and help you have a baby.

Be sure you understand the limitations of the various forms of treatment. For example, if your fallopian tubes are blocked, herbs and aromatherapy will almost certainly not open them. However, if you are taking hormonal medications to help you ovulate, you may find that aromatherapy and massage help to relieve your emotional stresses.

Whatever you decide to do, be sure that all of your caregivers are aware of any other treatments you may be taking. Working with both conventional and alternative medical practitioners will provide you with the best of both worlds. You may achieve your goal of having a baby sooner and with more comfort and serenity.

Summary

Here is a chapter summary that highlights the key concepts of this chapter.

Overview

- Most people prefer to try a natural approach to fertility, at least initially, before embarking on lots of uncomfortable and expensive procedures.

Diet and Nutrition

- A well-balanced diet helps to regulate your hormones and nourish your reproductive system.

- According to ACOG, the average woman needs about 2,200 calories per day and, once pregnant, needs about 300 additional calories daily.

- Choose your foods wisely to ensure that you receive the best possible vitamins and minerals from natural whole foods. The food guide pyramid serves as a guide for both men and women.

- Avoid these foods: raw or undercooked fish, meat and poultry, as well as fruits and vegetables that have been treated with potentially toxic chemical pesticides.

Healthy Weight

- Being at a healthy weight makes it easier for you to conceive because your metabolism and hormones are more likely to be in the proper balance.

- Doctors use the BMI as a reliable indicator of body fat. The BMI is a way of correlating your body weight to your height.

- Women that are either extremely thin or too heavy may experience difficulties becoming pregnant.
- To have the best chance of conceiving, aim for a BMI in the healthy midrange of about 19 to 25.

Keeping Fit

- Moderate exercise is a good way to naturally boost your fertility.
- Exercise helps to burn off excess body fat and allows hormones to reach their proper balance.

Reduce Your Stress

- Stress can be the cause of many common physical ailments, including causing your menstrual cycle and ovulation to become irregular.
- Although it's easier said than done, you need to figure out a way to reduce the stress in your life for your overall health and well-being.
- Consider joining a support group, learn stress-management techniques, try yoga or meditation, or explore other ways to release your burdens.

Vitamins and Nutrients

- Take a prenatal vitamin pill every day, even when you are just thinking about becoming pregnant. It provides you with a great source of vitamins and nutrients.
- Certain vitamins and nutrients have been studied and shown to help boost fertility, including these:
  - Vitamin A in the vegetable form (beta-carotene) is healthy for women.
  - Vitamin B may boost fertility in both men and women.
  - Vitamin C may boost fertility in both men and women.
  - Vitamin E may boost fertility in both men and women.
  - Zinc may boost fertility in both men and women.
  - Selenium may boost fertility in both men and women.
  - Essential fatty acids may boost fertility in both men and women.
  - L-arginine may boost fertility in men.
  - L-carnitine may boost fertility in men.

Lifestyle: Things to Avoid

- Caffeine
- Xenoestrogens
- Smoking
- Alcohol
- Street drugs
- Certain prescription medications
- Chemical toxins and radiation

Natural Ways to Monitor Your Own Fertility

- One of the best ways of naturally boosting your fertility is to pinpoint exactly when you are ovulating—that's when you're the most fertile.
- Several natural family-planning methods can help you figure out when you are ovulating, including rhythm, basal body temperature, and cervical mucus methods.
- You may decide that you want to try a slightly more sophisticated test called the home ovulation predictor test.

Other Natural Ways to Maximize Your Fertility

- Avoid artificial lubricants.
- Do not douche.
- Try the missionary position to maximize deep sperm penetration.
- Be sure to have sex during your most fertile time of the month.
- Make sure your male partner keeps his testicles slightly cooler than the rest of his body.

Alternative Medicine: Exploring Nonconventional Treatments

- In the United States, alternative medicine is a system of treatments that are not typically recognized by the traditional medical community.
- You may find that some therapies benefit you and boost your fertility, but you should understand the limitations of the various treatments.
- In all cases, you should be under the care of a qualified practitioner.
- Aromatherapy may help reduce emotional stress.

- Acupuncture has been shown in some studies to benefit both female and male fertility.
- Certain herbal remedies may be associated with fertility.
- Integrative medicine combines the best of both worlds—the high tech of conventional medicine with the high touch of alternative medicine.

CHAPTER 6

Fertility Drug Therapies

Most women who find their way into a fertility specialist's office will eventually end up taking some sort of fertility medication. This chapter explains some of the more common medications that you may encounter as you undergo your fertility treatments.

Fertility medications usually refer to drugs that regulate your hormones and induce ovulation. In addition, you may come across other medications that are designed to treat specific fertility problems or enhance other fertility medications.

Clomiphene Citrate (Clomid, Serophene, CC)

Clomiphene citrate is often referred to by one of its brand names Clomid but also goes by the names of Serophene and CC. Because Clomid has been used safely for more than 30 years, is easy to take, and is relatively inexpensive, it is often the first fertility medication prescribed.

Clomid is often recommended when you are not ovulating regularly or not ovulating at all. That's why it's the first-line medication used for women with ovulation disorders such as polycystic ovary syndrome (PCOS). On occasion, it is used along with other fertility medications.

HOW DOES CLOMID WORK?

Clomid is a medication that works on a woman's estrogen receptors and hormones and thereby causes her body to ovulate more efficiently and regularly. The effects of Clomid begin in the hypothalamus, a small gland at the base of the brain. There, Clomid causes the production of gonadotropin-releasing hormone. The GnRH prompts the brain's pituitary gland to produce more follicle-stimulating hormone and luteinizing hormone. The newly produced FSH and LH stimulate the ovaries into producing more follicles and eggs. In a nutshell, Clomid tricks a woman's body into secreting more ovulation-causing hormones and ultimately results in improved ovulation.

HOW DO I TAKE CLOMID?

Clomid is one of the few fertility medications taken orally. For that reason, many women prefer Clomid tablets to other medications, which are usually given by injection.

The dosage of Clomid varies but usually ranges from 50 mg to 200 mg daily. Most women start with a daily dosage of 50 mg, and if ovulation does not occur, the dose will be increased. Take your Clomid tablets at approximately the same time each day. Because Clomid works by interrupting your normal hormonal messages and feedback between your brain and ovaries, you should time your Clomid hormonal messages just right.

Clomid is typically given for approximately five days of each menstrual cycle. Many women are surprised to find out that they only take Clomid pills at the beginning of their cycle. The reason is because Clomid works at the beginning of your menstrual cycle to influence your hormones and determine your upcoming ovulation. Depending on your doctor's preferences, it may be prescribed from cycle day 3 through 7 or cycle days 5 through 9. (Remember that cycle day 1 is the first day of your normal menstrual bleeding.) Clomid usually induces ovulation at about day 14 of a regular 28-day cycle.

WHAT ARE THE POTENTIAL SIDE EFFECTS OF CLOMID?

Many women do not experience any side effects at all. However, our bodies and how they react to medication can vary, and thus some women do encounter unpleasant side effects.

Here is a list of some of the more common side effects that you may encounter while taking Clomid:

- Mood swings
- Hot flashes
- Abdominal discomfort or bloating
- Nausea and vomiting
- Tender breasts
- Blurred vision or other visual disturbances
- Headache
- Abnormal uterine bleeding or spotting

In addition, approximately 5 percent of women using Clomid will develop an ovarian cyst, which is an enlarged fluid-filled structure within your ovary. It may cause you some discomfort. However, in most cases, these cysts are completely benign and will go away without any treatment. If you suspect that you have an ovarian cyst, please see your doctor right away for an evaluation.

Ovarian hyperstimulation syndrome (OHSS) is an even rarer complication. This is a potentially serious condition, where your ovaries become enlarged, form large cysts, and can cause tremendous discomfort. Although OHSS may occur with Clomid, OHSS is more likely to occur if you are taking stronger ovulation-inducing medications. OHSS is discussed in more detail at the end of this chapter.

Be sure to notify your doctor if you experience any of these or any other unusual symptoms. You should also call your doctor if you are taking Clomid and do not have a menstrual period by cycle day 35. That's because you may have failed to ovulate or you may be pregnant! In either case, talk with your doctor to determine what is happening to your body.

HOW WILL I BE MONITORED WHEN I'M TAKING CLOMID?

Your doctor will probably recommend that you continue to monitor for ovulation. You will usually do this using either your temperature charts or an ovulation predictor kit.

If you have not become pregnant within three months of Clomid therapy, most doctors will want you to come in for a follow-up appointment. Your dosage of Clomid may be increased or other studies may be recommended, based upon your individual situation.

Sometimes your doctor may decide to monitor you more closely. In this circumstance, your doctor may order a series of pelvic ultrasounds to determine the number of ovarian follicles present and their rate of growth and to help pinpoint the time of ovulation. About 10 percent of women taking Clomid experience a thinning of their uterine lining. This can also be noted and monitored on pelvic ultrasound. Your blood may also be drawn and checked for a progesterone level. This test is usually performed on or about cycle day 21. The purpose of the blood test is to see if your progesterone levels are high enough after ovulation for a pregnancy to occur. Labs vary, but most doctors like to see a progesterone level of 15 or greater after ovulation.

WHAT ARE THE SUCCESS RATES AND OUTCOMES ASSOCIATED WITH CLOMID?

Data indicates that approximately 80 percent of women who take Clomid will ovulate. However, only about 30 to 40 percent of women who take Clomid will actually become pregnant. Clomid is sometimes combined with an intrauterine insemination procedure, which may increase the pregnancy rate by about 3 to 4 percent.

As with all fertility medication, an increased chance for multiple pregnancies exists. Multiple gestation pregnancies occur in approximately 8 to 10 percent of Clomid-induced pregnancies. The vast majority of these multiple gestations are twins. Triplets are considerably rarer.

WHAT ARE THE PROS AND CONS CONCERNING CLOMID?

Before taking Clomid or any medication, it's important to understand the pros and cons.

Pros

- Clomid has been used for more than 30 years as a safe and effective fertility medication. (The majority of concerns about ovarian cancer and birth defects have proven false under scientific scrutiny.)
- Clomid is easier to use than many other fertility medications because it is taken orally instead of by injection.

- Especially when compared with the cost of other fertility medication, Clomid is one of the more affordable and low-costs options available.

- This medication also has a generic equivalent available, for potential additional savings.

Cons

- Early research studies still quote an increased risk of ovarian cancer for women who use Clomid for longer than 12 cycles.

- Prolonged use of Clomid may lead to hostile cervical mucus, which can damage or kill sperm.

- Clomid may also thin the uterine lining, which can prevent egg implantation or cause an early miscarriage.

- In most cases, Clomid is not as strong or effective as alternative fertility medications, and therefore, fewer eggs will be formed.

IF I DON'T BECOME PREGNANT USING CLOMID, WHAT'S NEXT?

Research shows that if you aren't pregnant after six cycles of Clomid, you are unlikely to become pregnant from this medication. In fact, about 80 percent of pregnancies that occur with Clomid are conceived during the first three months of use.

In most situations, if you don't become pregnant after six months of taking Clomid, your doctor will recommend a different treatment. Many women go on to use other drug therapies, and some go directly to an assisted reproductive technology.

Gonadotropins (Follistim, Gonal-F, Bravelle [FSH] and Repronex, Menopur [FSH and LH])

Depending upon your particular medical circumstance, your specialist may recommend a stronger category of medication to induce ovulation: gonadotropins. The purpose in using a gonadotropin is to stimulate ovulation and encourage follicle development to produce more eggs.

Several types of gonadotropins are available. The most commonly used gonadotropin is man-made (from recombinant DNA technology) in a laboratory and is identical to your body's natural FSH. Examples of recombinant gonadotropins are Follistim and Gonal-F.

The other category is called urinary-based gonadotropins because these medications are made from the purified urine of menopausal women. Urinary-based gonadotropins fall into two types. The first type is almost as pure as the recombinant FSH and is sold under the brand name of Bravelle. The second type comprises nearly equal parts of FSH and LH. Brand-name examples of this type of gonadotropin are Repronex and Menopur. Some doctors prefer the pure FSH product, whereas others believe that LH helps the ovulation process.

HOW DOES A GONADOTROPIN WORK?

Gonadotropins work to stimulate ovulation in the same way that your body's hormones should. The injection of high levels of FSH (and sometimes also LH) into your bloodstream stimulates your ovaries to develop multiple follicles and eggs. By increasing the number of developing eggs, you maximize your chances of becoming pregnant.

Once your doctor determines that the eggs are ready, you will receive an injection of a different medication called human chorionic gonadotropin (hCG). This injection of hCG signals your body to release the developed eggs from your ovaries.

Depending on what form of fertility treatment you are doing, you will proceed from here. Your doctor may simply recommend that you and your partner have intercourse. In other situations, you will be scheduled for an insemination or egg retrieval.

HOW DO I TAKE GONADOTROPINS?

Gonadotropins are given to you by injection. Depending on your particular situation, the injections begin early in your menstrual cycle, usually about cycle day 2 or 3. (Remember that day 1 is the first day of normal bleeding.) Depending on your blood work and ultrasounds, you will typically receive injections for seven or more days.

If you are taking the recombinant form of gonadotropin, the injections can be given subcutaneously—that is, directly below the skin surface. That's because recombinant gonadotropins contain very few impurities and are unlikely to result in a skin reaction.

Urinary-based gonadotropins usually are injected deeper and into the muscle, because they sometimes contain irritants that could cause a skin rash.

No matter what type of gonadotropin you are taking, your doctor may recommend a deeper, muscular injection if your body mass index is greater than 30. The purpose of this is to maximize the absorption of the medication.

WHAT ARE THE POTENTIAL SIDE EFFECTS OF GONADOTROPINS?

Side effects and reactions to gonadotropins vary among women. Here is a list of some of the more common side effects that you may encounter while taking gonadotropins:

- Mood swings
- Abdominal discomfort or bloating
- Weight gain or swelling
- Backaches
- Headache
- Fatigue
- Tender breasts
- Increased vaginal discharge
- Discomfort at the injection site

Women taking gonadotropins have a slightly increased risk of developing an ovarian cyst, and ovarian hyperstimulation syndrome (OHSS) may rarely occur.

Be sure to notify your doctor if you experience any of these or any other unusual symptoms. Talk with your doctor to determine what is happening to your body.

HOW WILL I BE MONITORED WHEN I'M TAKING GONADOTROPINS?

While you are taking gonadotropins, you will be closely monitored by your fertility specialist.

Your blood will be checked for the level of estradiol, a form of estrogen that rises as your body produces more follicles and developing eggs. Tracking this rise in your estradiol levels will help your doctor follow your egg development.

Your fertility specialist will also perform regular vaginal ultrasounds on you. That's because it's important to keep a close eye on your ovaries. Frequent vaginal ultrasound can visualize the number of developing eggs, measure their size, determine their growth rate, and so on. Ultrasound can also discover an emerging ovarian cyst or another such problem that may require additional treatment.

WHAT ARE THE SUCCESS RATES AND OUTCOMES ASSOCIATED WITH GONADOTROPINS?

A medical study published in Fertility Sterility during 1999 and conducted by a university in Turkey showed that more than 80 percent of women who take gonadotropins will ovulate. It is also known that somewhere between 15 and 50 percent of women who take gonadotropins will actually become pregnant.

When gonadotropins are combined with intrauterine insemination, women with unexplained infertility who are age 36 or younger experience a pregnancy rate of between 5 and 15 percent per cycle. The pregnancy rate drops for older women, and in fact, by age 40, the pregnancy rates with this form of treatment are quite low. (In such a case, an assisted reproductive technology such as IVF may be considered.) As with all fertility medication, there exists an increased chance for multiple pregnancies, which occur in approximately 20 percent of those women taking gonadotropins. Of those multiple gestation pregnancies, about 75 percent are twins and the remaining 25 percent are triplets or higher-order multiples.

WHAT ARE THE PROS AND CONS CONCERNING GONADOTROPINS?

Before taking gonadotropins, it's important to know the pros and cons of this medication.

Pros
- Gonadotropins have been safely used for many years with minimal complications.
- The close monitoring of blood work and ultrasound helps to make the use of gonadotropins relatively safe.

Cons
- The chance of having twins, triplets, or higher-order multiples increases, as does the chance of premature delivery.
- The risk of ovarian hyperstimulation syndrome is slightly increased.
- Gonadotropins are relatively expensive.
- Medication must be injected instead of taken orally.

IF I DON'T BECOME PREGNANT USING GONADOTROPINS, WHAT'S NEXT?

Treatment with gonadotropins is typically considered practical and useful for about three to six months in women younger than 37. If you don't become pregnant by that time, you may wish to proceed to the next step, which is often IVF.

Gonadotropin-Releasing Hormone Agonists (GnRHa) (Lupron, Synarel, Nafarelin, Buserelin)

GnRHa is not really a fertility medication; however, it is often used as part of your IVF protocol. When used in this practice, GnRHa is given first to restrain your own body's hormones. Once your natural hormones have been suppressed, another medication (usually the gonadotropins discussed previously) will be given to induce ovulation. Using this protocol, the fertility specialist is able to precisely control the reproductive hormones and ovulation, thereby making conception more likely.

GnRHa can also be used as treatment for painful endometriosis. Your reproductive hormones are shut down, your periods stop, and the pain associated with endometriosis is gone. When GnRHa is used in this way, your body is transformed into a temporary menopausal state and pregnancy cannot occur during this time. This use of GnRHa is mentioned here because many women with fertility issues suffer from endometriosis. Therefore, it is possible that this treatment may be presented to you as temporary relief to your painful endometriosis symptoms.

HOW DOES GnRHa WORK?

GnRHa works by shutting down your body's reproductive hormones (FSH and LH), causing them to drop to almost zero. This subsequently causes a dramatic drop in your estradiol (estrogen) levels. Your normal menstrual cycle, hormones, and ovulation are all shut down.

When used as part of an IVF protocol, GnRHa suppresses your body's own hormones and improves the dependability and predictability of your IVF cycle, because when left to their own devices, your hormones may not always operate efficiently. For example, you might be producing only one dominant follicle or you may be prematurely ovulating, resulting in poor egg quality and a lower chance of success. If you first shut down your hormones with GnRHa and then give another medication (gonadotropins) to stimulate them, your hormones function normally and ovulation will occur in a more controlled and more predictable fashion.

When used in the treatment of endometriosis, the medication shrinks the endometriosis implants, which relieves the pain. GnRHa is sometimes used prior to surgery because it makes the endometriosis implants smaller and easier to remove. It also helps reduce the amount of scar tissue. Because of risks and side effects, GnRHa is typically only used for a short period of time, three to six months. The benefits of this treatment for endometriosis are often only a temporary solution, lasting for a few months. For others, pain relief lasts considerably longer.

HOW DO I TAKE GnRHa?

Several different forms of GnRHa exist. The most well known is Lupron, and it is injected under your skin. Nafarelin and Synarel are both nasal sprays that are sprayed into your nose. Buserelin is available in both nasal spray and injectable forms.

If you are taking a GnRHa as part of an IVF protocol, your doctor will discuss your treatment regimen with you. Depending on your medical history, age, and particular circumstances, you have several different IVF protocols to consider: long, short/flare, or stop protocol. All three protocols have the same goal: for you to become pregnant. They differ in the dose and timing of the medications given. You and your doctor will work together to determine which IVF protocol is best for your particular situation.

If you are taking a GnRHa for treatment of endometriosis, you will likely either receive a monthly injection or need to spray the medication into your nose twice daily. This form of treatment is typically limited to three to six months. This short time period is recommended because of the potential risks and side effects associated with long-term use of GnRHa.

WHAT ARE THE POTENTIAL SIDE EFFECTS OF GnRHa?

Side effects associated with GnRHa are similar to those experienced during menopause, because these side effects are caused by low estrogen levels. Here is a list of some of the more common side effects that you may encounter while taking a GnRHa:

- Mood swings
- Hot flashes
- Headache
- Vaginal dryness
- No menstrual periods
- Insomnia
- Bone pain and bone loss of up to 1 percent per month
- Tender breasts
- Insomnia
- Decreased sexual desire

These potential symptoms only last for as long as you are taking the GnRHa. Therefore, if you are taking this medication for only a few doses, as in the case of the IVF protocol, the side effects may be minimal. However, if you are taking the GnRHa for three to six months as treatment for endometriosis, the potential for discomfort is more profound. In such circumstances, your doctor may recommend that you also take a low-dose supplementation of estrogen and progesterone. This adding back of hormones can relieve some of your symptoms and also help prevent bone loss. Studies show that once the GnRHa therapy stops, most women will experience a complete recovery of their bone density loss.

HOW WILL I BE MONITORED WHEN I'M TAKING A GNRHA?

While you are taking a GnRHa as part of an IVF protocol, you will be closely monitored by your fertility specialist with frequent office visits, blood work, and pelvic ultrasounds.

If you are taking this therapy as endometriosis treatment, your doctor will probably want to see you about once per month. The purpose of this office visit is to determine your level of pain relief and also to discuss any side effects that you may be experiencing.

WHAT ARE THE SUCCESS RATES AND OUTCOMES ASSOCIATED WITH GNRHA?

When given to women undergoing in vitro fertilization, GnRHa makes the cycle more dependable and predictable and thereby increases the pregnancy rate.

When used as therapy for endometriosis, up to 90 percent of women report complete or partial pain relief after six months of therapy. Remember that GnRHa does not cure endometriosis, but it shrinks the endometriosis implants and provides substantial pain relief.

WHAT ARE THE PROS AND CONS CONCERNING GNRHA?

It's a good idea for you to be aware of the pros and cons before taking GnRHa.

Pros

- When used with an IVF protocol, GnRHa improves the dependability and predictability of your cycle to maximize your chance of becoming pregnant.
- When used for treatment of endometriosis, GnRHa is effective in reducing endometriosis implants and the associated pain.

Cons

- GnRHa therapy is very expensive.
- Approximately 20 percent of women treated with GnRHa for endometriosis will have pain return within one year after treatment.
- The side effects of GnRHa therapy are menopause-like and can be quite unpleasant.
- Loss of bone density associated with long-term GnRHa use could potentially place you at risk for osteoporosis.
- In some forms, GnRHa must be injected.

IF I DON'T BECOME PREGNANT USING GₙRHₐ, WHAT'S NEXT?

GnRHa is typically prescribed in conjunction with IVF treatment. If you don't become pregnant after several IVF cycle attempts, your fertility specialist will discuss which next step is best for you.

When GnRHa is given for treatment of endometriosis, the goal of treatment is pain relief, not pregnancy.

Gonadotropin-Releasing Hormone (GnRH) Antagonists (Cetrotide, Ganirelix)

This is a relatively new class of medications used as part of your IVF or other assisted reproductive program. The purpose of this medication is exactly the same as GnRHa, to suppress your own body's hormones. Also as in the case of GnRHa, once your natural hormones have been suppressed, another medication (gonadotropins) will be given to induce ovulation. Using this protocol, the fertility specialist is able to precisely control the reproductive hormones and ovulation, thereby making conception more likely.

Increasing numbers of doctors are now using a GnRH antagonist instead of a GnRHa. That's because GnRH antagonists work faster and are often more effective in shutting down a woman's natural hormones. Talk with your doctor to find out which category of medication would best suit your individual situation.

HOW DO GₙRH ANTAGONISTS WORK?

GnRH antagonists work directly on your pituitary gland to block the release of FSH and LH. This direct blockage works almost immediately. Compare this to the traditional GnRHa, which suppresses FSH and LH in the bloodstream and takes several days to stop ovulation. In contrast, the GnRH antagonist is effective at shutting down ovulation within an hour or two.

Remember that the purpose of traditional GnRHa and GnRH antagonists is the same. They are both used to suppress your body's hormones and improve the dependability and predictability of your IVF cycle.

HOW DO I TAKE GnRH ANTAGONISTS?

The two different medications under the classification of GnRH antagonists are Cetrotide and Ganirelix. These medications are given to you by injection. Your doctor will discuss the specific timing and treatment protocol with you.

WHAT ARE THE POTENTIAL SIDE EFFECTS OF GnRH ANTAGONISTS?

Because GnRH antagonists work quickly and are paired with ovulation induction medication, it's rare to experience low estrogen or menopausal-like symptoms. However, GnRH antagonist treatment has been associated with the following potential side effects:

- Headache
- Nausea
- Swelling
- Redness or itchiness at injection site

HOW WILL I BE MONITORED WHEN I'M TAKING A GnRH ANTAGONIST?

While you are taking a GnRH antagonist as part of an IVF protocol, you will be closely monitored by your fertility specialist with frequent office visits, blood work, and pelvic ultrasounds.

WHAT ARE THE SUCCESS RATES AND OUTCOMES ASSOCIATED WITH GnRH ANTAGONISTS?

When given to women undergoing in vitro fertilization, GnRH antagonists cause the IVF cycle to become more dependable and predictable and thereby increase the pregnancy rate.

WHAT ARE THE PROS AND CONS CONCERNING GnRH ANTAGONISTS?

Here's a list of pros and cons for you to review before taking GnRH antagonists.

Pros

- When used in an IVF protocol, GnRH antagonists work to control your hormones and ovulation to maximize your chance of becoming pregnant.
- GnRH antagonists work very quickly and efficiently and therefore require fewer injections and less expense when compared to GnRHa.

Cons

- GnRH antagonist therapy is expensive.
- The side effects of GnRH antagonist therapy can be unpleasant.
- This type of medication must always be injected.

IF I DON'T BECOME PREGNANT USING GnRH ANTAGONISTS, WHAT'S NEXT?

GnRH antagonists are prescribed in conjunction with IVF treatment. If you don't become pregnant after several IVF cycle attempts, your fertility specialist will discuss which next step is best for you.

Human Chorionic Gonadotropin (hCG) (Novarel, Pregnyl, Profasi, Ovidrel)

When you become pregnant, your body produces a pregnancy hormone called human chorionic gonadotropin (hCG). It is produced by the placenta and is responsible for the rise in your progesterone level and the cause of many changes during pregnancy, including morning sickness. In fact, hCG is the hormone that home pregnancy tests detect to determine whether you are pregnant.

In assisted reproductive technology procedures, an injection of hCG is often used as a way to trigger ovulation.

HOW DOES hCG WORK?

During various assisted reproductive technologies, your ovaries are stimulated to grow follicles and develop mature eggs. These eggs won't release from their follicles without a hormonal trigger. In a normal nonmedicated cycle, your own surge of LH is what triggers ovulation and release of the egg. Researchers have found that hCG is chemically very similar to LH. Therefore, hCG is injected and works as a hormonal trigger to release the eggs from their follicles. Ovulation typically occurs 36 hours after the hCG injection.

Depending on which assisted reproductive technology you are using, either you will be advised to have sexual intercourse or your fertility specialist will perform intrauterine insemination or egg retrieval. You must accurately time this event because precise timing is required for successful egg fertilization.

HOW DO I TAKE hCG?

HCG is given to you by an injection. Commercially prepared hCG is available under various brand names. Profasi, Pregnyl, and Novarel are derived from the urine of pregnant women. These forms of hCG may be given using either a subcutaneous or intramuscular injection. Ovidrel is made in the laboratory from genetic recombination technology. Its purity allows it to be injected just under the skin.

WHAT ARE THE POTENTIAL SIDE EFFECTS OF hCG?

HCG is used for only a short time and rarely causes significant side effects. However, some women experience discomfort. Here's a list of some possible side effects that you may encounter:

- Hot flashes
- Headache
- Fluid retention
- Abdominal discomfort or bloating
- Tenderness, bruising, redness at the injection site

Be sure to notify your doctor if you experience any of these or any other unusual symptoms.

HOW WILL I BE MONITORED WHEN I'M TAKING hCG?

As part of any assisted reproductive technology, you will be closely monitored by your fertility specialist with frequent office visits, blood work, and pelvic ultrasounds.

WHAT ARE THE SUCCESS RATES AND OUTCOMES ASSOCIATED WITH hCG?

HCG is extremely effective when used to trigger ovulation. Because hCG is used as part of an assisted reproductive technique, the success rate depends on many factors relating to your particular situation.

WHAT ARE THE PROS AND CONS CONCERNING hCG?

HCG injections have been associated with various pros and cons.

Pros

- There is just a one-time dose of hCG per cycle.
- HCG is a very precise and reliable method to trigger ovulation.
- There are few significant side effects.

Cons

- The use of hCG causes a positive pregnancy test even if you are not pregnant.
- Intramuscular injection causes some bruising at the injection site.
- The subcutaneous injection may cause the injection site to become red, swollen, and itchy.

IF I DON'T BECOME PREGNANT USING hCG, WHAT'S NEXT?

HCG is used in conjunction with various assisted reproductive technologies such as IVF. If you don't become pregnant after several cycle attempts, your fertility specialist will discuss which next step is best for you.

Bromocriptine (Parlodel)

Parlodel is a medication that slows or stops the production of the hormone prolactin in the brain's pituitary gland. It is very useful in treating women with abnormally high prolactin levels. Very high levels of prolactin may be due to polycystic ovary syndrome (PCOS), hormonal imbalance, or a benign tumor in the pituitary gland called a pituitary adenoma. Unfortunately, high prolactin levels interfere with the body's normal production of LH and FSH and thus hinder the ovulation process. Parlodel is prescribed to lower the prolactin level and therefore allow ovulation to occur.

Additionally, Parlodel is also prescribed to treat a wide variety of other medical conditions that are not related to fertility or women's health at all. Examples include Parkinson's disease, which is a neurological condition, and acromegaly, which is a rare condition where the body produces too much growth hormone.

HOW DOES PARLODEL WORK?

Parlodel inhibits the secretion of prolactin from your pituitary gland. In this way, it works by lowering and normalizing your body's prolactin level. Normal prolactin levels work to bring about the normal production of LH and FSH. With these key hormones now in balance, regular menstrual cycles and ovulation can function normally.

HOW DO I TAKE PARLODEL?

Parlodel is taken orally as either a capsule or tablet. Take your pills at approximately the same time every day. That's because Parlodel works by sending hormonal messages to your pituitary gland and you want to time these messages as best you can to maximize the benefit.

Most doctors recommend that you take Parlodel with food to avoid stomach upset. Depending on how your body responds, your doctor may adjust your dosage. Occasionally, your doctor may recommend that you take this medication vaginally. The reason for this is to minimize any potential side effects.

It typically takes several months to get the dosage just right and have your prolactin levels return to normal. Once your prolactin level is within the normal range, you will begin to have normal menstrual cycles and begin to ovulate regularly again. If recommended by your physician, you can continue to take Parlodel for a prolonged period of time, even several years if necessary.

When you become pregnant, you should stop taking Parlodel and notify your doctor right away.

WHAT ARE THE POTENTIAL SIDE EFFECTS OF PARLODEL?

Most side effects are usually most apparent as you begin treatment and then subside as your body adjusts to this medication. Many women find that taking Parlodel with meals helps to relieve their discomfort. Here is a list of possible side effects that you may encounter while taking Parlodel:

- Upset stomach with nausea and vomiting
- Diarrhea

- Drowsiness and fatigue
- Dizziness and lightheadedness
- Headache
- Rapid heart beat (rarely)
- Swelling of feet or ankles (rarely)
- Confusion (rarely)
- Watery discharge from nose (rarely)

Be sure to notify your doctor if you experience any of these or any other unusual symptoms. Rapid heart beat, extreme swelling, confusion, and watery discharge from your nose are extremely rare but require immediate medical attention.

HOW WILL I BE MONITORED WHEN I'M TAKING PARLODEL?

Your doctor will draw your blood and check your prolactin level before you begin treatment with Parlodel. If your prolactin level is elevated, you will probably undergo a magnetic resonance imaging (MRI) of your head. The purpose of that radiological study is to evaluate your brain's pituitary gland. Once you begin Parlodel, your doctor will order blood work to evaluate your response to the medication.

When you are going to have your blood prolactin level checked, remember these few important points:

- This test is usually performed in the morning, when a raised prolactin level is most apparent.
- This test should not be done for at least one day following a breast examination or sexual activity because these activities may increase your prolactin levels and result in a false positive reading. Ask your doctor for specific timeframe guidelines.

WHAT ARE THE SUCCESS RATES AND OUTCOMES ASSOCIATED WITH PARLODEL?

While taking Parlodel, approximately 90 percent of women will experience regular menstrual cycles and begin to ovulate regularly. Of those who ovulate, about 75 percent will become pregnant.

It should also be noted that Parlodel does not increase your risk of becoming pregnant with a multiple (twins, triplets, and so on) pregnancy.

WHAT ARE THE PROS AND CONS CONCERNING PARLODEL?

Like all medication, it's important for you to understand the pros and cons of taking Parlodel.

Pros

- This medication has a high success rate for ovulation and pregnancy.
- This medication is not expensive, especially when compared to other fertility medications.
- Parlodel does not increase your risk of having multiples.
- This medication is easy to take because it is taken orally in either capsule or tablet form.

Cons

- Side effects associated with Parlodel are sometimes quite uncomfortable.

IF I DON'T BECOME PREGNANT USING PARLODEL, WHAT'S NEXT?

If you don't ovulate within a few months of starting Parlodel, your doctor may increase your dosage accordingly. If you still don't ovulate, some doctors prescribe Clomid along with Parlodel to increase your chances of ovulation and pregnancy.

If you don't become pregnant after several cycles of both of these medications, your doctor will recommend additional treatment based upon your particular situation. Some women go on to use other drug therapies or some go directly to assisted reproductive technology.

Progesterone (Progesterone in Oil, Vaginal Suppositories, Crinone Gel, Prometrium, Provera)

Progesterone is one of your body's naturally occurring reproductive hormones. If your progesterone level is too low, you may encounter problems becoming pregnant because of menstrual irregularities and problems with ovulation. In some cases, you may be able to get pregnant but will continue to experience miscarriage. In these situations, supplemental progesterone may be recommended. Supplemental progesterone is also used during some assisted reproductive technologies.

HOW DOES PROGESTERONE WORK?

During your regular monthly cycle, progesterone is made by the ovarian follicle (called the corpus luteum) just after ovulation. This progesterone circulates through your bloodstream and helps to stabilize and maintain your uterine lining (endometrium) so that it will be ready for a fertilized egg. If pregnancy occurs, progesterone is required to maintain the pregnancy. If you don't become pregnant during that cycle, the progesterone levels decrease and eventually cause the lining of your uterus to shed, resulting in menstrual bleeding. Progesterone plays an important role in your menstrual cycle, hormonal balance, and ovulation. Supplemental progesterone can be helpful if you suffer from these fertility conditions.

During an assisted reproductive technology, progesterone supplementation may also be given. In this case, supplemental progesterone is given to mimic and reinforce your body's naturally occurring progesterone. The purpose is to thicken and prepare the uterine lining for the fertilized egg(s) and help to maintain the pregnancy.

HOW DO I TAKE PROGESTERONE?

Progesterone therapy usually begins two or three days after ovulation has occurred. Therapy continues until your menstrual period begins. If you become pregnant, progesterone therapy will continue, oftentimes until you have completed your first trimester of pregnancy. However, the length of time that you take progesterone will depend on your medical history, your specific fertility condition, and the recommendation of your specialist.

Progesterone as a supplemental hormone is available in several forms:

- Synthetic progesterone (Provera) available in pills and for injection
- Natural progesterone tablets (Prometrium)
- Natural progesterone vaginal suppositories
- Natural bio-adhesive vaginal gel (Crinone)
- Natural progesterone in oil for injection

It's important to distinguish between those progesterone supplements already discussed with natural progesterone creams that are available over the counter. Natural progesterone creams contain small amounts of progesterone but not in high enough dosages to treat fertility and other related hormonal issues.

WHAT ARE THE POTENTIAL SIDE EFFECTS OF PROGESTERONE?

The side effects associated with progesterone therapy depend on the form of progesterone therapy that you receive and how your body reacts to it. Here is a list of possible side effects that you may encounter while taking progesterone:

- Mood swings
- Bloating
- Tender breasts
- Fatigue
- Nausea
- Headache
- Vaginal discharge (with suppositories)
- Tenderness at injection site (with injections)

Most side effects will diminish as your body gets used to this medication.

HOW WILL I BE MONITORED WHEN I'M TAKING PROGESTERONE?

Your doctor will draw your blood and check your progesterone level before you begin treatment. Laboratories vary, but most doctors want to see a progesterone blood level of at least 10 ng/ml and preferably 15 ng/ml after ovulation. Your specialist will continue to check your blood level of progesterone. Your dosage of progesterone will be adjusted to get your level within the desirable range.

WHAT ARE THE SUCCESS RATES AND OUTCOMES ASSOCIATED WITH PROGESTERONE?

The pregnancy rate depends on why you are taking progesterone therapy. Studies show that if you are taking progesterone due to a hormonal imbalance, the pregnancy rate is about 77 percent.

WHAT ARE THE PROS AND CONS CONCERNING PROGESTERONE?

Here are some key pros and cons regarding progesterone supplementation.

Pros

- Natural oral progesterone (Prometrium) is convenient because it is taken orally as a tablet.
- Suppositories target only your pelvic region, and thus you have fewer side effects throughout your body.
- Progesterone gel (Crinone) comes in an easy-to-use tamponlike applicator. The gel targets only your pelvic region, and thus you have fewer side effects.
- Progesterone in oil is highly effective at correcting hormonal imbalances and correcting menstrual and ovulation problems.

Cons

- Unlike natural progesterone, synthetic progesterone (Provera) is not safe to use once you become pregnant.
- Natural oral progesterone (Prometrium) may be associated with lower success rates than found with some other forms of progesterone.
- Natural oral progesterone (Prometrium) has side effects of dizziness or sleepiness.
- Progesterone suppositories are made by specialty pharmacies, which may be difficult to find in your area.
- Some women find the vaginal discharge associated with suppositories to be very unpleasant.
- The gel (Crinone) sticks so well in the vagina that some women experience vaginal irritation as a result of the buildup. Sometimes the accumulated gel must be removed every few days.
- Progesterone in oil must be injected, and a larger needle is required because of the thickness of the medication.

No one single form of progesterone is best for all women. Talk with your doctor about your particular situation and determine which method is best for you.

IF I DON'T BECOME PREGNANT USING PROGESTERONE, WHAT'S NEXT?

If you don't become pregnant and maintain the pregnancy after several cycles of progesterone, your specialist will recommend additional treatment based upon your particular situation. Some women go on to use other drug therapies or some go directly to an assisted reproductive technology.

Aspirin and Heparin

You are probably familiar with aspirin as an over-the-counter medication that has traditionally been used to relieve minor pain and fever. In recent years, aspirin has become well known for its blood-thinning properties. Heparin is a prescription medication that has long been used to thin out the blood and prevent the formation of blood clots.

Aspirin and heparin are used alone or together in the treatment of some fertility conditions. These medications may be prescribed to reduce the risk of miscarriage, especially when you have experienced miscarriages in the past. These medications are often recommended when you have been diagnosed with a blood-clotting disorder, such as antiphospholipid antibodies (APAs). Aspirin and heparin are also sometimes used during an IVF cycle to prevent pregnancy loss.

HOW DO ASPIRIN AND HEPARIN WORK?

If you have had prior miscarriages, they possibly were caused by a blood-clotting problem. Aspirin and heparin are both able to thin your blood and help to prevent the formation of blood clots.

Women with antiphospholipid syndrome (see Chapter 2) possess an increased tendency to form clots within their blood vessels. This is especially troublesome during pregnancy when clotting problems occur within the placenta. This places the baby at risk and increases the chance of miscarriage and/or stillbirth. Aspirin therapy reduces these risks by maintaining good placental blood flow between the mother and fetus.

When heparin is added to the treatment regimen, the blood-thinning properties are increased, because heparin works by interfering with your blood's natural clotting abilities, resulting in blood that is less sticky and can't bind together as easily.

HOW DO I TAKE ASPIRIN AND HEPARIN?

Aspirin comes in tablet form and is taken orally, usually in baby aspirin dosage of 81 mg. Heparin is given through an injection, often starting with a dosage of regular heparin 500 twice daily. Instead of using regular heparin, your fertility specialist may choose to prescribe a special type of low molecular weight heparin called Lovenox, which is also administered in the form of an injection. Your doctor will adjust the dose and discuss which treatment regimen is best for you.

WHAT ARE THE POTENTIAL SIDE EFFECTS OF ASPIRIN AND HEPARIN?

Many people think that aspirin is harmless because it has been an over-the-counter medication for decades. However, many doctors say that, if aspirin were to be discovered today, it would be available only by prescription. If you have any of the following conditions, please be sure to talk with your doctor before beginning aspirin therapy:

- Allergy to aspirin
- Medical history of stomach ulcers, gastric irritation, gastric bleeding
- Hemophilia, severe anemia, blood disorder

Heparin is somewhat controversial in the treatment of fertility problems, so it's especially important for you to be under the care of a competent fertility specialist who understands the side effects and possible complications associated with its use. Potential side effects associated with heparin use are:

- Back pain
- Stomach pain
- Skin rash
- Bone loss, which may lead to osteoporosis
- Excessive bleeding (nose bleeds, eye bleeds, heavy menstrual bleeding)
- Hair loss

HOW WILL I BE MONITORED WHEN I'M TAKING ASPIRIN AND HEPARIN?

Your doctor will draw your blood and check your blood-clotting factors to ensure that you are receiving the proper dosage. Report any side effects or unusual symptoms to your doctor right away.

WHAT ARE THE SUCCESS RATES AND OUTCOMES ASSOCIATED WITH ASPIRIN AND HEPARIN?

Recent clinical studies conclude that aspirin therapy is effective in treating women who have been diagnosed with various blood-clotting disorders. Aspirin therapy also appears to improve the pregnancy rate in patients undergoing IVF.

Heparin is somewhat more controversial; however, studies show that heparin appears to improve the chances of carrying a pregnancy to term. When heparin and aspirin are taken together, the live birth rates are approximately 70 percent.

WHAT ARE THE PROS AND CONS CONCERNING ASPIRIN AND HEPARIN?

Before taking aspirin and/or heparin, you should be aware of their pros and cons.

Pros

- Aspirin and heparin appear to be useful and effective treatments for patients who are undergoing fertility treatments.
- Both medications are relatively inexpensive.

Cons

- Aspirin and especially heparin have been linked to potentially dangerous side effects.
- Aspirin and heparin have not been approved by the Food and Drug Administration for use as blood-thinning therapy for IVF patients.

If you are considering using aspirin or heparin as part of your fertility treatment, be sure to discuss all of the risks and benefits with your fertility specialist.

IF I DON'T BECOME PREGNANT USING ASPIRIN AND HEPARIN, WHAT'S NEXT?

If you don't become pregnant and maintain the pregnancy after several cycles of aspirin and heparin treatment, your specialist will recommend additional treatment based upon your particular situation.

Risks: Ovarian Hyperstimulation Syndrome (OHSS)

OHSS occurs when your ovaries become overly stimulated from ovulation-induction medications. Studies show that approximately 4 percent of women undergoing assisted reproductive technologies may develop OHSS. The ovaries begin to enlarge and form multiple fluid-filled cysts. The excessive fluid can leak into your abdominal and chest cavity and cause serious complications.

Symptoms usually begin about four or five days after the stimulated ovulation has occurred. A woman with OHSS might notice pain and bloating in her abdomen. She may have difficulty urinating and experience a sudden weight gain of up to 10 pounds. Rarely, the symptoms can become excruciatingly painful and accompanied by nausea, vomiting, and shortness of breath.

Any patient who undergoes ovulation induction is at risk of developing OHSS. However, the reason why some women are more likely to develop OHSS than others is not completely understood. Here's a list of women who seem to be at higher risk of developing OHSS:

- Women who become pregnant during that cycle
- Women with polycystic ovary syndrome (PCOS)
- Women who are young
- Women with high estrogen levels and a large number of eggs
- The use of a GnRH agonist (GnRHa)

In mild cases, OHSS may be managed with rest and doctor visits. It will resolve by itself in a few days. Severe cases of OHSS require urgent hospital admission and may last for several weeks. Hospital treatment focuses on restoring your fluid and electrolyte balance and controlling your pain. In life-threatening situations, you may need cardiac support and blood transfusions.

OHSS is certainly one of the most serious complications that a fertility patient can encounter. Fortunately, it is quite rare and most cases are mild. The severe form of OHSS occurs in less than 1 percent of women affected. However, any woman undergoing ovulation induction should understand the symptoms and potential risks of OHSS.

Conclusion

Of course, most women don't relish the idea of taking fertility medications. They are expensive and often have various unpleasant side effects. That said, isn't it good to know that a variety of effective and safe medications are available? Almost certainly one or more of them will suit your needs and enable you to become pregnant. Hopefully, this chapter has provided you with the knowledge to understand what's available and some pros and cons for each medication. Ask your fertility specialist how these medications might be used for your particular situation. By working together, you can hopefully anticipate and minimize side effects and fully benefit from what these medications have to offer you.

Summary

Here is a summary of the medications discussed in this chapter.

Clomid

- This is often the first medication that fertility patients receive because it helps to regulate ovulation and is relatively inexpensive.

- Clomid is one of the few fertility medications taken orally.

- Approximately 80 percent of women taking Clomid will ovulate.

- If you don't become pregnant after about six cycles of using Clomid, you are unlikely to become pregnant from this medication.

Gonadotropins

- The purpose of using a gonadotropin medication is to stimulate ovulation and encourage follicle development to produce more eggs.

- Gonadotropins are available either in a man-made form produced from recombinant DNA technology or from the purified urine of menopausal women. Your doctor will determine which is best for you.

- Medical research shows that more than 80 percent of women taking gonadotropins will ovulate.

Gonadotropin-Releasing Hormone Agonists (GnRHa)

- This medication is often used as part of your IVF protocol to suppress your own body's hormones. Once they are shut down, gonadotropins are given to induce ovulation. This technique allows your doctor to precisely control your hormones and ovulation.

- Another use for this medicine is for the treatment for painful endometriosis. Once GnRHa has shut down your hormones and stopped your periods, the unpleasant endometriosis symptoms stop. However, you cannot become pregnant during this time; therefore, this is seen as temporary relief treatment.

Gonadotropin-Releasing Hormone Antagonists (GnRH antagonists)

- Just like GnRHa, this relatively new class of medications may be used as part of your IVF cycle to suppress your own body's hormones. Afterward, the gonadotropins will be administered to induce ovulation.

- Some doctors prefer GnRH antagonists instead of GnRHa because they are thought to work faster and more effectively. Other doctors disagree.

Human Chorionic Gonadotropin (hCG)

- This hormone is produced naturally by your body when you become pregnant. However, it is used as a medication during fertility treatments for the purpose of triggering ovulation within your ovary.

Bromocriptine (Parlodel)

- High levels of the hormone prolactin hinder the ovulation process. This medication slows or stops the production of the prolactin so that ovulation may occur.

- Women with abnormally high levels of prolactin may include those with polycystic ovary syndrome, various hormonal imbalances, or a benign tumor in the pituitary gland.

Progesterone

- Progesterone is one of your body's naturally occurring hormones. If your progesterone level is too low, you may experience problems becoming pregnant because of irregular menses or problems with ovulation. Or you may experience repeat miscarriages, perhaps linked to low progesterone levels. In these situations, supplemental progesterone may be recommended.

- Progesterone may also be prescribed as part of an assisted reproductive technology. The purpose would be to stabilize and maintain the uterine lining so that the egg can implant and grow.

Aspirin and Heparin

- Aspirin and heparin are sometimes prescribed to treat those diagnosed with recurrent miscarriages or known blood-clotting abnormalities.

Ovarian Hyperstimulation Syndrome (OHSS)

- OHSS is a medical condition that may occur, though rarely, when your ovaries have been overly stimulated by various fertility medications.

- Approximately 4 percent of women undergoing assisted reproductive technologies may develop OHSS.

- During OHSS your ovaries enlarge and form many fluid-filled cysts. This fluid can leak into your abdomen and chest, causing potentially serious complications and symptoms. Talk with your doctor if you believe that you are experiencing any of the following symptoms so that you can be quickly diagnosed and treated:

- Pain and bloating in your abdomen
- Difficulty urinating
- Sudden weight gain of up to 10 pounds
- Rarely, extreme pain, nausea, vomiting, shortness of breath

CHAPTER 7

Assisted Reproductive Technologies (ARTs)

Assisted reproductive technologies (ARTs) involves the sophisticated treatment and processing of human eggs and sperm to help you become pregnant. The treatments that you receive will depend on a variety of issues, including your health and that of your partner, your concerns and desires, and your particular fertility situation.

Examples of ART include intrauterine insemination (IUI), which is commonly referred to as artificial insemination, and in vitro fertilization (IVF), which results in what some people call test tube babies. Depending on your circumstance, you may be offered various other specialized techniques, such as intracytoplasmic sperm injection (ICSI), embryo assisted hatching, and cryopreservation of sperm and embryos. Each of these ART procedures is discussed in detail in this chapter.

If you are seriously considering assisted reproduction, you need to understand what medical conditions or circumstances you have and why natural conception has not worked for you. You'll want to set realistic goals and understand your chances of success with each available option. The Centers for Disease Control and Prevention (CDC) reveals the pregnancy success rates for many U.S. clinics on its website, cdc.gov. Be sure to discuss pregnancy success rates with your doctor and find out how it applies to your particular situation. In general, it's usually best to try the least invasive procedures first. This may save you time, money, and emotional concern.

Intrauterine Insemination (IUI)

IUI is a procedure in which your doctor inserts washed and concentrated sperm directly into your uterus at the time that coincides with your ovulation.

WHY DOES IUI WORK BETTER THAN NATURAL INTERCOURSE?

During normal intercourse, only a small fraction of sperm makes it up into the woman's uterus and into the fallopian tubes, where fertilization takes place. With IUI, concentrated amounts of sperm are inserted directly into your uterus. This significantly increases the number of sperm that can make it into your fallopian tubes to fertilize the egg.

CAN IUI HELP YOU?

To be a candidate for IUI, you must be able to meet these conditions:

- Have a normal uterine cavity
- Have open fallopian tubes
- Be ovulating normally or be responsive to ovulation-stimulating medications

You might be helped with IUI if you are experiencing one of these fertility problems:

- Hostile cervical mucus or another problem concerning cervical mucus
- Mild endometriosis but no distortion or scarring within your uterus
- An ovulation disorder, provided you respond to fertility ovulation drugs

- Unexplained infertility
- Antisperm antibodies in you or your male partner

WHAT ABOUT THE MAN'S ROLE IN IUI?

The sperm used during your IUI procedure may come from either your partner or a sperm donor.

Most women prefer to use sperm from their partner. However, your partner must have adequate sperm function. This means that his sperm must have the natural ability to fertilize an egg. This is typically measured in terms of adequate sperm quantity, movement of sperm, and shape of sperm. If your partner's sperm count is just a little low, his sperm may still be used because they will be washed and concentrated in the laboratory. However, in cases of zero or very low sperm count or abnormally functioning sperm, a sperm donor will likely be recommended.

Sperm from a donor is frozen ahead of time and checked for medical problems such as certain genetic disorders and sexually transmitted diseases (STDs). Ask your doctor which specific tests are performed at your laboratory.

HOW IS IUI PERFORMED?

Your fertility specialist will perform your IUI in the doctor's office. Important preparations must be taken ahead of time to maximize your chances of becoming pregnant. The following points, each of which is discussed immediately following, highlight the significant aspects of the IUI procedure.

- Ovulation
- Monitoring and timing
- Semen collection and preparation
- Insertion
- Follow-up after IUI

Ovulation

Depending on your particular situation, you may be given fertility medication to stimulate ovulation or you may ovulate naturally. If you will be ovulating naturally, your doctor will use blood or urine tests to calculate your ovulation time, which will be identified by the rise in your LH.

Many doctors prefer to perform IUI in conjunction with ovulation induced by fertility medication. That's because an overwhelming amount of research has shown that the best pregnancy rates are achieved when IUI is coupled with ovulation-induced fertility medication. Therefore, your doctor may recommend fertility medication to induce your ovulation, even if you don't have an ovulation disorder.

Monitoring and Timing

Of course, the IUI procedure must coincide with ovulation. If you will be ovulating naturally, your doctor will calculate your ovulation time based on blood or urine tests, typically the rise in your LH.

If you will be taking fertility medication (often either Clomid or a gonadotropin) to induce ovulation, further monitoring is required. The combination of ultrasound and blood work will help the doctor monitor your treatment cycle, adjust medication dosages, and reduce possible side effects.

You will have several pelvic ultrasounds during this treatment cycle to monitor and measure the growing follicles, the fluid-filled sacs around the eggs within your ovaries. Because the actual eggs are too small to be seen on ultrasound, the fluid-filled sacs (the follicles) around the eggs are measured and monitored. They must be monitored closely to ensure that only two or three follicles are developing. If too many follicles develop, too many eggs may be released and increase the risks of multiple pregnancy. Your doctor may also measure the estrogen concentration in your blood. That's because usually the more eggs, the higher the estrogen level in your bloodstream.

Once the ultrasound has shown that two or three follicles have reached the proper size, ovulation will be triggered with hCG. The IUI is typically performed between 24 and 48 hours after the hCG injection because that is the most likely time period for ovulation to occur.

Semen Collection and Preparation

Whether you are using sperm samples from your partner or a donor, the sperm sample is collected from the man on the morning of your IUI procedure. The fresh semen is taken to the laboratory, where it is washed. Then the sperm are separated from the liquid portion of the semen. The washed sperm are placed into a sterile medium and then concentrated into a small volume. This small amount of concentrated washed sperm will be used in your IUI procedure later that same day. (Unwashed sperm should never be placed directly into the uterus because they can cause a potentially serious allergic reaction.)

Insertion

For the procedure itself, you will be placed on the examination table with your feet in stirrups, much like the position you are in for a Pap test. The doctor will insert a very thin and flexible catheter into your vagina and through your cervix. Once the catheter is in place, the washed and concentrated sperm will be inserted high into your uterus. This high placement is closer to your fallopian tubes and increases the chance of successful fertilization.

Follow-Up After IUI

Your doctor will give you instructions about what activities you should and should not do after your IUI. In most cases, you can return to work and go about your normal activities. You may be instructed not to have sexual intercourse for a couple of days.

The doctor will ask you to make a follow-up appointment for pregnancy testing and early ultrasound monitoring after your IUI procedure.

DOES IUI HURT AND WHAT ARE THE RISKS?

Most women say that IUI is fairly painless and compare it to having a Pap smear. Some women note that after the procedure they have cramping, which usually goes away with a mild pain reliever.

Risks are usually infrequent with the IUI procedure, but you need to be aware that they could occur. Risks include:

- Infection
- Multiple pregnancy
- Ovarian hyperstimulation syndrome (OHSS)

Infection with a bacteria or virus could occur during the IUI procedure, from contaminated equipment, catheter, or the sperm itself.

If you are using fertility medication to induce ovulation, you have an increased risk of multiple pregnancy. Multiple pregnancies tend to have higher rates of miscarriage, low birth weight babies, and greater social difficulties. Therefore, if your doctor notices more than three maturing follicles on ultrasound prior to the procedure, the IUI may be canceled for that treatment cycle.

Ovulation-induction fertility medication also places you at an increased risk to develop OHSS. This is a potentially serious complication, where the ovaries become overstimulated and enlarged, resulting in pain and a collection of fluid in your abdomen and chest. (For a more detailed discussion of OHSS, see Chapter 6.) If your doctor suspects OHSS, the IUI will be canceled for that treatment cycle.

HOW SUCCESSFUL IS IUI?

Overall, the success rate of IUI is between approximately 10 and 18 percent per cycle, when combined with ovulation-induction medications. Of course, individual rates will vary based on a number of factors. In general, you will encounter a higher success rate with the IUI procedure under these conditions:

- You produce several follicles instead of just one follicle.
- You have the IUI procedure performed more than once per treatment cycle.
- The sperm count is higher than average.

In Vitro Fertilization (IVF)

IVF is the procedure where the woman's ovaries are stimulated to produce eggs, the eggs are removed and fertilized with the male partner's sperm in a laboratory, and the resulting embryos are transferred into her uterus after several days.

WHY DOES IVF WORK BETTER THAN NATURAL INTERCOURSE?

IVF is more effective than natural intercourse because of the following:

- Fertility medications are used to produce more eggs than would develop naturally.
- Instead of your having to wait for the eggs to ovulate naturally, with IVF the eggs are retrieved manually by your doctor.
- IVF bypasses the fallopian tubes because the eggs are retrieved directly from the ovaries and transferred directly into the uterus.
- Sperm are specially prepared in the laboratory so they can avoid the many hurdles that sperm encounter in a natural setting, such as cervical mucus and long difficult swims.
- Most IVF programs transfer several fertilized eggs back into your uterus to improve the chances of a successful pregnancy outcome.

CAN IVF HELP YOU?

For the most part, IVF is an effective treatment for all causes of infertility. One exception to this would be if the woman has major abnormalities within her uterus, such as severe adhesions.

You might be helped with IVF if you are experiencing one of these fertility conditions:

- Hostile cervical mucus or another problem concerning cervical mucus
- Blocked or scarred fallopian tubes
- Endometriosis
- Unexplained infertility
- Male factor infertility (such as low sperm count, low mobility, poor quality)

WHAT ABOUT THE MAN'S ROLE IN IVF?

The sperm used during your IVF procedure may come from either your partner or a sperm donor. Most women prefer to use sperm from their partner. Unless your partner has a very low sperm count or extremely poor sperm quantity, his sperm can probably be used during the IVF process. That's because his sperm will be washed and concentrated and also specially treated in the laboratory to enhance their ability to fertilize your eggs. If he has very poor sperm function, he may need to produce several semen samples over a few days for the laboratory to have enough good-quality sperm for use on the day of fertilization.

Of course, if a sperm donor is required, this will be arranged in advance. Sperm from a donor is frozen ahead of time and checked for medical problems such as certain genetic disorders and STDs. Ask your doctor which specific tests are performed at your laboratory.

HOW IS IVF PERFORMED?

Your fertility specialist will perform your IVF in either the doctor's office or an outpatient surgery facility. To increase your chances of success, the IVF procedure must be very well organized and perfectly timed. Most IVF programs follow these important steps. Each of these stages is discussed in more detail immediately following the list.

- Ovulation stimulation
- Egg retrieval
- Semen collection and preparation

- Fertilization
- Embryo monitoring
- Embryo transfer
- Follow-up after IVF
- Cryopreservation after IVF

Ovulation Stimulation

You will be given fertility medication to develop multiple eggs and stimulate ovulation. The usual protocol involves three types of medication: a GnRH agonist or antagonist to suppress your natural hormones, a gonadotropin to stimulate follicle and egg development, and hCG to finalize egg development and trigger ovulation. Your doctor will discuss the exact medications and timing with you.

Hormonal blood levels and pelvic ultrasounds are performed every few days to monitor the progress of the developing follicles. The doctor notes the number of developing eggs and records the size of each follicle. Once the follicles have reached their goal size and there are between 10 and 30 developing follicles, the egg retrieval process will be scheduled.

Egg Retrieval

When the follicles are mature, the ultrasound guided egg retrieval procedure is performed. The purpose of this step in the procedure is to remove the eggs from your ovaries. The egg retrieval procedure is performed either in the doctor's office or in an outpatient surgery facility. The average time to perform this procedure is about 20 minutes. For your comfort, you will usually be given an anesthetic for this procedure.

Your doctor will introduce a long ultrasound probe into your vagina. This probe will transmit a clear image of your ovaries on the ultrasound monitor. The doctor will then pass a sterile needle alongside the ultrasound probe through the top of your vagina and into the ovary and gently suction each developing egg.

You'll be asked to recover and rest for about an hour following the egg retrieval. During this time, your doctor's lab employee, the embryologist, will examine the collected eggs and let you know how many high-quality eggs were collected. In most cases, you can return to your normal routine the following day.

Sperm Collection and Preparation

Most laboratories need the sperm specimen within a few hours after egg retrieval. The fresh semen is taken to the laboratory, where it is washed and separated from the liquid portion of the semen. The washed sperm are placed into a sterile medium and then concentrated into a small volume.

The sperm are then treated in the laboratory with a variety of techniques to enhance their ability to fertilize an egg. The sperm are treated and incubated in a special medium that alters the membrane covering the sperm, increasing enzymes that will be needed for egg penetration and fertilization. The sperm are also processed in a centrifuge, which allows the laboratory to isolate the highest quality and concentration of sperm. Some labs have the sperm swim through special tubing to isolate only the most vigorous and healthy sperm. Occasionally, labs will add a caffeinelike substance to the sperm to invigorate the sperm and make them more active and mobile. The purpose of all of these sperm preparations is to ensure that the best, highest quality, and greatest concentration of sperm is available to fertilize your eggs.

Fertilization

In the laboratory, your recently collected eggs are placed in a Petri dish and combined with the healthy sperm. The Petri dish contains a nourishing liquid that bathes and nourishes the eggs and sperm, just as it would occur in nature within your own body fluids and reproductive tract. The egg and sperm Petri dish mixture is then placed in an incubator and closely monitored to see which eggs become fertilized.

Fertilization, which is the actual entry of the sperm into the egg, usually occurs within a few hours. A typical goal for most labs would be that each collected mature egg has a better than 70 percent chance of fertilization. The fertilized eggs are left in the incubator to continue to grow and develop into embryos.

Embryo Monitoring

The embryos continue to grow and develop in the incubator set at normal body temperature, which is the same temperature of your uterus. The laboratory serves as a temporary womb and ensures that the newly fertilized eggs are nourished and monitored closely. Those that are growing and developing properly will typically consist of four to eight cells within two or three days. This level of development serves as a guide to determine which of the embryos are developing normally and which will be the best candidates for transfer back into your uterus. At this point, the newly formed embryos are prepared for transfer to your uterus.

Embryo Transfer

You should be as comfortable as possible during the embryo transfer. Many doctors offer a relaxing medication or sedative for this stage of IVF. Fortunately, the procedure is not uncomfortable and it only takes a few minutes to perform.

For the procedure itself, you will be placed on the examination table with your feet in stirrups, very much like the position you are in for a Pap test. Sometimes the table is tilted somewhat with your head down. Your doctor will use an ultrasound to guide the placement of the very thin and flexible catheter through your vagina and cervix and into your uterus. The lab assistant will load the embryos into the catheter, and your doctor will carefully inject the embryos into your uterus. Once the catheter is withdrawn, the lab assistant examines the catheter in the laboratory to make sure that all the embryos have been properly transferred.

Although embryo transfer is the shortest step in the IVF procedure, it is a very important and critical element of the entire process.

You'll be asked to stay reclining for between 30 minutes and an hour. During this time, you may experience mild abdominal or pelvic cramping. You may also notice a slight vaginal discharge after the procedure, which is likely due to the supplies and equipment used during the procedure itself.

Once transferred, the developing embryos should begin to implant into your uterine lining within the next couple of days.

Follow-Up After IVF

Your doctor will give you instructions about what activities you should and should not do after your IVF. Many women prefer to take it easy and rest for the remainder of the day.

Depending on your medical history and your doctor's preferences, you may be started on progesterone hormone supplementation to maintain and stabilize the uterine lining for the next few weeks, just in case you are pregnant. Some IVF programs wait until they can confirm a pregnancy and then begin hormonal therapy to help support and maintain the pregnancy. Still other IVF programs do not prescribe any hormones at all after the transfer. This controversial issue has no clear-cut answer. Ask your doctor which method would work best for you.

The doctor will ask you to make a follow-up appointment after your IVF procedure for pregnancy testing and early ultrasound monitoring. A positive blood test may indicate the possibility of a pregnancy. However, pregnancy will be confirmed by ultrasound, usually three weeks after the embryo transfer.

Cryopreservation After IVF

After your IVF treatment cycle, you could possibly have some leftover embryos. That is, healthy fertilized eggs were not transferred to you because you already received the proper amount. Many couples choose to freeze their leftover embryos, a process called cryopreservation. For more about this technique, see the section specifically on cryopreservation near the end of this chapter.

DOES IVF HURT AND WHAT ARE THE RISKS?

You are typically sedated during the egg retrieval process and again during the embryo transfer process and therefore quite comfortable. Most women say that the procedure is painless and compare it to having a Pap smear. Some women note that after the procedure they have cramping, which usually goes away with rest and a mild pain reliever.

Risks are infrequent with the IVF procedure, but you need to be aware that they could occur. Risks include:

- Infection
- Bleeding
- Multiple pregnancy
- Ovarian hyperstimulation syndrome (OHSS)

Infection with a bacteria or virus could occur during the IVF procedure from contaminated equipment or the sperm itself.

Bleeding is unlikely but could occur during the egg retrieval portion of the procedure. If this occurs, a blood transfusion or surgery may be required to correct the situation.

Because you are using fertility medication to induce ovulation, you have an increased risk of multiple pregnancy. However, in the case of IVF, your doctor will determine how many embryos to transfer back to your uterus and thereby keep it to a reasonable number. Talk with your doctor about the number of embryos that you will have transferred back to your uterus. You'll also want to address, ahead of time, what to do with any leftover embryos that cannot be transferred back during that treatment cycle.

If your doctor suspects OHSS, the IVF will be canceled for that treatment cycle. (For a more detailed discussion of OHSS, see Chapter 6.)

There has been some speculation about the possibility of linking IVF to an increased incidence of birth defects. It is known that chromosomal abnormalities increase as a woman ages or if a man has abnormal sperm. However, minimal evidence exists to support the suggestion that the IVF procedure itself increases the risk of birth defects.

HOW SUCCESSFUL IS IVF?

Overall, the success rate of IVF is between 25 and 50 percent per cycle. Rates vary based on a number of variables. In general, a higher success rate is more likely under these conditions:

- You are young and produce a high number of good quality of eggs.
- Your uterus is normally shaped and free of scarring or abnormalities.
- The sperm quality is good.
- You are willing and able to undergo the complete IVF procedure several times.
- Your IVF team is talented, skilled, and experienced.

Intracytoplasmic Sperm Injection (ICSI)

ICSI is a special fertilization technique that is sometimes used along with the other ART procedures. It involves the injection of a single sperm directly into the center of an egg. The resulting embryos are placed back into the woman's uterus, using a technique exactly like IVF.

WHY DOES ICSI WORK BETTER THAN NATURAL INTERCOURSE?

ICSI is more effective than natural intercourse because:

- Fertility medications are used to produce more eggs than would develop naturally.
- Instead of your having to wait for the eggs to ovulate naturally, with IVF the eggs are retrieved manually by your doctor.
- IVF bypasses the fallopian tubes because the eggs are retrieved directly from the ovaries and transferred directly into the uterus.
- Your eggs are treated in the laboratory, and their outside protective layer is removed to make them more easily penetrated and fertilized by sperm.
- Sperm are specially prepared in the laboratory and then injected directly into each of your pretreated eggs to greatly improve the chances of fertilization.
- Most IVF programs transfer several fertilized eggs back into your uterus to improve the chances of a successful pregnancy outcome.

CAN ICSI HELP YOU?

Although IVF can be successfully used for men with mild sperm abnormalities, ICSI has brought a new dimension of therapy for men with severe male factor infertility issues. Indications for ICSI include:

- Extremely low sperm count
- Poor sperm quality (abnormal shapes and poor movement)
- Presence of antisperm antibodies
- History of poor fertilization during one or more prior IVF attempts
- Any reason why the man's sperm cannot easily penetrate the woman's egg

WHAT ABOUT THE WOMAN'S ROLE IN ICSI?

Because ICSI is really designed for severe male factor infertility, as a woman, you may or may not have a fertility condition yourself. But as a couple, of course, you are both affected. As a woman, you will likely undergo IVF or another similar ART procedure to become pregnant.

HOW IS ICSI PERFORMED?

The ICSI procedure refers to the process of how the sperm fertilizes the egg and is typically performed in conjunction with another ART, such as IVF. The remainder of the steps are usually identical to IVF or another ART technique that your doctor may recommend.

Because most of the time ICSI is performed in conjunction with IVF, the steps of these procedures are almost identical.

- Ovulation stimulation
- Egg retrieval
- Sperm collection and preparation
- Fertilization
- Embryo monitoring
- Embryo transfer
- Follow-up after ICSI
- Cryopreservation after ICSI

Ovulation stimulation and egg retrieval follow the same steps as in the IVF procedure.

Sperm Collection and Preparation

The sperm used during your ICSI procedure almost always comes from your partner as opposed to a sperm donor. After all, the primary purpose of ICSI is to assist men with severe male fertility issues. So even if your partner has very poor sperm quality or quantity, his sperm are often still used successfully.

As with most other techniques, sperm are usually obtained via masturbation and ejaculation. If that is objectionable to you or your partner for religious or other reasons, talk to your doctor about a special condom that may be used to collect sperm during intercourse.

The laboratory needs the semen specimen within a few hours after egg retrieval. The fresh semen is taken to the laboratory, where it is washed, concentrated, and specially treated so each healthy sperm has the best potential to successfully fertilize your eggs. Sometimes in the case of severe male fertility problems, sperm cannot be obtained through masturbation or sexual intercourse. In this situation, sperm can sometimes be captured with direct testicular biopsy.

Sperm Aspiration. Sometimes sperm can't be collected with routine methods of masturbation or a special collection condom during sexual intercourse. This may be because of an abnormality of the male reproductive tract that your partner was born with or the result of a serious injury. It may also be the case with men who have had a prior vasectomy. New microsurgical techniques have been developed to obtain the sperm directly from either the testicles or the epididymis when it cannot be collected by the usual methods.

- **Testicular sperm extraction (TESE):** Sperm can be directly obtained from the testicles using a special testicular biopsy technique. A very small piece of testicular tissue is taken to the laboratory, where sperm are extracted and evaluated.

- **Microsurgical epididymal sperm aspiration (MESA):** Sperm can be directly obtained from the epididymis using a specialized needle collecting system. You'll recall that the epididymis is a thin, hollow coiled system within the scrotum that receives the maturing sperm from the testicles. The fluid from the epididymis is collected and then sent to the laboratory, where sperm are removed and evaluated.

The emergence of these techniques has been of great benefit for male fertility problems. Men who could not use their sperm in the past are now able to do so with these specialized procedures. The collected sperm can be used in various ART procedures. With these important microsurgical techniques, men who thought they would never be able to father a child are now able to do so.

Fertilization

Your collected eggs will be examined in the laboratory and will be specially treated to remove the surrounding membrane, thereby making the egg easier to penetrate and fertilize.

Each egg is held in place with a specially designed instrument, and one sperm is injected into each egg's center. The inseminated eggs are then placed in an incubator and checked the next morning to determine which have successfully fertilized. The fertilized eggs are left in the incubator to continue to grow and develop into embryos for the next day or two.

The next steps—embryo monitoring, embryo transfer, follow-up, and cryopreservation—are the same as those in the IVF procedure.

DOES ICSI HURT AND WHAT ARE THE RISKS?

The man experiences essentially no risk or discomfort when sperm is collected, usually through masturbation or sexual intercourse with a special collection condom. However, as previously stated, in the case of severe male fertility problems, a testicular biopsy may be required to obtain sperm.

Risks are infrequent with ICSI, but you need to be aware that they could occur. Risks include:

- Infection
- Bleeding
- Multiple pregnancy
- Ovarian hyperstimulation syndrome (OHSS)

Some fertility experts speculate that a link exists between ICSI and an increased incidence of birth defects. However, extensive research has shown no increase in the rate of birth defects or other abnormalities due to the ICSI procedure.

Some concern also exists that ICSI might increase the incidence of male infertility in male offspring. The thinking behind this theory is that in nature, the most viable and healthy sperm reaches and fertilizes the egg. However, with ICSI, the sperm are manually selected and injected and thereby bypass the natural selection process. Thus if rare sexual chromosomal abnormalities exist within the sperm, they might be passed to the male offspring. More research is needed to further evaluate and understand this theory.

HOW SUCCESSFUL IS ICSI?

The success rate for ICSI is usually about 30 percent. This is essentially the same pregnancy rate as with IVF. However, this is a significant achievement because ICSI is primarily used in cases of severe male infertility.

The success of the ICSI technique takes the anonymous sperm donor out of the picture, which eases much of the emotional difficulty that couples have when dealing with an outside third-party sperm donor.

Of course, even more than with some of the other ART procedures, a high level of technical expertise is required to successfully perform ICSI, an exquisitely delicate and intricate technique.

Embryo Assisted Hatching

Assisted hatching is a special technique to help the embryo implant into your uterus. The technique is typically used in conjunction with IVF or ICSI. The thought is that thinning or making a small hole in the embryo's outer shell (called the zona pellucida) may help the embryo to progress and successfully implant in your uterine lining.

Some fertility specialists and clinics choose to use assisted hatching with all of their IVF patients because they believe that it increases pregnancy success rates. Others decide to use assisted hatching under certain conditions, such as:

- Older women using their own eggs
- Couples with poor quality embryos
- Embryos that have a thick outer shell
- Couples who have failed implantation in previous IVF or ICSI cycles

Assisted hatching is done just prior to embryo transfer during your IVF or ICSI treatment cycle. The procedure is usually performed on day 3 of the embryo's development and usually when the embryo is at the eight-cell stage. The methods used to place the tiny hole in the outer shell vary and may include the use of acid, a micro needle, or laser. The embryos are then placed back in the incubator, and the embryo transfer is performed shortly thereafter.

Unfortunately, a few risks are involved with this procedure:

- The procedure itself will damage or destroy about 1 percent of the embryos.
- Infection risk for the embryo is greater because the procedure deprives the embryo of its outer protective layer.
- Assisted hatching has been linked with a slightly higher chance of identical twins.

Pregnancy rates vary from clinic to clinic. Many fertility programs report an increased pregnancy rate for IVF with assisted hatching technique when compared to IVF without hatching. Ask your doctor if this technique could benefit you.

Cryopreservation

Cryopreservation is the technology of using subzero freezing on human cells. This technique can be used on sperm or embryos. They can remain frozen indefinitely, but most people choose to eventually thaw them and implant them for another pregnancy.

The technique used to freeze either sperm or embryos is basically the same. The sperm or embryos are placed in a special cryoprotectant solution, sort of like anti-freeze. The purpose of this substance is to insulate and protect the fragile human cells. The sperm or embryos are then suctioned into a small plastic freezing straw, and the straw is sealed at both ends. The filled straws are then placed in a tank of liquid nitrogen and gradually frozen.

SPERM

A man may decide to freeze his sperm under these situations:

- He has difficulty producing sperm at any given time.
- The sperm were obtained using a microsurgical technique (such as testicular biopsy), and he wants to avoid having to go through another invasive procedure.
- He is planning to undergo cancer treatment, such as chemotherapy or radiotherapy, which could damage his sperm.
- He may want to donate his sperm for use by other couples.

When sperm is needed, it can be thawed and used for various ART procedures that same day.

EMBRYOS

You may choose to freeze embryos under these situations:

- You have leftover embryos after an embryo transfer cycle and would like to use these in a future cycle. This would save you from having to undergo another egg retrieval procedure.
- You are facing cancer treatment with chemotherapy or radiation, which could permanently damage your eggs.
- You are approaching menopause and won't be able to produce viable eggs in a few years.
- You would like to donate your embryos to other people looking to become pregnant.

When the frozen embryos are needed, they are typically thawed just prior to or on the day of the scheduled embryo transfer. The newly thawed embryos will be assessed for survival and development and only the healthy embryos will be transferred. Rates vary, but about 15 percent of the frozen embryos will be lost during the freeze-thaw process.

Embryo cryopreservation has revolutionized the IVF process and positively affected pregnancy rates. That's because it reduces the incidence of multiple pregnancy since a more reasonable and safer number of embryos will be transferred to your uterus and the remainder will be frozen. It also gives patients an additional chance to become pregnant without having to undergo another complete IVF cycle, which is expensive and time consuming and may be emotionally difficult.

EGGS

Although cryopreservation is a useful technique for embryos, it has not thus far been very successful on unfertilized human eggs. Clinical research studies are currently being conducted. Hopefully, a freezing technique will be found that works well on human eggs in the near future.

What About Gamete Intrafallopian Transfer (GIFT) and Zygote Intrafallopian Transfer (ZIFT)?

GIFT is a procedure where the eggs and sperm are placed directly into the woman's fallopian tube during a laparoscopy procedure. The ovaries are stimulated with fertility medications, and the mature eggs are retrieved during an ultrasound guided procedure, much like IVF. However, with GIFT, the eggs are mixed with the washed, enhanced sperm and then placed directly into the fallopian tube during a laparoscopy. The eggs are (hopefully) fertilized within the woman's body, unlike IVF, which fertilizes the eggs in a laboratory.

ZIFT is a combination of GIFT and IVF. For the ZIFT procedure, fertilized eggs are placed directly into the woman's fallopian tube during a laparoscopy procedure. As with the other techniques, the ovaries are stimulated with fertility medications, and the mature eggs are retrieved during an ultrasound guided procedure. Then, like IVF, the eggs are mixed with the washed, enhanced sperm in the laboratory and monitored for fertilization. The only difference is where the embryos are placed after the procedure. In IVF they are placed into the uterus without the need for surgery, but for ZIFT they are placed within the fallopian tube with a laparoscopy procedure.

WHAT EVER HAPPENED TO GIFT AND ZIFT?

GIFT was introduced in 1984 and enjoyed widespread popularity for many years. ZIFT also was widely used during the 1980s and 1990s. Both GIFT and ZIFT report very similar pregnancy success rates when compared to IVF. However, GIFT and ZIFT are rarely performed anymore.

The major reason is that both GIFT and ZIFT require a laparoscopy surgical procedure and general anesthesia. This makes GIFT and ZIFT considerably more expensive and more physically demanding than IVF. Given the additional costs and potential physical risks of surgery and anesthesia, it's difficult to justify GIFT or ZIFT in preference to IVF.

Talk with your doctor to determine if GIFT or ZIFT is a realistic fertility treatment choice for you. Some doctors believe that it may be useful in certain situations. However, for the most part, many doctors say that GIFT and ZIFT are about ready to be reassigned to the history books.

Conclusion

If you are about to embark on an ART procedure, it's a big deal. Not only does it require a big financial commitment, but it also can take a lot out of you both mentally and physically. That's why this chapter aims to educate you about the various ART procedures that you may encounter. By understanding your options and what's happening to your body, you'll be better equipped to handle the uncertainties that may come your way. You'll be armed with the knowledge and be able to a have a more informative discussion with your fertility specialist. That way, you can work together to select the most appropriate ART procedures for your special set of circumstances.

Summary

Here is a summary of the key concepts discussed during this chapter.

Overview

- ART involves the sophisticated treatment and processing of human eggs and sperm to help you become pregnant.
- Which treatments you receive will depend on a variety of issues, including your health and that of your partner, your concerns and desires, and your particular fertility situation.
- If you are seriously considering assisted reproduction, you must understand what medical conditions you have and why natural conception has not worked for you.
- You must understand the risks, benefits, pros, and cons of each technique.

Intrauterine Insemination (IUI)

- IUI is a procedure in which your doctor inserts washed and concentrated sperm directly into your uterus at the time that coincides with your ovulation.

- This technique significantly increases the number of sperm that can make it into your fallopian tube to fertilize the egg(s).

- Many fertility specialists use ovulation-inducting medication along with the IUI procedure to increase your odds of becoming pregnant.

- Individual rates will vary, but overall the pregnancy rate of IUI is between 10 and 18 percent per cycle when combined with ovulation-induction medication.

In Vitro Fertilization (IVF)

- IVF is a procedure in which your ovaries are stimulated to produce eggs, the eggs are removed and fertilized with the man's sperm in a laboratory, and the resulting embryos are transferred into your uterus several days later.

- The IVF technique is performed in various stages:
  - Ovulation stimulation
  - Egg retrieval
  - Semen collection and preparation
  - Fertilization
  - Embryo monitoring
  - Embryo transfer
  - Follow-up afterward
  - Cryopreservation afterward

- Individual rates will vary, but overall the pregnancy rate of IVF is between 25 and 50 percent per cycle.

Intracytoplasmic Sperm Injection (ICSI)

- ICSI is a special fertilization technique that is sometimes used along with the other ART procedures. It involves the injection of a single sperm directly into the center of an egg.

- The resulting embryos are placed back into your uterus, using the same techniques as for IVF.

- ICSI is particularly beneficial for men with severe male factor infertility issues including:

- Extremely low sperm count
- Poor sperm quality
- Presence of antisperm antibodies
- History of poor fertilization during one or more prior IVF attempts
- Any reason why the man's sperm cannot easily penetrate the woman's egg

- The ICSI technique is performed in various stages:
  - Ovulation stimulation
  - Egg retrieval
  - Semen collection and preparation
  - Fertilization
  - Embryo monitoring
  - Embryo transfer
  - Follow-up afterward
  - Cryopreservation afterward

- Individual rates will vary, but overall the pregnancy rate using ICSI is about 30 percent per cycle. This is a significant achievement because ICSI is primarily used in cases of severe male infertility.

- Sometimes sperm can't be collected using the routine methods. This may be because of a birth abnormality, serious injury, or previous vasectomy.

- New microsurgical techniques have been developed to obtain sperm directly from the testicles or the epididymis.

Embryo Assisted Hatching

- The technique is based on the idea that thinning or making a small hole in the embryo's outer shell may help the embryo to successfully implant in your uterine lining.

- This technique may be used in conjunction with your IVF or ICSI procedure.

- Some fertility specialists use this hatching technique with all of their IVF patients, but others reserve assisted hatching for certain patient situations, such as:
  - Older women using their own eggs

- Couples with poor quality embryos
- Embryos that have a thick outer shell
- Couples who have failed implantation in previous IVF or ICSI cycles

Cryopreservation

- Cryopreservation is the technology of using subzero freezing on human cells. They can remain frozen indefinitely, but most people choose to eventually thaw and implant them for another pregnancy.
- This technique is currently being used to freeze sperm and embryos.
- Thus far, cryopreservation techniques for unfertilized human eggs have not been very successful. Scientists are currently working to find a freezing technique that will work well on unfertilized human eggs.

CHAPTER 8

Moving On: Alternatives for the Infertile Couple

Perhaps you've already endured the time, expense, and physical and emotional difficulties of fertility treatments and still did not become pregnant. Now you can have renewed hope for becoming a parent. When traditional technologies are no longer a viable option, third-party reproduction offers an exciting and promising way for you to welcome a baby into your home. Third-party reproduction means that you would use eggs, sperm, or embryos that have been donated by a third person. The third-party donor may be someone you know or may be anonymous. In this chapter, we'll take a look at various third-party options, including:

- Sperm donation
- Egg donation

- Embryo donation
- Traditional surrogacy
- Gestational surrogacy
- Adoption

Sperm Donation

Although most women prefer to use their own partner's sperm to conceive a baby, that's not always possible. You may be a single woman who desires pregnancy but lacks a male partner. Or you may have a male partner who has abnormal sperm. The emergence of the ICSI procedure has enabled many men, who previously were unable to do so, to father a child. Even so, ICSI does not work for all cases of male infertility. It may be that your male partner has an extremely low sperm count or exceptionally poor sperm quality, or he may carry a genetic disorder. In any of these situations, donor sperm may be the answer to your dilemma.

SELECTING YOUR SPERM DONOR

Selecting your sperm donor is a pretty big step and can be very exciting, too. Most sperm banks offer a catalog of all their sperm donors. You can look through the listings and note the physical and intellectual characteristics of each potential donor. You may want to select someone who is very similar to you or your own male partner. Or you may want to focus on certain traits and talents that you hope your baby may inherit. Your doctor and fertility clinic will offer some guidelines about selecting the best sperm donor for you. In addition, here are some things for you to consider when selecting your sperm donor:

- **How old is the donor?** Sperm donors should be of legal age and ideally less than 40 years old. Although rare, some studies indicate that birth defects and chromosomal abnormalities may increase as a man ages. One such study was conducted at France's Hospital Caremeau in 2004 and published in *Progres en Urologie*. The researchers concluded that there is an age-related deterioration of male fertility and also an increased genetic risk for the offspring for chromosomal mutations and abnormalities.

- **Is the donor available for a second child?** This may or may not be important to you. If you are planning to have more than one child using donor sperm, you may want to consider using the same sperm donor with each child so the children are all biologically related.

- **Once you've narrowed it down, is there additional information about your top picks?** Sperm banks often provide baby and adult pictures of the donors. Some clinics even offer video- or audiotapes from the donors. There may also be a personal statement or questionnaire from the donor that highlights his education, hobbies, interests, and personal habits.

- **Once your child reaches legal age, is this donor open to contact from the child that was conceived using his sperm?** Of course, this is a very personal decision and varies from woman to woman. You certainly don't have to decide if and how you will tell your child about his or her biological heritage at this point. However, it is helpful to find out right now whether contact with the biological father is even an option at some time in the distant future.

THE SPERM BANK

Your fertility specialist can introduce you to a reputable sperm bank. Your doctor and someone from the fertility clinic will talk with you about how the process works. Additionally, here are some things for you to consider when working with a sperm bank:

- **What types of screening tests do they perform to check the health of the donors?** The American Society for Reproductive Medicine (ASRM) recommends initial and follow-up testing for both anonymous and known donors. This includes:

  - Complete medical history (including donor's family, personal, and sexual history)

  - Physical exam

  - Testing for STDs (at donation and every six months)

  - Routine blood work (such as blood type)

  - Genetic testing that is ethnically based (for example, sickle cell for those of African descent)

- **How long do they freeze and quarantine the sperm before thawing and using?** ASRM recommends a minimum six months of freezing and quarantine before the donor sperm is thawed. At the time of thawing, the specimen is again tested for STDs to assure that results are still negative.

- **Do they limit the number of pregnancies per donor?** Large numbers of offspring from one donor would increase the risks that these children might someday meet and reproduce without realizing they are related.

Egg Donation

Of course, you'd prefer to use your own eggs, but that's not always possible. It could be that you've already tried to use your eggs during IVF procedures but had poor results. Or perhaps you no longer have any viable eggs because of menopause, chemotherapy, radiation, or another medical condition. In some cases, you may carry a genetic defect that you don't want to pass along to your offspring. In any of these situations, receiving eggs from another woman may be the answer to your fertility concerns.

Egg donation allows you to carry a pregnancy and deliver the baby. The donor provides the eggs, the eggs are fertilized by your partner's sperm, and then the newly formed embryos are placed within your uterus for you to carry the pregnancy.

Some women choose this option over adoption because it allows them to physically and emotionally experience pregnancy. They also like that the baby is genetically related to their male partner. It's important to understand that the baby is not genetically related to you, since your eggs were not used. However, you obviously have an extremely important role in this baby's life as its mother.

SELECTING YOUR EGG DONOR

Choosing a woman to donate her eggs is a big deal, and it's both exciting and overwhelming. Two ways to go about finding an egg donor are by asking someone that you already know or using an anonymous donor.

Some women ask a family member or close friend to donate their eggs. Family members may be highly regarded because they carry genes that are similar to yours. Friends are valued because you know and care for them, and they possess desirable traits that your baby may inherit.

Other women prefer to use anonymous donors. Some fertility clinics have egg donation programs, where women donate their eggs in exchange for money. Also, many fertility clinics encourage patients undergoing IVF to donate their leftover eggs to be used by another woman. By donating their leftover eggs, these patients generally receive a price break for their own IVF services. In either case, the fertility clinic will have information about the woman so that you will be able to read about her physical and intellectual characteristics. Another option is for you to place an ad in the newspaper and find a donor on your own.

Your doctor and fertility clinic will provide you with guidelines for selecting the best egg donor for you. In addition, here are some things for you to consider:

- **How old is the donor?** Ideally, egg donors should be between the ages of 21 and 34. The minimum of 21 is recommended because the donor must be of legal age, and also hopefully they are mature enough to understand the ramifications of egg donation. A maximum age of 34 is recommended because younger women typically respond better to ovulation induction by producing more high-quality embryos and consequently higher pregnancy rates than those older than 35. Also, women age 35 or older have a somewhat higher risk of chromosomal abnormalities, such as Down syndrome.

- **Once you've narrowed it down, is additional information about your top picks available?** Egg donation programs usually require that the donors complete a personal statement or questionnaire that highlights her education, hobbies, interests, and personal habits. It may also include her reason for wanting to donate her eggs and provide some insight into her personality.

- **Once your child reaches legal age, is this donor open to contact from the child that was conceived using her egg?** Of course, this is a very personal decision. You certainly don't have to decide if and how you will tell your child about his or her biological heritage at this point. However, it is helpful to find out right now whether contact with the biological mother is even an option at some time in the distant future. Some parents do not want any contact with the donor. However, others want their children to be able to locate the donor once they become adults.

THE EGG DONATION PROGRAM

Your doctor and staff member from the fertility clinic will explain to you how their egg donation program works. Additionally, here are some things for you to consider:

- **What types of screening tests do they perform to check the health of the donors?** ASRM recommends initial and follow-up testing for both anonymous and known donors. This includes:

  - Complete medical history (including donor's family, personal, and sexual history)

  - Physical exam

  - Testing for STDs (must be negative within 30 days before egg donation)

  - Routine blood work (such as blood type)

  - Genetic testing that is ethnically based (for example, cystic fibrosis for those of Caucasian descent)

- **Is there a legal contract between the egg donor and the recipient?** Be sure you have a legally binding contract with the egg donor. Even if the fertility clinic provides you with a form, it's best to have a reproductive law attorney review it. The important point is that the agreement states that the donor gives up all rights to the eggs and any children conceived from them.

- **Is psychological counseling offered or required?** Most health care professionals recommend professional counseling for the donor, the recipient, and their partners. Egg donation and the IVF process can be physically and emotionally difficult for both parties. There are also ethical and social issues to explore. It's best to understand all of these demands prior to embarking on this difficult process.

- **What are your pregnancy success rates with the egg donation process?** Ask about the pregnancy success rates at your particular fertility clinic. According to ASRM, the average live birth rate per transfer is about 43 percent for all egg donor programs.

- **How many embryos do you transfer into my uterus?** Be sure to find out your doctor's practices. The major risk for egg donation programs is multiple gestations. In fact, the multiple pregnancy rate is about 30 percent, most of those being twins. The current trend is for the doctor to limit the number of embryos transferred to two in an effort to reduce high-order multiple pregnancies.

HOW THE EGG DONATION PROCEDURE WORKS

The procedure for egg donation is considerably more complicated than for sperm donation. Part of this is because eggs cannot yet be effectively frozen. Therefore, the donor and the recipient must have their hormonal cycles adjusted so they coincide with one another. That way, eggs can be removed from the donor and implanted into the intended mother within a few days of each other. Egg donation is also more complicated than sperm donation because eggs are considerably more difficult to obtain. Whereas sperm can be easily obtained from ejaculate on any given day, ovaries must be hormonally stimulated to induce ovulation and then an egg retrieval procedure must be done to harvest the eggs.

Adjusting the Hormonal Cycles of the Donor and Recipient

Both women must undergo hormonal preparation to synchronize their cycles. Fertility medicines are used to stimulate ovulation in the donor. The recipient must also take fertility medicines to prepare her uterine lining to receive and hopefully implant the transferred embryos. Your fertility doctor will explain the exact medications, their timing, and the necessary protocol requirements. The goal is to hormonally prepare the donor for egg production and retrieval and to prepare your uterus to receive the embryos that will be transferred. Ultrasound and blood tests may be performed to ensure that both the donor and recipient are properly prepared and ready to proceed.

Egg Retrieval from the Donor

Once the eggs are developed, the donor will undergo an egg retrieval procedure. The standard IVF technique with ultrasound and needle is used to extract the eggs through the donor's vagina. Once the eggs have been harvested, they are taken to the laboratory, where they are evaluated for maturity and quality. The healthiest eggs are then inseminated with the male partner's sperm using the same fertilization technique as in IVF. (For a detailed description of the IVF process, see Chapter 7.)

Embryo Transfer to the Recipient

The embryos are transferred into the recipient's uterus within a few days after fertilization in the laboratory. The technique used for embryo transfer is the same as for IVF, where a special catheter and syringe are passed through the cervix and the embryos are inserted into the uterus. Hormones are given to help the embryos implant, grow, and develop. Pregnancy tests and ultrasound are performed within a couple of weeks to confirm pregnancy.

Embryo Donation

You may be in a situation where your best choice of carrying a baby is to receive a donated embryo. Embryo donation may be an option for you if you and your partner have both been diagnosed with untreatable infertility. It is also sometimes used in cases where a woman has experienced recurrent miscarriage thought to be caused by problems with the embryo. Another reason that embryo donation is used is because you or your partner have a genetic disorder and do not want to pass it to your baby.

Embryo donation is a procedure whereby embryos are transferred to your uterus for pregnancy and delivery. The embryos may have been created by other couples undergoing fertility treatment or they may have been created from donor sperm and donor eggs for the specific purpose of embryo donation.

Like adoption, the baby that is born to you will have no genetic link to either you or your partner. However, some couples prefer this option over adoption because it allows them to physically and emotionally experience pregnancy. By being pregnant with the baby, you have control over the baby's uterine environment, diet, lifestyle, and habits. And although no actual genetic link exists, you and your partner will have a very meaningful role in this baby's life as its parents.

SELECTING YOUR EMBRYOS

Unfortunately, most recipients don't have much of a choice when it comes to embryo donations. That's because there usually aren't many embryos available for donation. Couples who have undergone their own fertility procedures and have leftover frozen embryos do not always feel comfortable donating them to another couple.

Fortunately, some fertility clinics do arrange for embryo donations. These programs do their best to match donors and recipients based upon ethnicity and physical traits.

THE EMBRYO DONATION PROGRAM

In addition to trying to match donor and recipient's ethnic background and physical characteristics, the program also works to ensure that other important standards are met. Your doctor and fertility clinic will explain to you how the embryo donation programs works. In addition, here are some things for you to consider:

- **What types of screening tests are performed to check the health of the donors?** The Food and Drug Administration recommends that the donors were young and healthy without serious medical conditions or health concerns. Also, the embryos should undergo the proper health screening and testing required for all egg and sperm donors. (This includes medical history, physical exam, STD check, routine blood work, and ethnically relevant genetic screening.)

- **Is there a legal contract between the embryo donors and the recipient?** It's very important that you have a legally binding agreement between you and the embryo donors. Some fertility clinics will provide you with a form or suggested format for a contract. That is helpful and may serve as a good starting point. However, most people agree that this is such an important step in your life that it's best to involve a reproductive law attorney. The key feature is that you have a legally binding contract stating that the donor(s) give up all rights to the embryos and any children conceived from them.

- **Is psychological counseling offered or required?** Embryo donation and the IVF process can take a toll on everyone involved, both from a physical and an emotional standpoint. That's why many medical professionals recommend professional counseling for both the donors and the recipient couple. The counseling process will address various ethical and social issues and your own set of particular circumstances. This is such a complex time in your life; it's in your own best interest to gain as much support and understanding as possible.

- **What are your pregnancy success rates with the embryo donation process?** You'll need to ask your particular fertility clinic about their pregnancy success rates. No national statistics exist on the pregnancy success rates of embryo donation because of the small number of embryo donation cases performed nationwide.

- **Once the child reaches legal age, are the donors open to contact from the child who was conceived using her egg and his sperm?** Of course, this is a very personal decision. You certainly don't have to decide if and how you will tell your child about his or her biological heritage at this point. However, it is helpful to find out right now whether contact with the biological parents is even an option at some time in the distant future.

HOW THE EMBRYO DONATION PROCEDURE WORKS

The embryo donation procedure is somewhat less complicated than the egg donation process. That's mainly because the hormonal cycles of the female donor and female recipient do not need to be carefully synchronized. In this case, the embryos are already frozen and ready for use.

Preparing the Recipient for the Embryos

As the recipient, you must take fertility medicines to adjust your hormones and prepare your uterine lining for the upcoming embryo transfer. Your fertility specialist will discuss which fertility medications and protocols are necessary for your particular situation. Additionally, you will likely undergo various blood tests and pelvic ultrasound to make sure that your hormone levels and uterine lining are prepared and ready to receive the new embryos.

Embryo Transfer to the Recipient

When the timing and indications are right, the frozen embryos are thawed in the laboratory and transferred into the recipient's uterus. The technique used for embryo

transfer is the same as for IVF, where a special catheter and syringe is passed through the cervix and embryos inserted into the uterus. Hormones are given to help the embryos implant, grow, and develop. Pregnancy tests and ultrasound are performed within a couple of weeks to confirm pregnancy.

PROS AND CONS OF EMBRYO DONATION

Because embryo donation is relatively rare, it's especially important for you to know as much about it as possible. Here are some pros and cons for you to consider:

Pros

- You typically become a parent faster than when waiting for the adoption process.
- Embryo adoption offers more privacy than adoption.
- Because you are the one that is pregnant, you control the environment of the developing fetus.
- You experience pregnancy, delivery, and breast-feeding.
- You may be able to have genetic siblings if there are enough embryos from the same donor couple.
- You typically receive complete medical information about the donor couple.
- Embryo donation is usually cheaper than paying for an egg donor or a surrogate.
- The legal risk is fairly low if the contract is properly executed by a reproductive law attorney.

Cons

- The supply of embryos is not large, and therefore the selection is limited.
- You probably will not know or meet the biological parents of the embryo and may not even see a photo of them.
- Donors tend to be people who have fertility problems themselves, and thus their embryos may have some problems.
- Donors tend to be somewhat older, and their embryos may have genetic abnormalities or be of lower quality.
- Your child from embryo donation may have genetic siblings in the world without ever knowing about them.

Surrogacy

Surrogacy is probably the most controversial of all the assisted reproductive technologies currently in use. A surrogate is a woman who carries a pregnancy for you. The two types of arrangements with surrogates are called traditional surrogacy and gestational (carrier) surrogacy. Traditional surrogacy refers to a woman whose own egg is inseminated with sperm from your male partner. Gestational surrogacy involves a woman who carries an embryo created from the joining of your egg and your partner's sperm. Both types of surrogacy arrangements have pros and cons. However, perhaps most importantly, surrogacy is an option that allows you to become parents when you can't carry a pregnancy on your own.

TRADITIONAL SURROGACY

In traditional surrogacy, the surrogate's own eggs are used and are inseminated with your male partner's sperm. The resulting child will have a genetic link to both the surrogate and your male partner. A contract is signed and agreed upon that after this baby is born, you and your partner will adopt the child and have full legal parenting rights.

This option may arise when your male partner is fertile but you are not. It may also be indicated when you possess a genetic condition that you don't want to pass to your child.

The procedure is carried out using various assisted reproductive technologies previously discussed. If conception occurs, the surrogate will carry the resulting pregnancy and turn the baby over to you once it has been delivered.

Traditional surrogacy arrangements are often considered somewhat controversial because the baby is genetically linked to the surrogate. This can cause considerable psychological and legal issues for both you and the surrogate. Because of these concerns, the majority of surrogacy in the United States involves the gestational surrogacy arrangement.

GESTATIONAL (CARRIER) SURROGACY

Remember Phoebe on the TV show "Friends"? She was a gestational surrogate for her brother and his wife. She carried triplets for them! Those babies were the creation of her brother's sperm and his wife's eggs and therefore not directly genetically linked to her. That's how gestational surrogacy works. The surrogate is only used to carry the pregnancy and the baby is not genetically connected to the surrogate. The baby is the combination of genetic material from you and your male partner. In essence, you are only borrowing the surrogate's uterus. That's why this process is sometimes referred to as uterine borrowing. Because the surrogate is carrying and delivering the child, a legal contract that states the baby belongs to you and your partner is still necessary.

Gestational surrogacy may be an option if you have normally functioning ovaries but do not have a uterus. You may lack a uterus because you were born that way or perhaps you've had a prior hysterectomy. This type of surrogacy may also be indicated when you possess untreatable scarring or other such abnormalities within your uterus. Another reason to choose gestational surrogacy could be if you have a medical condition where pregnancy would be dangerous to you (severe heart disease is one example).

The procedure for gestational surrogacy is carried out using IVF techniques previously discussed. In fact, the only difference is that the transferred embryos are placed into the surrogate's uterus instead of your own. That means ovulation stimulation and egg retrieval for you and sperm collection and preparation for your partner. The surrogate's hormonal cycle must be synchronized with yours and her uterus must be prepared with hormones for it to be receptive to embryo implantation. The surrogate will carry the resulting pregnancy and turn the baby over to you once it has been delivered.

Gestational surrogacy is considered more complicated than traditional surrogacy because it requires IVF to create the embryos. Despite this, gestational surrogacy is more commonly used in the United States because it is considered to be legally and psychologically more acceptable to all parties.

SELECTING A SURROGATE

No matter which type of surrogacy arrangement you choose, you will need to select your surrogate. The surrogate may be someone you know, such as a close friend, a sister, or another relative, who is willing to carry the pregnancy for you. Sometimes the surrogate is someone you don't know but who has been identified through an agency. These agencies specialize in recruiting surrogates, prescreening them, and then matching them with the intended parents. Following are some criteria that you should consider when selecting your surrogate. You'll note that these criteria are similar to those used in selecting an egg or embryo donor. However, in the case of the surrogate, she must have a normal uterus and must have delivered a full-term infant in the past.

- She should undergo a diagnostic test to prove that she has a normal uterus.
- She should be at least 21 years old and already have delivered a full-term infant in the past.

- She should be healthy, not have any underlying medical conditions, and be able to pass a thorough physical examination.

- She should be tested and found to be negative for infectious diseases and STDs.

- She should have her blood drawn and tested, and her blood type should be noted.

- She should undergo a complete psychological evaluation.

COUNSELING

Both the surrogate and the intended parents should undergo psychological counseling.

The surrogate should undergo a complete psychological evaluation to make sure that she is up to the physical and emotional demands of surrogacy. It's also important for the surrogate to be able to cope with any attachment issues that she may develop with the fetus. She will also need to know how to deal with the impact of this pregnancy on her own children, spouse, family, friends, and coworkers. Of course, she'll also benefit from guidelines on managing a relationship with you, the intended parents.

You and your partner can also benefit from counseling. Work with the counselor and the surrogate to determine what type of relationship you would like to maintain.

If you don't already know each other, you and the surrogate should become better acquainted. You'll both want to feel comfortable with one another. After all, surrogacy involves a large degree of trust. Enter into this arrangement only if both sides feel comfortable with the arrangements.

LEGAL AGREEMENTS

Be sure you have a legal contract with your surrogate. Surrogacy agreements are usually rather complicated, so have a reproductive law attorney advise you. The most important feature for you is that the surrogate and her partner revoke all parental rights to you and your partner. In most cases, the surrogate will have a separate legal counsel who will represent her rights and interests.

Adoption

You may reach a point when you decide that you are finished with fertility and assisted reproductive technologies and want to pursue adoption. Of course, this is a difficult decision and not one that you come to easily or quickly—it's a personal decision that is best made after careful consideration and usually much conversation

with your partner. You may also wish to discuss this with your fertility specialist and a close friend or family member.

On the other hand, some people decide to continue their fertility and ART options and begin the adoption process at the same time. You certainly have the right to pursue both options simultaneously. That way, if either one or both work out, you are delighted and able to enjoy your new and growing family. Do keep in mind that both fertility treatments and adoption are expensive and emotionally draining. That's why most people choose to pursue only one option at a time.

Here are some thoughts and concerns you may want to consider as you decide how best to make your decision:

- What does your fertility specialist have to say about your chances of becoming pregnant?
- How important is it for you to have a genetic link to your child?
- What is your financial situation, and what is the cost of fertility treatments versus the cost of pursuing adoption?
- What is the physical and emotional toll that you are taking on yourself and your partner?
- How does this fit in with your current life situation (your age, health, lifestyle, career, relationships, and so on)?

If you decide to choose adoption as a means of building your family, you will probably find that it is not as easy as it once was. The declining birth rate in our society makes finding a baby to adopt a somewhat difficult task. If you want a healthy, Caucasian baby, the waiting list may be years long. That's why many couples are now open to the possibilities of adopting a baby from another culture or nation or choosing a child with special needs. If you are willing to accept these differences, your waiting time will be considerably shorter.

Most adoptions in the United States occur through social adoption agencies. Other options include private adoptions in which a doctor or lawyer makes the necessary arrangements. You will want to use your fertility specialist, your family doctor, your reproductive lawyer, and any social workers that you have worked with as resources to begin your adoption quest. You may also want to use the Internet as a way of gaining information about the adoption process and also about placement of babies and children in need of families and homes.

You should feel happy about adopting a child and see it as a positive experience. It may be helpful for you to speak with others who have undergone the adoption process. Many people find that joining a support group is a good way to share their experiences with like-minded people. Having the support of friends and family also helps you as you adjust to this new change in your life.

Finally, the decision to move from fertility treatments to adoption does not have to be a permanent one. You might begin the adoption process and then decide that you really want to go back and try some additional fertility procedures. That's OK, too. There is no one correct path. Just do your best to assess your situation at the present time and make the best choice that you can.

Conclusion

By the time you've reached this point in your fertility journey, you've already endured a lot. And now you are considering moving on to other alternatives, such as third-party reproduction or adoption. You may find that some of your well-meaning family and friends are questioning your decisions and just don't seem to understand. That's right—they don't understand, because they haven't walked in your shoes. It can be difficult, but try to be patient and explain your feelings to them. Sometimes family and friends are so wrapped up in their own lives, they don't understand the full impact of your situation. Family and friends who love you will want what's best for you. Once they understand, they'll support and do all they can to help you.

This chapter has given you lots of information about the various alternatives available. Of course, they each have their own pros and cons, strengths and weaknesses. Trust your instincts. The best you can do is to work together with your doctor and partner to come up with the best fertility answer for you.

Summary

Here is a summary of the key concepts.

Overview

- Now there are some exciting new alternatives and renewed hope for you to become a parent.
- Third-party reproduction involves using eggs, sperm, or embryos that have been donated by a third person.
- You should consider the numerous emotional, physical, social, and financial factors when thinking about these alternatives.

Sperm Donation

- It's not always possible or logical to use your partner's sperm. Sometimes receiving sperm donation from a third party is your best alternative.

- Factors to consider when selecting a sperm donor:
  - Has this donor been properly screened by the sperm bank for medical history and a physical exam?
  - What are the donor's physical and intellectual characteristics?
  - What is the donor's age? (The donor must be of legal age, but ideally younger than 40 is optimum.)
  - Is this donor available for a second child?
  - How many other pregnancies have occurred using this donor's sperm?
  - Is the donor open to contact from the child once the child reaches legal age?

Egg Donation

- Most women prefer to use their own eggs, but for various reasons, this is not always the best course of action or even an option. For such cases, egg donation provides a good alternative, because you are still able to carry the pregnancy and deliver the baby.
- Remember that this baby will not be genetically related to you because your eggs were not used. However, you will still play a supremely important role in this child's life as its mother.
- Factors to consider when selecting an egg donor:
  - Some women ask a family member or close friend to donate their eggs, whereas other women prefer to use anonymous donors.
  - What is the donor's age? (Ideally, egg donors should be between the ages of 21 and 34.)
  - Some women like to know a little about the egg donor; such information may be found in the form of a personal statement made by the donor that highlights her education, hobbies, interests, and personal habits.
  - What are the donor's physical and intellectual characteristics?
  - Be sure that your donor has been properly screened by the fertility clinic for her medical history and physical exam.
  - Is this donor available for a second child?
  - Is the donor open to contact from the child once the child reaches legal age?
- Involve a reproductive law attorney to ensure that a legal contract is in place between you and the egg donor and that the donor gives up all rights to the eggs and any children conceived from them.

- Many fertility specialists recommend psychological counseling for the donor, the recipient, and their partners. That's because this is a very physically and emotionally difficult time for everyone involved.

- As part of the egg donation procedure, the donor and the recipient must have their hormonal cycles adjusted so they coincide with one another. This is done with various fertility medications and close monitoring by your fertility specialist.

- Once your two cycles are synchronized, the eggs will be retrieved from the donor, fertilized in the laboratory, and transferred into your uterus using the same techniques as for IVF.

Embryo Donation

- You might encounter a situation where your best choice of carrying a baby is to receive a donated embryo. The embryos are transferred into your uterus for pregnancy and delivery.

- The embryos are often already created by other couples undergoing fertility treatments. Sometimes they have been created from donor sperm and donor eggs for the purpose of embryo donation.

- This baby will not be genetically related to you or your partner. But of course, you will maintain a very important role in this child's life as its parents.

- Factors to consider when selecting an embryo donor:

  - Unfortunately, most recipients don't have much of a selection for embryo donors because there usually aren't many embryos available for donation.

  - Some fertility doctors and clinics arrange for embryo donations and do their best to match donors and recipients based upon ethnicity and physical traits.

  - Be sure that your donor couple has been properly screened by the fertility clinic for medical history and a physical exam.

  - Are the donors open to contact from the child once the child reaches legal age?

- You'll also want to engage the services of a reproductive law attorney. Have a legally binding contract between you and the donor couple. The key point is that the donor couple surrenders their rights to the embryos and any children conceived from them.

- Psychological counseling is usually recommended for all parties involved. Both the donor and recipient couples must understand the relevant ethical and psychosocial issues. You may also wish to explore additional circumstances with a fertility counselor.

- During the embryo donation procedure, you will be given various fertility medications to prepare your uterus for receiving the embryos. Your fertility specialist will monitor you by using pelvic ultrasound and blood tests.

- When the timing is right, the frozen embryos will be thawed in the laboratory and transferred into your uterus using the same techniques as with IVF.

Surrogacy

- A surrogate is a woman who carries a pregnancy for you. The two types of surrogacy arrangements are traditional and gestational (carrier).

- Traditional surrogacy is when the surrogate woman's own egg is fertilized with sperm from your male partner. The baby is genetically related to the surrogate and your male partner. This is more controversial because of the baby's genetic link to the surrogate and the greater ensuing psychological and legal issues.

- Gestational surrogacy is when the surrogate carries an embryo created from the joining of your egg and your partner's sperm. The baby is not genetically related to the surrogate. Sometimes called carrier surrogacy or uterine borrowing, gestational surrogacy accounts for the majority of surrogacy arrangements in the United States.

- Factors to consider when selecting a surrogate:

  - The same criteria used when selecting an egg donor is a good guideline.

  - In addition, a potential surrogate should undergo testing to prove that she has a normal uterus.

  - Also, it's best when the surrogate has already delivered a full-term infant in the past.

- As with all third-party reproduction, you should utilize a reproductive law attorney and also participate in psychological counseling.

Moving from Fertility to Adoption

- You may get to a point where you want to stop all fertility and ART procedures and turn to adoption.

- Share your thoughts with someone you can trust, such as your partner, a fertility specialist, a close friend, or a family member, to help you with your decision making.

- Some people pursue both fertility treatments and adoption, but most don't do them simultaneously because both are expensive and emotionally draining.

- In the United States, many couples are now turning to other cultures and nations or are adopting a child with special needs because their waiting time is considerably shorter.

CHAPTER 9

Emotional Issues

Few things in life rival the emotional and hormonal roller coaster that the fertility patient must endure. It's difficult enough to come to terms with the shocking diagnosis of infertility. Most women see infertility as a major life crisis and experience significant feelings of loss. Add to that the numerous doctor visits, various medications, multiple unpleasant tests and procedures, and perhaps also surgeries. The financial burden of paying for this medical care, most of which is not covered by your health insurance plan, can also add significant stress.

Is it any wonder that most fertility patients occasionally feel overwhelmed, discouraged, and depressed? The American Society for Reproductive Medicine (ASRM) states that it is normal for you to experience an array of emotions:

- Shock
- Anxiety
- Sadness

- Anger
- Shame
- Fear
- Loneliness
- Resentment

These feelings seem to touch all aspects of your life. They certainly affect how you feel about yourself and also have an impact on your relationships with others. How you deal with these feelings will depend on your own personality and your life experiences thus far. From time to time, you may experience some of these:

- Depression and loss of interest in your usual activities
- Feeling isolated and having strained relationships with your partner, family, friends, and coworkers
- Preoccupation with fertility and difficulty thinking about anything else
- Physical symptoms such as a change in your sleeping and/or eating patterns
- Inability to concentrate and more difficulty with decision making
- Thoughts of your own death or dying

While it is perfectly normal to struggle with these thoughts and feelings, there comes a point when these emotions may get out of hand and become potentially dangerous. Seek help from a mental health professional if you are feeling significant symptoms of depression over a prolonged period of time. Be aware of these warning signs of depression:

- Extreme sadness and hopelessness
- Lack of interest or motivation to perform your normal activities
- Inability to concentrate
- Decreased energy
- Insomnia or sleeping too much
- Unintended significant weight gain or loss
- Obsession and preoccupation with fertility
- Increased anxiety
- Extreme anger and resentment
- Persistent thoughts of suicide or death

Again, it's normal to experience any or all of these symptoms from time to time. However, if you experience them severely or for a prolonged period of time, please talk with your doctor or a mental health professional.

Dealing with Others

It's often difficult enough to deal with your own emotions. Dealing with family and friends, even those with good intentions, can also be challenging.

COUPLES

Many couples say that coping with the decisions and uncertainties of infertility brings about the most stressful life crisis that they have ever encountered. It's not surprising that men and women often react differently to these stresses.

Women generally view themselves as the emotional caretakers of the relationship. Therefore, it's normal for you to try to protect your spouse from pain and feelings of failure by taking on most of the responsibility yourself. Holding yourself responsible for this entire ordeal can take an emotional toll on you—no wonder you may experience intense feelings of anger, pain, fear, and frustration. Over time, these feelings turn into anxiety and depression.

In most situations, men see themselves as the financial breadwinner and also the protector of the family. Men who usually see themselves as physically and emotionally strong may feel threatened if asked to express their feelings. It's not unusual for the man to feel overwhelmed by your emotions and not know what to do. Even if they have been trained to be decision makers and problem solvers, they often find themselves helpless to make the situation better for you, and so out of frustration, they may say that you are too emotional or acting crazy, hoping that this will calm you down. Of course, it doesn't. So they change their focus on things where they can be more successful, such as their work, sports, or hobbies.

If the reason for the infertility is because of a problem with the man, he takes on added emotional problems. Some men feel that their masculinity is now in question. They are worried that others will find out and ridicule them. Some men feel so inadequate that they don't even understand why you would stay with them. They may feel such embarrassment and shame that they turn down all offers of medical intervention or emotional support.

In addition to these stressors, it's also not unusual for you both to stop enjoying sex. What used to be spontaneous and enjoyable may have turned into a technical, well-timed, baby-making chore, and sexual intercourse can even be resented as it begins to represent failure.

You can both do some things to better deal with the emotional difficulties of infertility.

- **Understand:** Emotions and disagreements may become magnified during this trying time.

- **Communicate:** On a regular basis, discuss your emotions and fears with your partner. It won't always be easy, but having each other's support now is critical.

- **Support:** Know that you are both doing your best during this stressful time, no matter how you each deal with it on the outside.

- **Participate:** Go to doctor appointments together, and use a teamwork approach to deal with the decisions, tests, and procedures that you will both endure.

- **Enjoy:** Make dates to have "fun sex" during nonfertile times of your cycle, find new hobbies or activities that you can do together, and focus time and energy on your relationship.

- **Get counseling:** Seek professional counseling to help you get through the many challenges that you both face. Work together and provide one another with emotional support. Many couples find that it not only alleviates some of the stress but actually makes your relationship stronger and brings a new sense of closeness as you learn to lean on one another for needed reassurance and encouragement. You may come to realize that if you can get through the physical and emotional demands of fertility treatments, you can probably conquer anything that life throws your way. Being able to endure these overwhelming demands may leave you with a renewed sense of respect and confidence in your relationship.

LESBIAN COUPLES

The increasing number of lesbian couples choosing to bring children into their relationship represents a growing trend. They are now finding greater acceptance in society and are often part of a supportive community. It's only natural that this public acceptance has made sharing a pregnancy together a more feasible option.

As with any couple facing a pregnancy, one of you may feel more ready and enthusiastic than the other. You must be able to openly communicate your thoughts and emotions so that you can reach a sound decision together. You'll want to share and enjoy this experience together. Participate in the planning and doctor visits together. Don't get so wrapped up in the baby preparation that you neglect your own relationship as a couple—enjoy each other and plan fun dates and activities.

You'll also have to deal with other difficulties that heterosexual couples don't usually face, such as finding a sperm donor willing to father your child. Friends, family, and coworkers may not greet your decision to have a baby with the same joy and response that they would for a traditional couple. Also, the coparenting relationship that you share may not be as legally protected as that of a married heterosexual couple. Because of this, many lawyers advise drawing up a legal agreement that clearly defines and protects your parenting roles.

SINGLE WOMEN

Having and raising a child can be difficult even when you are part of a couple. It's especially an ambitious undertaking when you decide to consider motherhood without a partner.

For most women, it's wise for you to first come to terms with your life circumstances. Many women must deal with the sadness that their first choice of finding "Mr. Right" and living happily ever after may not be a reality. This may involve a grieving process, given that most of us were conditioned from childhood that we should find love, marriage, and a baby carriage, in that order.

Once you have come to the decision that you are ready to be a single parent, you must face some other issues. First you need to find a sperm donor who is willing to father your baby. You may use a friend or perhaps need to use an anonymous donor via a sperm bank. It's also important that you are financially able to support this child. How might having a child affect your current job? How much time can you take off? Will you need to use a day care or hire a nanny? What about health insurance for the child?

You will need emotional support from family, friends, and coworkers. A support group may help you deal with some of your uncertainties and concerns. The organization Single Mothers by Choice (http://mattes.home.pipeline.com) can also provide you with much-needed advice and emotional support.

DEALING WITH FAMILY AND FRIENDS

Starting a family is supposed to be a personal and enjoyable experience. However, for couples with infertility issues or unconventional situations, such as lesbian couples or single women, it can be a very difficult situation. You come face-to-face with family and friends who may not be sensitive to your situation. They may or may not have good intentions, but they seem to believe that you will benefit from their thoughts and opinions. They just don't seem to realize how emotionally challenging it can be on you.

Because most people view their infertility as a personal issue, they are often hesitant to share their experiences openly with family and friends. To a couple that has been diagnosed with infertility, unknowing friends and family may ask:

- "So, when are you two going to get busy and start a family?"
- "What are you waiting for? You'd be such good parents."
- "You don't have any children—don't you like children?"

This situation can end up driving a wedge between you and those close to you. Consequently, many couples suffer in silence and end up feeling lonely and isolated.

Lesbian couples and single mothers often encounter another form of reprimand from friends and family. In these situations, others may say to you:

- "How could you bring a child into the world under these circumstances?"
- "Are you planning to mess up and confuse your child for life?"
- "How will you ever be able to manage and financially support this baby?"

They don't seem to consider that you have been dealing with these complex issues and have put much more thought and planning into the situation than they could possibly fathom. Obviously, bringing a baby into the world is not something that you are doing frivolously or impulsively. Caring friends and family should give you more credit than that. You just may need to spend a little effort to educate them about your circumstances. If they are true loving friends and family, they will come around and become more supportive and understanding.

EMOTIONS AND FERTILITY TREATMENTS

It's perfectly normal to experience a wide variety of emotions as you endure fertility treatments.

ASSISTED REPRODUCTIVE TECHNOLOGY (ART)

The assisted reproductive technologies include such procedures as intrauterine insemination (IUI), in vitro fertilization (IVF), and intracytoplasmic sperm injection (ICSI), to name a few. When you reach a decision to undergo one of these ART procedures, you may feel the conflicting emotions of both excitement and dread. It's normal to be excited, because this scientific approach offers tremendous breakthroughs and success in the world of fertility. With such high pregnancy rates and successful outcomes, it's only natural that you feel optimistic and joyful. At the same time, ART procedures require a big commitment from you and your partner. You'll both undergo many invasive tests and procedures. You'll be subjected to numerous medications, each with its own potential side effects. Add to that the financial burden associated with ART, and it's no wonder that you feel anxious and apprehensive.

Most women agree that this can be difficult from an emotional, physical, and financial standpoint. Plus, you have to come to terms with the fact that you probably aren't going to be able to conceive a child on your own without some kind of medical intervention. That's probably not an easy statement for you to accept, especially on an emotional level. Share with your partner and decide how much you want to reveal to other people about what you're going through. Some people find comfort in sharing all of the details with close friends and family. Other people are more private and choose to keep matters to themselves. You're likely to cope better if you have a supportive and understanding partner, considerate close friends and family, and a support group where you can vent to like-minded women.

THIRD-PARTY REPRODUCTION

Third-party reproduction means that you would use sperm, eggs, or embryos donated by a third person to have a baby. It also encompasses surrogacy and adoption, because an outside party is used to conceive or carry the baby. Many emotional and ethical complexities are associated with third-party reproduction. Have a candid discussion with your partner about the types of medical assistance that you are both willing to accept. Your partner may feel differently from you when it comes to sperm donors, egg donors, embryo donors, surrogates, and adoption. Keep in mind that the way you feel now may change as you and your partner move through the assorted fertility treatments. If you do not experience good success with the standard fertility treatments, your earlier objections to third-party reproduction may very well change.

Before reaching a decision, here are some additional thoughts for you to consider:

- How many more disappointments can you endure as you strive to become a parent?
- How important is it that the child is genetically yours?
- Will you want to have an open relationship with the donor or do you prefer that this remain private and anonymous?
- How will you handle this situation as your child gets older?

Only you as potential parents can answer these questions since they really depend on your own values and life experiences.

If you decide to pursue third-party reproduction, it will require a big commitment from you and your partner. You'll both undergo many invasive tests and procedures. You'll both need to go through the difficult task of selecting a donor. Depending on the circumstance, you may be subjected to numerous medications, each with its own potential side effects. You'll also need to seek counsel from a reproductive law attorney. Add to that the substantial financial burden, and it's no wonder that you feel overwhelmed and anxious. On the other hand, you'll soon have a beautiful baby to take home, and your dream of having a family will have come true.

Once you've decided to pursue third-party reproduction, take the time to feel good about your decision. You are going to be a parent! Take a moment to revel in this feeling and enjoy this as a wonderful and positive experience. Continue to share your concerns and your joy with your partner. Family and friends can also help you adapt to your upcoming role as a parent. Many women also find tremendous encouragement in support groups, which provide them the opportunity to interact with other women who are experiencing the same concerns and emotions.

Fertility Counselors

Almost all fertility doctors and fertility clinics have at least one fertility counselor as part of their patient care team.

WHEN TO SEE A FERTILITY COUNSELOR

Of course, everyone deals with stress in their own way. Some women cry, others pray, some take up unhealthy habits, others are stoic. Even so, at some point, you may feel the need to seek out a mental health professional to provide you with an objective sounding board for your thoughts and feelings.

The counselor can assess the degree of nervous tension that you are feeling and how it's affecting your relationship with your partner and with others. The counselor can help you come to terms with realistic expectations. You'll also explore new ways to manage and cope with your stress.

If you are having difficulty deciding whether to talk with a counselor, consider that it almost assuredly won't hurt you and it very well might help you. Many women find it beneficial to seek professional help to manage their emotions and also when they feel that they have reached a decision-making crossroad and need guidance regarding taking the next step in treatment. You may exhibit certain signs that indicate you could benefit from talking with an infertility counselor. Here's a checklist that you may find helpful:

- Persistent feelings of sadness, guilt, or worthlessness
- Persistent feelings of bitterness, anger, or resentment
- Loss of interest in activities that you once enjoyed
- Depression that lasts for more than a couple of weeks
- Agitation and high levels of anxiety
- Complete immersion in and preoccupation with infertility
- Friction and strain within your relationship with your partner
- Difficulty concentrating and trouble accomplishing tasks that you could once do
- Increased use of alcohol or drugs
- Change in appetite, weight, or sleep patterns
- Thoughts about suicide or death

Consider counseling when you are feeling stuck and need to sort out your fertility treatment options and alternatives. Here are some possible scenarios that you may be facing:

- How can you best go about gathering the information that you'll need to make the best treatment decisions for you?
- Should you partake in an ART procedure? How will you deal with the emotional, physical, and financial burdens?
- What coping and relaxation skills can you learn to deal with your upcoming diagnostic tests, invasive procedures, and surgeries?
- How can you cope with the losses and disappointments associated with infertility and still continue on with more treatments?
- What about moving on to third-party reproduction? How would you deal with a third-party donation of sperm, egg, or embryo?
- What are the implications of surrogacy and/or adoption in your life?
- How can you and your partner resolve your differences when it comes to dealing with fertility treatments?

HOW TO SELECT YOUR FERTILITY COUNSELOR

It's very important that your counselor be trained and well versed in the issues of fertility, both the causes and the treatment options. That way the counselor can truly understand the range of physical issues and emotions that you are facing.

Start by talking with your own fertility specialist and medical staff at your fertility clinic. Fertility clinics may have counselors who are associated with the clinic and ready to help you, and if not, they likely have already compiled a list of good fertility counselors for your consideration. Some clinics also offer special relaxation and stress reduction programs to help you manage your overwhelming feelings. If these choices don't work, try the ASRM website: asrm.org. They have a list of mental health professionals who specialize in fertility issues. Another alternative would be to contact a national support group such as RESOLVE (resolve.org) or the American Fertility Association (theafa.org).

When narrowing down your search for a fertility counselor, feel free to interview several and see who best fits with your needs and values. Make sure you choose a counselor who is familiar with the emotional experience of infertility. It is also recommended that they have:

- A graduate degree in a mental health profession
- A license to practice counseling
- Experience in the medical and emotional aspects of infertility, including such topics as ART, third-party reproduction, pregnancy loss, and adoptions
- Other patients that they are currently treating for fertility issues

Conclusion

The most important thing to remember is that you always have choices. The best thing you can do is work with a competent and caring fertility specialist and educate yourself about the different choices you can make. If after a certain amount of time you have not become pregnant, you still have options. Depending on your circumstances and desires, you may choose to continue treatment. Or you may decide that it is no longer a realistic alternative for you and your partner. With time, patience, support, and knowledge, you'll find the best course of action for you.

Summary

Here is a chapter summary that emphasizes the key concepts discussed.

Your Emotions

- It is completely normal for you to experience a wide range of emotions as you deal with the stresses of fertility.

- According to ASRM, here are some common emotions experienced by fertility patients:
  - Shock
  - Anxiety
  - Sadness
  - Anger
  - Shame
  - Fear
  - Loneliness
  - Resentment
- While it's normal to struggle somewhat with your thoughts and feelings, there comes a point when these emotions may get out of hand and potentially become dangerous. Here are some warning signs of depression:
  - Extreme sadness and hopelessness
  - Lack of interest or motivation to perform your normal activities
  - Inability to concentrate
  - Decreased energy
  - Insomnia or sleeping too much
  - Unintended significant weight gain or loss
  - Obsession and preoccupation with fertility
  - Increased anxiety
  - Extreme anger and resentment
  - Persistent thoughts of suicide or death
- Be sure to seek help from your doctor or a mental health professional if you are feeling significant symptoms of depression over a prolonged period of time.

Dealing with Others

- The many decisions and uncertainties associated with fertility diagnosis and treatment often bring about great stress in the life of the couple.
- In most cases, women and men react very differently to stress; those differences can lead to additional conflicts and frustrations.
- Here are some actions that you and your partner can do to help deal with these difficulties:

- **Understand:** Emotions and disagreements may become magnified during this trying time.

- **Communicate:** On a regular basis, discuss your emotions and fears with your partner. It won't always be easy, but having each other's support now is critical.

- **Support:** Know that you are both doing your best during this stressful time, no matter how you each deal with it on the outside.

- **Participate:** Go to doctor appointments together, and use a teamwork approach to deal with the decisions, tests, and procedures that you will both endure.

- **Enjoy:** Make dates to have "fun sex" during nonfertile times of your cycle, find new hobbies or activities that you can do together, and focus time and energy on your relationship.

- **Get counseling:** Seek professional counseling to help you get through the many challenges that you both face.

- Lesbian couples are finding greater acceptance in society, and more are choosing to make public their decision to have children together.

- Unfortunately, lesbian couples often must deal with additional difficulties not encountered by heterosexual couples, such as finding a sperm donor, dealing with closed-minded family and coworkers, and obtaining legal rights to clearly define both parenting roles.

- Single women may face additional hardships, such as finding a sperm donor, having financial and career concerns, and receiving criticism from various aspects of society.

- Dealing with family and friends can be quite difficult, even if they have good intentions. Their insensitive and harsh words may make you feel bad, causing you to suffer in silence, feeling lonely and isolated.

- If they are truly loving friends and family, once you explain your situation to them, they'll come around and become your top supporters during this difficult time.

Emotions and Fertility Treatments

- Going through ART can be exciting but also exhausting. Most people agree that it requires a huge commitment from you and your partner and can be draining—physically, emotionally, and financially.

- People are different, of course, but you're likely to cope better if you have a supportive partner, considerate close friends and family, and a support group where you can reach out to like-minded women.

- Many emotional and ethical complexities are associated with third-party reproduction, and your feelings may change as you journey onward with your fertility treatments.

- Keep an open line of communication with your partner to make sure that you both see eye to eye concerning the various third-party reproduction alternatives.

Fertility Counselors

- Everyone deals with stress in their own way. Certainly, some days will seem drearier than others. That said, many women benefit from talking with an infertility counselor.

- Signs that you might benefit from talking with an infertility counselor:

  - Persistent feelings of sadness, guilt, or worthlessness

  - Persistent feelings of bitterness, anger, or resentment

  - Loss of interest in activities that you once enjoyed

  - Depression that lasts for more than a couple of weeks

  - Agitation and high levels of anxiety

  - Complete immersion in and preoccupation with infertility

  - Friction and strain within your relationship with your partner

  - Difficulty concentrating and trouble accomplishing tasks that you could once do

  - Increased use of alcohol or drugs

  - Change in appetite, weight, or sleep patterns

  - Thoughts about suicide or death

- When selecting your fertility counselor, make sure that he or she is a licensed mental health professional and has experience treating couples with fertility issues.

CHAPTER 10

New and Emerging Technologies

Fertility and the field of reproductive medicine have many new and emerging technologies. Some of these exciting new techniques are already available or currently in investigational FDA clinical trials. Others are not yet available but show great promise for the near future.

Preimplantation Genetic Diagnosis (PGD)

Preimplantation genetic diagnosis (PGD), a technique used for the early diagnosis of genetic disorders in developing embryos, involves conducting a biopsy of the embryo to identify which cells may contain the disorder. Couples undergoing IVF procedure may have their embryos screened for an assortment of genetic disorders,

and only genetically normal embryos will then be used for embryo transfer back into the woman's uterus. The purpose of PGD is to select only healthy embryos for transfer to the uterus with the goal of achieving more healthy pregnancies, fewer miscarriages, and fewer genetically abnormal offspring.

HOW IS PGD PERFORMED?

PGD is done in conjunction with IVF. Normally during the IVF cycle, the eggs are retrieved from your ovaries and fertilized with your partner's sperm. If PGD is performed, the lab embryologist observes the embryo until it reaches the six- to eight-cell stage. At that time, one or two cells are removed and biopsied. The removal of one or two cells does not damage the embryo's development.

The biopsied cells are tested using sophisticated techniques to determine which embryos contain genetic defects. The cells from the embryo are also analyzed to ensure that they have the proper number of chromosomes. Any embryos found to be genetically defective or to have an abnormal number of chromosomes are discarded. Healthy and genetically normal embryos are allowed to further develop and will eventually be transferred back to your uterus as a normal step in the IVF process.

WHO MIGHT BENEFIT FROM PGD?

In a perfect world, we would test every single chromosome of every embryo to ensure that the embryo is healthy and normal. However, PGD technology is expensive, and at this point scientists are only able to check for the major nine chromosomes (out of 24) that affect the embryo's health. Most clinics limit that use of PGD technology to situations where it can detect those with the highest risk for genetic problems. Patients who might benefit from the PGD technique include:

- A woman or her partner who is a known carrier of a genetic disorder
- Women over the age of 35, because of the increased incidence of genetic abnormalities as women become older
- Women who have experienced recurrent miscarriages
- Women who have in the past conceived a baby with known genetic abnormalities
- Couples who have experienced several IVF failed attempts
- Men who have such a low sperm count that a surgical procedure is needed to retrieve their sperm

WHICH GENETIC DISORDERS CAN BE DETECTED DURING PGD?

PGD can detect many though not all genetic diseases or defects. Following is a partial list of those that can be identified using the PGD technique. If you and your partner are not affected by one of these but instead are carriers, you could still pass the disorder on to your child. Here's a list of genetic disorders that can be detected using PGD:

- Tay-Sachs disease
- Cystic fibrosis
- Thalassemia
- Sickle cell disease
- Down syndrome
- Hemophilia
- Duchenne muscular dystrophy
- Marfan syndrome
- Spinal muscular atrophy
- Turner's syndrome
- Fragile X syndrome
- Huntington's chorea

Other genetic disorders can also possibly be identified with PGD. Be sure to ask your fertility specialist if you have concerns about a specific disease.

WHAT ARE THE RISKS ASSOCIATED WITH PGD?

PGD does carry with it a few risks and limitations that you should be aware of and understand. These are generally considered rare. One such risk involves the rare but controversial subject of mosaic embryos. In a mosaic embryo, not all of the cells within the embryo are genetically identical; some cells may carry the disease and others do not. Because the PGD technique selects one or two cells at random, the disease may not be diagnosed if the embryo is a mosaic embryo. Even so, most people believe that the benefits from PGD outweigh the risks.

Damage to the Embryo

Every cell of the embryo at the six- or eight-cell stage is genetically identical to every other cell. Any and all of these cells will have the genetic potential to develop

into a normal embryo. Because one or two cells can be safely removed and the embryo can go on to develop normally, the risk of accidental damage to an embryo during the embryo biopsy is very low, about 0.6 percent.

Implantation Rates

How PGD affects embryo implantation rates remains an area of controversy. A report from the Kentucky Center for Reproductive Medicine & IVF suggests that the implantation rate may be slightly lowered as a result of the embryo biopsy. This means that embryos that have been biopsied may not be as likely to properly implant within your uterus. Therefore, early miscarriage may be more likely.

However, a Spanish study done in 2003 and published by Reproductive Biomedicine Online concluded that implantation rates may actually increase when PGD is used in IVF patients that have experienced implantation failures in the past. This improvement is thought to be caused by transferring only tested and proven genetically normal embryos into the IVF patient's uterus.

Delay in Embryo Development

PGD may cause the biopsied embryos to slow their growth and development for a few hours. After this time, the embryo appears to recover and continues to develop normally. While PGD may delay the embryo development for a short time, this is merely a temporary delay and does not harm the embryo in the long run.

USING PGD TO DETERMINE THE SEX OF YOUR BABY

When PGD was first offered to the public, it was intended for couples whose offspring were at high risk of inheriting a genetic disorder. Today as more fertility clinics offer PGD, this technology has become more available to those desiring it. However, at the current time, the majority of fertility centers in the United States do not offer this as an elective service.

If you are looking to use PGD technology to choose the gender of your child, find out ahead of time if this is an option at your fertility clinic. Couples may desire a child of a specific gender for a variety of reasons. The euphemistic term for this gender selection is *family balancing.*

PGD for the purpose of sex selection is performed in the same way as for PGD when used for genetic screening. As part of the IVF cycle, the eggs are retrieved from your ovaries and fertilized with your partner's sperm. The embryos are observed until they reach the six- to eight- cell stage. At that time, one or two cells are removed and biopsied.

The biopsied cells are tested using sophisticated techniques to identify sex chromosomes within each embryo. Sex chromosomes, also referred to as X or Y chromosomes, will determine whether the child will be a boy or a girl. These sex chromosomes are easy to distinguish in the laboratory. Embryos with two X chromosomes are female, and those with one X and one Y chromosome are male.

When PGD is used for sex selection, only those embryos of the desired sex are transferred back into your uterus. The other embryos are destroyed, cryopreserved, or donated. For many people, this practice raises serious ethical concerns. Some doctors may not be willing to perform PGD for the sole purpose of sex selection.

WHAT ARE THE PROS AND CONS CONCERNING PGD?

Here's a list of pros and cons for your consideration regarding PGD technology.

Pros

- If you or your partner is the carrier of a genetic disorder, this procedure can provide you with tremendous peace of mind.

- This procedure allows couples to avoid passing a serious genetic condition to their child.

- Because genetic abnormalities are a common cause of miscarriage, this procedure reduces the risk of miscarriage by transferring only healthy embryos.

- For some, this technique is preferable to abortion when a fetus is discovered to have a serious genetic disorder.

- For those who find it ethically acceptable, this procedure allows you to select the gender of your child.

Cons

- This procedure only tests for a limited number of genetic disorders; thus you may still transfer a genetic problem to an embryo that PGD is unable to detect.

- PGD is not considered a routine part of IVF, and thus an extra fee will be charged for those partaking in this procedure.

- People who oppose the destruction of human embryos are typically opposed to this procedure.

- Disability rights advocates have been critical of widespread use of this procedure because they point out that the definition of *disease* or *disorder* may be somewhat subjective.

- Many people are ethically opposed to using PGD as a form of gender selection. They are also concerned that this may pave the way for even more frivolous choices, such as a future child's looks or behavioral traits.

- The PGD technique is not 100 percent accurate, and false results have been known to occur.

MicroSort

MicroSort is an emerging scientific technique that increases the odds for a couple who want to select the gender of their baby. A special sperm-sorting machine is used to separate the sperm according to X (female) and Y (male) chromosomes. Once the sperm have been separated, the couple can choose to become pregnant using only the sperm with their desired gender.

At the time of this writing, MicroSort is still conducting clinical trials because it is a new technology and is still being evaluated for safety and outcomes by the FDA.

MicroSort is only available at two MicroSort Clinics. One is located in Fairfax, Virginia, and the other is in Laguna Hills, California.

HOW IS MICROSORT PERFORMED?

Your partner's sperm is evaluated at one of the two MicroSort clinical facilities. It is then placed in the flow cytometer machine, which will sort and separate the sperm into those with X chromosomes and Y chromosomes.

For the sorting to be performed, sperm are first treated with a dye that temporarily attaches itself to the DNA within each sperm. Although the size of the actual sperm is the same, the size of the genetic material (DNA) that they contain is different, because the X chromosome is larger than the Y chromosome. When a special fluorescent light is shined on the treated sperm, those with X chromosomes show up brighter and pink because they contain larger DNA. The sperm with the Y chromosomes don't shine as brightly, and they give off a green tint. The flow cytometer machine picks up these differences in brightness and color and then separates the sperm as they move through the machine.

Once the sperm have been sorted for gender selection, they can be used with assisted reproductive technology (ART) to bring about a pregnancy. Most women use the MicroSort technique in conjunction with intrauterine insemination (IUI). Women who will be conceiving using IUI must go to one of these two facilities.

Patients who plan to conceive using IVF can elect to have their sperm sorted at one of the two MicroSort facilities and then frozen and shipped to a collaborating fertility clinic in or near their hometown.

WHO MIGHT BENEFIT FROM MICROSORT?

Many couples would prefer to have a child of one gender or the other. Perhaps they already have one or more children of one gender and would like to have a child of the other gender. As fertility patients, they have already endured a great deal to have a baby. They realize that they may only be able to endure fertility treatments one or two more times, so they may desire to choose the sex of their planned upcoming pregnancy.

In some cases, a person may be the carrier of a gender-linked genetic disease that they don't want to pass along to their offspring. An example of this is the genetically inherited condition of hemophilia, in which the male is most susceptible to the disease. The gene for hemophilia is carried on the X chromosome. A female baby would inherit one X that contains the hemophilia gene and one X that is normal. The normal X balances out the abnormal X so she does not have hemophilia but is a genetic carrier. A baby boy is born with one X and one Y chromosome. If his X chromosome contains the hemophilia gene, he is stricken with this life-threatening disorder, because his Y chromosome is too small and not able to counterbalance the diseased X. You can see why couples who are carriers of hemophilia often prefer to have only female children.

In each of these situations, MicroSort can be used to shift the odds in favor of the parents' becoming pregnant with a child of their desired gender.

QUALIFICATIONS FOR ENROLLMENT IN THE MICROSORT CLINICAL TRIAL

Because this promising technology is still under FDA investigation, prospective patients must meet certain guidelines and qualifications before they can participate in the program. The basic qualifications for enrollment in the MicroSort clinical trial are discussed next.

For Genetic Disease

New patients who wish to participate in the program for the purpose of reducing the probability of transmitting a genetic disease to their offspring must meet the following minimum qualifications:

- They must be a married couple.
- Either partner must be a known carrier of X-linked disorder such as hemophilia.
- The husband and wife (donor if applicable) must test negative for HIV and hepatitis B and C.

For Family Balancing

New patients who wish to participate in the program for the purpose of family balancing must meet the following minimum qualifications:

- They must be a married couple.
- The couple must already have at least one child.
- The couple will sort for the less represented sex of children in the family.
- The wife (donor if applicable) is 18 to 39 years of age.
- The husband and wife (donor if applicable) must test negative for HIV and hepatitis B and C.

WHAT ARE THE RISKS ASSOCIATED WITH MICROSORT?

Because MicroSort is a relatively new technique and still in the process of FDA clinical trials, only limited information about the risks and outcomes is available. If you choose to become part of the clinical trial, you are required to sign an informed consent form stating that you understand that the potential risks and benefits are still largely unknown.

WHAT IS THE CHANCE OF GETTING YOUR DESIRED GENDER?

MicroSort sperm separation for female gender selection (XSort) has resulted in an average of 88 percent X (female) bearing sperm in the sorted specimen. Thus far, 91 percent of babies born using this method have been female (295 out of 325).

MicroSort sperm separation for male gender selection (YSort) has resulted in an average of 73 percent Y (male) bearing sperm in the sorted specimen. Though the data is still limited, 76 percent of babies born using this method have been male (39 out of 51).

A child of the desired gender cannot be guaranteed, because the current technology does not completely eliminate either female or male sperm cells from the sorted sample. So while MicroSort cannot offer a 100 percent guarantee, their method does offer better odds than you would find naturally, which are 50-50.

WHAT ARE THE PROS AND CONS CONCERNING MICROSORT?

Here is a list of pros and cons when considering using the MicroSort technology.

Pros

- If you or your partner is the carrier of a sex-linked genetic disorder, this procedure enables you to choose the sex that is not affected.
- For those who find it ethically acceptable, this procedure greatly increases the chances of selecting the desired gender of your child.
- MicroSort increases your odds over mere chance of giving birth to a baby of your desired gender.
- MicroSort is still emerging and coming up with exciting new innovations and promises additional growing technologies.

Cons

- MicroSort is still an emerging technology and participating in FDA clinical trials. Thus only limited information is available on pregnancy rates, risks, and outcomes.
- You must meet strict guidelines to qualify for the MicroSort program at this time.
- Only two MicroSort clinical facilities exist in the United States. Because of limited capacity, there is a waiting list (usually several months) for services.
- While MicroSort increases your odds for the desired gender, it is not guaranteed.
- This procedure is expensive and not covered by insurance.

Ovarian Tissue and Egg Freezing

At present, technology has become proficient at freezing sperm and embryos to be thawed for later use. However, because eggs and ovarian tissue (which contain many eggs) are extremely sensitive and delicate, they often cannot survive the methods used during traditional freezing and thawing. New breakthroughs in the field of freezing ovarian tissue and eggs are showing great promise. This is significant because it allows a woman to preserve her fertility for years to come.

Scientists in Japan have pioneered a revolutionary method called egg vitrification. The technique was initially used for female cancer patients, and the same principles are now being applied to preserve any woman's fertility. This new tech-

nique can be used on individual eggs or on a piece of ovarian tissue. Once perfected, the dreaded biological clock becomes a worry of the past.

HOW IS OVARIAN TISSUE AND EGG FREEZING PERFORMED?

The original problem with freezing ovarian tissue and eggs was due to damage from ice crystal formation in the inner layers of these cells. Now with the new vitrification process, the inside of the cell is not frozen. The new procedure is based on the insight that all of the eggs in each ovary live in the outermost layer of tissue. Japanese scientists discovered a successful way to "flash freeze" only this thin outer layer; results have been remarkably effective. Medical researchers in the United States are working with the Japanese scientists, and clinical research trials have begun. Dr. Sherman Silber of the Infertility Center of St. Louis has partnered with the Kato Ladies Clinic in Tokyo to bring some of these emerging technologies to the United States.

To obtain the eggs that will be frozen, the procedure is the same as for IVF egg retrieval. Fertility medication is given to stimulate and induce ovulation, ultrasound and blood tests monitor when the eggs are mature, and then ultrasound-guided egg retrieval is performed. Obtaining ovarian tissue requires a brief outpatient laparoscopy procedure for the purpose of ovarian biopsy. Through the use of microsurgical techniques, only the thin outer layer of the ovary is removed, frozen, and eventually grafted back at a later date, much like a skin graft.

WHO MIGHT BENEFIT FROM OVARIAN TISSUE AND EGG FREEZING?

All women are born with a limited supply of eggs. These eggs continue to dwindle in supply as we grow older. One recent study indicated that 98 percent of women are fertile through their early 20s. However, by their mid-30s, the percentage of those who are still fertile drops to about 70 percent. This biological clock phenomenon continues to tick until a woman reaches menopause and all of her eggs are depleted. Given that, the preservation of eggs and ovarian tissue by means of freezing can be of great benefit for many women who:

- Have not yet found a partner and want to delay pregnancy until they do
- Prefer to delay pregnancy because of school, career, personal issues, and so on
- Want to preserve their leftover eggs from an IVF cycle for future use

- Are facing the loss of their ovarian function because of approaching menopause, disease, or planned complete hysterectomy
- Have a diagnosis of ovarian cancer
- Are receiving radiation or chemotherapy treatment

Emerging Technologies Not Yet Available in the United States

New scientific studies and technologies are being tested all over the world. As these emerging technologies are proven to be safe and effective, they will likely be available in the United States also.

IN VITRO MATURATION OF EGGS

At the present time, a woman must undergo various fertility medications, ultrasounds, and blood work to stimulate her ovaries and induce ovulation. The net result is typically somewhere between 10 and 50 mature eggs. This is an expensive and physically demanding procedure for such a relatively small payback.

As a result, much research is being focused on in vitro maturation of eggs. What this means is that immature eggs are removed from your ovaries, taken to the laboratory, and treated with special techniques to cause them to further develop and mature. The mature eggs could subsequently be used with various assisted reproductive technologies. This saves you from the discomfort of fertility medications and the physical demands of many tests and procedures and you gain substantial financial savings.

This technique could be used by women who have:

- Premature ovarian failure
- Reached menopause
- Serious ovulation problems
- Cancer and are facing chemotherapy or radiation
- A desire to donate eggs to others
- Fertility issues that require IVF
- A wish to delay childbearing

Once the technique of in vitro maturation of eggs becomes refined and available, it will likely revolutionize IVF.

OVARIAN TISSUE DONATION AND TRANSPLANT

It may soon be possible to transplant ovarian tissue from one woman to another. This would allow one woman to donate a piece of her ovary and have it transplanted into another woman. The recipient would use the donor ovarian tissue to ovulate and become pregnant using natural sexual intercourse. The eggs would have the genetic material from the donor, but the pregnancy would be fertilized and grown within the body of the recipient. Ovarian tissue transplant is generally acceptable even for women who are forbidden to receive egg donation for religious reasons because it is viewed as an organ transplant and not a human egg or embryo donation.

As with donors of sperm, eggs, or embryos, a legal agreement must be in place between the donor and recipient.

At the present time, ovarian donation and transplant has only been successful in animals, but research continues and appears promising for the future.

CYTOPLASMIC TRANSFER

To understand this procedure, you should know a little about cytoplasm. Cytoplasm is the liquid portion of the egg that surrounds the central nucleus. (Is this bringing back thoughts of high school biology?) It may help to think of a regular chicken egg. For example, the yellow yolk would be the nucleus, and the white liquid part that surrounds it is the cytoplasm. In human eggs, the nucleus is also the center part of the egg and contains the genetic material, DNA. The surrounding cytoplasm functions to supply the rest of the egg with nutrition and energy.

Women who have experienced several IVF cycle failures because of poor embryo development may have had these losses because of defective cytoplasm. In most cases, receiving an egg from a donor usually becomes the next step. Although egg donation is a viable option, many women are reluctant because the baby is genetically linked to the donor and not to them.

Cytoplasmic transfer is an experimental laboratory technique that injects the cytoplasm from a healthy donor egg into your recipient egg. Because the egg still has your nucleus and DNA, the resulting baby will, too. Cytoplasmic transfer offers an alternative to egg donation but is actually better because the baby is genetically linked to only you and your male partner.

As of this writing, cytoplasmic transfer is banned in the United States because the FDA is requiring further clinical studies. The FDA may eventually approve the procedure, but it will likely take many years of trials and evaluations. In the meantime, couples desiring the procedure can have it performed outside of the United States. Among the various countries that offer cytoplasmic transfer are Israel, Lebanon, and Taiwan.

NUCLEAR TRANSFER

The nucleus is the central part of the egg that contains the genetic material, DNA. Nuclear transfer is an experimental laboratory technique that removes the nucleus of one egg and replaces it with the nucleus from another egg. Because the nucleus contains the DNA, the baby that is formed will have the newly transplanted DNA.

This procedure could be beneficial for women who are not able to produce their own viable eggs. In such a case, a donor egg would be obtained and the nucleus removed. Then the intended mother's nucleus, containing her DNA, would be implanted into the donor egg. The egg would then contain the intended mother's genetic material but would also contain the cytoplasm and other structures from the donor. Because the nucleus with DNA is what determines the baby's genetic makeup, the baby would be genetically linked to the intended mother and not to the donor.

Another interesting option for this procedure is to replace the nucleus of the donor egg with the nucleus from a sperm. The new nucleus egg could then be fertilized by sperm from a different man. The resulting child would be genetically linked to both men. This technique would likely be of great interest within the gay community.

The nuclear transfer procedure has been attempted with human eggs but has not yet been successful. Research studies continue to refine the techniques and methods.

CLONING

Cloning is a process that creates an organism that is an exact genetic copy of the original. This means the original cell and the newly cloned cell have the same DNA. Certainly, cloning has been the topic of much debate and has received a lot of media coverage in recent years. Cloning is typically considered to be the most controversial of all the assisted reproductive technologies.

Actually, different types of cloning exist and are distinct from one another. The two main types of cloning are human reproductive cloning and therapeutic cloning.

Reproductive Cloning

Reproductive cloning is performed for the purpose of producing a genetic duplicate of a living being. This is the type of cloning that you see dramatized in the

movies or when you jokingly say that you wish you had a clone to help you accomplish all of your duties and responsibilities. You might remember Dolly the sheep, from 1997, as an example of reproductive cloning. Did you know that she died prematurely as a result of lung cancer and arthritis? Apparently, serious health problems and untimely deaths are thought to be associated with reproductive cloning.

The American Society for Reproductive Medicine (ASRM) is opposed to any attempt at human reproductive cloning.

Therapeutic Cloning

As the name suggests, therapeutic cloning is performed to treat and even cure severe health problems. Here's a basic step-by-step guide to the therapeutic cloning procedure:

- The nucleus is removed from a donated human egg in the laboratory.

- A cell from your body (for example, a skin cell) is taken to the laboratory, and that cell's nucleus (which contains your DNA) is injected into the egg.

- Because the skin cell's nucleus already contains your complete set of DNA, the egg does not need to be fertilized.

- The cells begin to grow and divide, during the first few days of development, the cells that form are referred to as stem cells.

- Stem cells have unique and important properties. They're unique because at this point they have not yet developed into any particular type of cell (such as skin, muscle, fat, nerve, and so on). Instead, they have the amazing ability to develop into almost any type of cell.

- Let's say you need a new liver. Instead of dealing with an organ transplant, scientists can stimulate these stem cells to grow into liver cells.

- Now you've essentially grown your own new liver! There's no chance of tissue rejection or other such problems because all of the cells possess your DNA.

Medical researchers and scientists foresee tremendous promise for stem cells. These incredible cells can be stimulated to develop into various types of cells or tissues and lead to lifesaving therapies. The controversy arises because donated human eggs are used in this technique.

ASRM supports research for therapeutic cloning. However, at this time, it is illegal to use federal research funds in the United States to clone human embryos. Debate continues concerning the moral and ethical limits of cloning. At some point in the future, cloning may become a viable option.

Conclusion

Certainly, the field of fertility and reproductive medicine has many new and emerging technologies that indicate great promise. Some innovations are already available in the United States; others are undergoing the scrutiny of investigational FDA clinical trials or may not yet be obtainable. You, the fertility patient, will benefit from this growing area of scientific technology.

This chapter aims to educate you about new options that are available to you now or coming soon. However, because this is such an ever-changing field, you need to keep your eyes and ears open for other exciting procedures as they become available. Check with your fertility specialist, read newspapers and magazines, and check out the television and Internet for the latest and greatest options.

Summary

Here is a recap of the important concepts discussed in this chapter.

PGD

- PGD is a technique done in conjunction with IVF. PGD is used for the early diagnosis of genetic disorders in developing embryos.

- To perform PGD, the lab embryologist removes one or two cells from the developing embryo and evaluates them for genetic content.

- The purpose of PGD is to select only healthy embryos for transfer back to the uterus during an ART procedure.

- Currently, scientists are only able to check for particular chromosomes that affect the embryo's health; thus only certain genetic disorders can be identified.

- You should be aware of the risks associated with PGD, but most people agree that the benefits outweigh the risks.

- Some fertility clinics will use PGD to select the sex of your embryo; however, the majority will not unless there is a medical reason to prefer a specific gender.

- There are numerous ethical concerns involving PGD.

MicroSort

- MicroSort is a new scientific technique that increases the odds for selecting the gender of your baby. At present, MicroSort is still conducting FDA clinical trials.

- This technique uses a special sperm-sorting machine to separate the sperm according to X (female) and Y (male) chromosomes. The separated sperm are used during various ART procedures.

- People with a known gender-linked genetic disease (such as hemophilia) may greatly benefit from this emerging technique.

- Some people are interested in MicroSort to shift the odds in their favor of becoming pregnant with a child of their desired gender.

- Various ethical implications are involved in selecting the sex of your child.

- This is still an expensive and emerging technology. The results are not 100 percent accurate or guaranteed.

Ovarian Tissue and Egg Freezing

- New breakthroughs in the field of freezing ovarian tissue and eggs are promising.

- Research studies are being conducted in a joint effort between the United States and Japan to further advance this technology.

- Because women are born with a limited supply of eggs, this technology would revolutionize the fertility world and provide a huge reproductive advancement for women. In essence, the biological clock would no longer be of such importance.

Emerging Technologies Not Yet Available in the United States

- In vitro maturation of eggs
- Ovarian tissue donation and transplant
- Cytoplasmic transfer
- Nuclear transfer
- Cloning

CHAPTER 11

Ethical Considerations and Decision Making

The study of ethics refers to a set of moral principles and values and is concerned with the basic principles of right and wrong, good and bad. Your own standards of ethics may come from or be influenced by an individual, a professional organization, a culture, or a religion.

Of all the various fields of medicine, the specialty of fertility is brimming with many unanswered ethical questions and concerns. Some people view the field of fertility as "playing God" because it is able to help create human life, using unnatural techniques. Others believe that this technology has been made available to us for a reason and that we should use it to the best of our abilities.

The way that you view the many ethical considerations of fertility will have to do with your own experiences and outlook on life. It will also probably include your principles based on your education, religion, and culture as well as viewpoints of family and friends.

Assisted Reproductive Technology (ART)

The scientific field of ART brings with it a host of many ethical concerns.

OBJECTIONS TO TECHNOLOGY

Some couples have a moral dilemma or religious objection to using any type of ART. Certainly, couples should come to terms with these concerns and apprehensions before embarking on any type of advanced fertility treatment. It helps to establish what you and your partner are willing and unwilling to do. You may find that it's easier to come to a decision when you are educated and well informed about your options. Talk openly with your fertility specialist. Many couples also benefit from talking with a mental health counselor who specializes in fertility matters. You may also find comfort and answers by speaking with your minister, priest, or rabbi. By exploring all possible options, you can find an approach that best suits your particular needs and situation.

WHAT TO DO WITH ANY LEFTOVER EMBRYOS

Depending on which ART you use, you may be faced with the ethical dilemma of what to do with your leftover embryos. If you have decided that you will not be using them for your own family building, you face several options:

- You may donate your embryos so that another couple may use them.
- You may donate your embryos for medical science and research.
- You may have your embryos destroyed.

Of course, these decisions are not easy and are very personal. You'll need to explore your thoughts about this topic from a personal, religious, and emotional standpoint. You and your partner should come to a decision that is acceptable to both of you.

RAISING AN ART CHILD

As if raising a child isn't difficult enough, parents who conceive using ART may face additional challenges.

First, you must decide if you will explain your child's conception to him or her. Especially in cases where no outside donor is involved, some parents never tell their child that ART was used to achieve the pregnancy. Other parents feel obliged to explain the child's conception when the time seems right. If you do choose to tell your child, remember to explain only what your child can handle at his or her current age. Young children won't be able to fully grasp the concept of ART. Try to break it down into easy-to-understand terms. As your child matures, you'll be able to fill in the blanks and answer more questions because you've already opened this path of discussion.

You might also want to discuss your wishes with close family members and friends. Explain to them whether or not you will be telling the child about the ART conception. Set the tone and the ground rules so that your family and friends don't violate your wishes. For example, you might say that you and your partner are the only two people who can discuss this topic with your child. Certainly, if you don't plan to tell your child, let your friends and family know and ask them to honor your wishes to keep this a secret.

Third-Party Reproduction: Sperm, Egg, and Embryo Donation

There are certainly many ethical considerations surrounding the subject of third-party reproduction.

EGG DONATION: SHOULD THERE BE AN UPPER AGE LIMIT?

Is there an age when a woman becomes too old to become a mother? It's well known that a woman's egg supply diminishes as she ages. Also, with advancing age comes an increased risk of genetic abnormalities, such as Down syndrome. For these reasons, most doctors recommend that the egg donor be young, preferably under age 35.

However, what about the case of the egg recipient? Should there be an age limit for her? Consider that the average woman now enjoys an average life expectancy of approximately 80 years. As a postmenopausal woman, she is likely to have greater financial stability, wisdom, and life experiences. On the other hand, she may be at higher risk of physical ailments and diseases. Some people believe that postmeno-

pausal women (women in their 50s and older) should be banned from receiving donor eggs. Opponents point out that younger women with cancer or other potentially life-threatening conditions such as diabetes or muscular dystrophy are not denied donor eggs. All the while, these younger women may have a shorter life expectancy than the postmenopausal woman.

PAYMENTS TO DONORS

Questions often arise about the practice of paying donors for their services. Although close friends or family may agree to donate their genetic material as an act of kindness, most donors expect to be financially compensated.

Sperm donors are typically paid for their services by the sperm bank or clinic. These fees are passed along to you as part of your fertility treatment.

Egg donors usually receive greater compensation. That's because they must endure the physical and emotional demands of fertility medications, invasive tests, and procedures. Unfortunately, these steps are required to stimulate the ovaries, induce ovulation, and ultimately recover and harvest the eggs. Most people believe that these sacrifices are deserving of considerable financial compensation. However, there are those who argue that egg donation should not be permitted at all. These people reason that a woman should not be subjected to potentially dangerous medications and procedures for another woman who is not actually ill in the true sense of the word.

Many clinics offer a price break for women undergoing ART who are willing to donate a portion of their retrieved eggs to other women in the program. Proponents of this arrangement state that women who would be unable to afford ART can be offered treatment and a chance at becoming a parent. It also provides eggs to other women who desire to become mothers. Those who disagree with this situation argue that this practice could lead to coercion for those unable to pay. It would also likely reduce the chance of the woman becoming pregnant given that she has fewer eggs because she's given up some of her own eggs for another woman.

RAISING A CHILD CONCEIVED WITH DONOR MATERIAL

The challenge of raising an ART child has been discussed previously. Raising a child that has been conceived with donor material forces you to tackle even more ethical considerations.

Of course, you must decide if you will explain your child's conception to him or her. And you'll also want to discuss your wishes with close family members and friends so that they will abide by your wishes.

In the case of donor sperm, eggs, or embryos, you'll also need to decide if you want to explain this to your child. If you do decide to be open about the conception, consider how much information to share with the child. Some people choose to portray the donor in the same way as a biological parent who placed the child for adoption. Others explain that the donor was more of a helper who assisted in conception but has no further role. At some point, will the child be able to find out about the donor? Should they meet and form a relationship? Many agencies keep this information on file, and so it may become available to the child once he or she reaches age 18. Ideally, this type of information should be spelled out in your donor agreement prior to conception. At the very least, the child should know about the donor's medical history because it is part of the child's genetic makeup and medical family history.

Surrogacy

The topic of surrogacy brings about many ethical considerations.

WHAT ARE THE PROS AND CONS CONCERNING SURROGACY?

Here are pros and cons to consider regarding surrogacy.

Pros

- Surrogacy allows a couple to have a baby when they would otherwise be unable to do so, except by adoption.

- Surrogacy allows a genetic link with at least one parent, which is very important for some prospective parents.

- Surrogacy may be used for practical reasons because of the scarcity of adoptable babies in this country.

- Some women who serve as surrogates do so because they want to help others and derive great satisfaction from the gift of their services.

Cons

- According to the American College of Obstetricians and Gynecologists (ACOG), the main arguments against surrogate motherhood are based on the harm it could produce. These include potential physical and emotional harm that pregnancy may bring to the surrogate mother herself, possible emotional harm to the child that is born, and impending harm to the surrogate's existing children.

- If no legal agreement exists or the surrogate mother changes her mind and decides to dispute the agreement, a difficult custody battle may ensue.

- Because of the hormonal changes of pregnancy and the associated emotions and mood swings, some people believe that the surrogate cannot possibly understand the implications of giving up her child until after the birth has occurred.

PAYMENT TO THE SURROGATE

Several ethical issues arise when it comes to financial payment to the surrogate. Although close friends or family may agree to donate their genetic material as an act of kindness, most surrogates expect to be financially compensated.

Most people agree that financial compensation should be made to the surrogate for her time and effort in initiating and carrying the pregnancy, her acceptance of the hazards of pregnancy and childbirth, delivering the baby, and her possible loss of employment opportunities. Do not compensate the surrogate for delivering an "acceptable product." This means that payment to the surrogate should not be contingent upon her delivering a healthy live-born baby because this would seem to devalue human life and turn surrogacy into a financial baby buying business.

Another matter of concern is that surrogacy payment may lead to the exploitation of potential surrogates. In most cases, women who agree to be surrogates have less education, financial resources, and power when compared to the intended parents. This is why it is imperative that the surrogate have her own independent legal and psychiatric counseling professionals. Otherwise, the surrogate may be at risk for being treated as an impersonal commodity.

SEPARATE PROFESSIONAL TEAMS FOR SURROGATE AND INTENDED PARENTS

While both the surrogate and the intended parents share some common goals, such as the goal of creating and delivering a baby, they could find themselves with opposing viewpoints and concerns. For this reason, the surrogate and the intended parents should have their own separate professional teams for legal, medical, and counseling advice and treatment. This way both parties can be properly represented should a conflict occur.

Of course, the fertility specialist must deal with both the surrogate and the intended parents because that doctor will perform the ART as part of the surrogacy services. However, the surrogate should obtain obstetrical care from a physician who is not involved with the intended parents in any way. This allows the surrogate to feel comfortable during pregnancy and delivery with a doctor of her own choosing.

Sex Selection

The field of fertility raises many ethical questions, but perhaps no other brings about as much interest and debate as choosing the sex of your child. Patients may wish to determine the sex of their offspring for various reasons—some are medically indicated and others are not.

MEDICALLY INDICATED SEX SELECTION

The medical reason for sex selection is to prevent sex-linked genetic disorders, as discussed in Chapter 10. Ideally, the best way to screen for a genetic disorder would be to test for the specific gene that is causing the disorder, but unfortunately, science and technology have not yet reached that point for many diseases. Therefore, the only way to prevent a known sex-linked genetic disorder is to choose to give birth to a baby of the sex that is not affected. For example, if a woman carries the gene for hemophilia, then 50 percent of her sons will have hemophilia, a life-threatening disease. Girls born to this woman will not have the disease, though they could be carriers of hemophilia. To ensure that her children will not have hemophilia, the woman either decides to abort male fetuses or chooses not to transfer male embryos back into her uterus. Of course, this is not ideal, because healthy male embryos may be discarded. Though still a new technology, MicroSort, which helps to select the sex prior to fertilization through sperm sorting, is more favorable than discarding or aborting the embryo after it has begun to develop and grow.

The American Society for Reproductive Medicine (ASRM) committee on ethics states that the practice of sex selection for the purpose of preventing sex-linked genetic disorders is ethically permissible.

NONMEDICALLY INDICATED SEX SELECTION

Patients sometimes desire to choose the sex of their child for nonmedical reasons, which may be due to social, economic, religious, cultural, or other personal reasons. For example, parents may want their only or first-born child to be of a certain sex. Or they may already have children of one sex and desire to have children of the opposite sex for family balancing. Surveys indicate that the majority of couples in the United States who seek to choose the sex of their baby want a male child.

Proponents of sex selection argue that if the technology is available, it should be used. They also state that it could decrease population growth because couples often have more children than they actually want because they keep trying for their desired gender baby.

The ASRM ethics committee discourages sex selection of already existing embryos for nonmedical reasons. They do not believe that it is ethically appropriate to destroy and discard embryos for the sole purpose of "family balancing." However, as the technology of MicroSort becomes more refined and available, ASRM believes that sex selection for nonmedical reasons would be more ethically permissible.

Selective Reduction in Multiple Pregnancies

Most women who undergo an ART procedure are thrilled and can successfully carry a twin pregnancy. However, pregnancies with triplets and especially a higher number of fetuses carry increased risks of birth defects and premature delivery. Risks for the mother include greater chance of high blood pressure, gestational diabetes, uterine bleeding, and complications associated with a C-section delivery.

For these reasons, most fertility clinics limit the number of embryos transferred into the woman's uterus to two or three. Sometimes three or more babies implant and grow; in this circumstance, the parents and the fertility specialist are faced with a heart-wrenching decision. Do they continue the pregnancy as is and accept the many increased risks to mother and babies? Or do they decide to destroy one or more of the fetuses in an effort to save the others?

Selective reduction is the process of destroying one or more fetuses with the purpose of reducing the pregnancy, usually to twins. In such a case, selective reduction could be ethically acceptable, because it is aimed at optimizing the quality of life after birth. Even so, those against selective reduction argue that it is ethically wrong and note that it may even, though rarely, result in a loss of the entire pregnancy (2 to 7 percent of cases).

Cloning

Many people believe that cloning should be differentiated into separate categories. For example, reproductive cloning is performed to exactly duplicate an existing animal. Many medical ethicists find this procedure to be morally wrong, as it disregards the sanctity of human life. On the other hand, therapeutic cloning is done to harvest stem cells from early embryos for the purpose of curing disease and helping others. Even with the potential benefit of replacing diseased organs and curing disease, some people still find this type of cloning to be morally wrong.

The results of a 2006 poll conducted by International Communications Research concluded that:

- 83 percent of Americans are opposed to human cloning to provide children for infertile couples

- 81 percent are opposed to human cloning to produce embryos that would be destroyed in medical research

Similar polls conducted in recent years confirm that the American public is concerned about the moral issues of cloning. Given the current state of opinions, it is doubtful that cloning will become a popular method of fertility treatment in the near future.

Interesting Ethical Scenario

In the early 1980s, a plane crash cut short the lives of an infertile couple, leaving two frozen embryos orphaned. Several important ethical and legal questions arose:

- Who would have decision-making powers over the fate of the embryos?
- Should there be provisions for the embryos in the couple's will?
- Did the embryos have a right to be born?
- If so, would the embryos inherit the couple's estate?
- Who would serve as a surrogate to grow and deliver these babies?
- Who would raise these children and would they be compensated financially from the deceased parents' estate?

Conclusion

At the present time in the United States, no standard practices exist when it comes to ethics concerning fertility issues. Each fertility clinic essentially has free reign with regard to their ethics and morality. Several national organizations represented by the federal government, fertility medicine professional associations, and various religious groups are working to agree upon and establish a set of ethical standards.

In the meantime, it's up to you. The best choices you can make are based on understanding your options and thereby making an informed decision. Read and learn as much as you can about your fertility situation, and understand the pros and cons of your options. It's extremely important to have an open line of communication with your partner. Choose your fertility specialist as someone who is not only competent but also communicative and caring. You may also want to have a reproductive attorney and a mental health counselor who specializes in fertility to gain better understanding and sound advice. After gathering all of the information and taking into consideration the advice of experts, you will be able to make your best personal decision. Then you'll be assured that you've made a truly caring and wise choice.

Summary

Here is a summary of the major points discussed during this chapter.

Overview

- Ethics is the study of moral principles and values. Your own standards of ethics may come from or be influenced by an individual, a professional organization, a culture, or a religion.
- The way that you view the many ethical considerations of fertility will be based upon your own life experiences and outlook on life.

ART

- Some people have objections to ART because of moral or religious values.
- Depending on which ART you use, you may be faced with the ethical dilemma of what to do with your leftover embryos.
- Raising a child conceived from an ART raises the issue of if and how you might eventually tell your child about his or her conception.

Third-Party Reproduction

- Regarding egg donation, should there be an upper age limit for the egg recipient?
- While close friends or family members may donate their genetic material for free, most donors expect to be paid. Questions often arise about the practice of paying donors for their services.

- Raising a child conceived from third-party involvement may be complicated by explaining the role of this donor to the child. At the very least, the child should know about the donor's medical history because it is part of the child's genetic makeup and medical family history.

Surrogacy

- Numerous pros and cons abound regarding the issue of surrogacy.
- Ethical issues may be raised when it comes to financial payment of the surrogate.
- Because they could find themselves with opposing viewpoints, the surrogate and the intended parents should have their own separate professional teams for legal, medical, and counseling advice.

Sex Selection

- Some cases of gender selection are medically indicated because of a known sex-linked genetic disorder.
- More controversial is the topic of nonmedically indicated sex selection techniques.

Selective Reduction in Multiple Pregnancies

- Fertility clinics usually limit the number of embryos transferred into the woman's uterus to two or three because of the many complications and risks associated with higher-order pregnancies. However, sometimes three or more babies implant and grow.
- Selective reduction is the process of destroying one or more fetuses with the purpose of reducing the pregnancy, usually to twins.
- This presents a moral and ethical dilemma and is a heart-wrenching decision.

Cloning

- Reproductive cloning involves the exact duplication of an existing animal. Many medical ethicists believe it is morally wrong because it disregards the sanctity of human life.
- Therapeutic cloning involves harvesting stem cells from early embryos for the purpose of curing disease. People are divided on the issue.

GLOSSARY

Abscess: A collection of pus due to infection that can occur in any part of the body.

Abstinence: The refusal to partake in sexual intercourse.

Adhesions: Scar tissue that forms within the body as a result of surgery, infection, or disease.

Amenorrhea: The lack of menstrual periods.

Androgen: Male hormones—for example, testosterone—produced by the testicles and responsible for male characteristics.

Anesthesia: The relief of pain and loss of sensation due to special medication or techniques.

Antibiotics: Medications that are used to treat and cure infections.

Antibody: A protein found in the bloodstream that has been produced by the immune system as a reaction to a foreign substance.

Assisted reproductive technology (ART): All treatments, procedures, and medical assistance that involve the handling of human eggs and sperm for the purpose of helping a woman become pregnant.

Autoimmune disease: A medical condition whereby the body attacks its own tissues.

Azoospermia: The complete absence of sperm during ejaculation.

Basal body temperature (BBT): The body temperature taken upon awakening first thing in the morning, prior to any activity.

Biopsy: A minor surgical procedure to remove a small piece of tissue, which is then taken to the laboratory, where it is examined and analyzed under a microscope.

Blighted ovum: An egg that does not develop properly and is typically miscarried.

Cervical mucus: The normal secretions formed by the glands within the cervix. They change in texture and consistency with the hormone fluctuations of the menstrual cycle.

Cervix: The lower and narrow end of the uterus that protrudes into the vagina and connects the uterus to the vagina.

Chlamydia: A sexually transmitted disease that can cause infection, pelvic inflammatory disease, infertility, and various problems during pregnancy.

Chromosome: A tiny structure within the cell's center (nucleus) that contains the genetic material which determines a person's physical traits.

Cloning: An involved scientific technique that creates a duplicate copy of a cell.

Corpus luteum: After ovulation, the empty follicle that once encased the egg. This tiny structure produces hormones and typically has a life span of about two weeks, at which time the menstrual period begins. If a pregnancy occurs, this structure will continue to produce hormones for many weeks.

Cryopreservation: The process of freezing and storing (in liquid nitrogen) eggs, sperm, or embryos for future use.

Cytoplasm: The material within a cell that surrounds the nucleus and provides the cell with energy.

Cytoplasmic transfer: A technique that removes the cytoplasm from a donor egg and injects it into the intended mother's egg.

Diethylstilbestrol (DES): A synthetic estrogen used between 1940 and 1970 to prevent miscarriage. Its use was discontinued because it has been linked with causing certain birth defects in the offspring.

Dilation and curettage (D&C): A procedure in which the cervix is opened and the inner contents and lining of the uterus are scraped or suctioned.

Donor eggs: Eggs that are taken from the ovaries of a fertile woman and donated to another woman to be used for an ART procedure.

Dysmenorrhea: Painful or crampy menstrual period.

Ectopic pregnancy: A pregnancy that is growing outside of the uterus, such as in the fallopian tubes, the abdomen, the cervix, or an ovary.

Eggs: The female sex cells produced by the ovaries. When fertilized by sperm, they produce embryos.

Ejaculation: Semen that is emitted from the male's penis during sexual climax.

Embryo: The term for a developing fertilized egg during the first six to eight weeks of pregnancy. After this time, it is typically referred to as a fetus.

Endometriosis: A condition where the tissue that lines the uterus implants outside of the uterine cavity in such locations as the ovaries, fallopian tubes, and other pelvic structures. It can grow with hormonal stimulation, cause pain, scar tissue, and lead to infertility.

Endometrium: The inner lining of the uterus that grows and sheds according to hormonal stimulation during the menstrual cycle.

Epididymis: The long, thin, hollow duct system within the scrotum, where maturing sperm leave the testicles and continue to develop until they are ready to fertilize an egg.

Estrogen: A female hormone responsible for many female physical traits.

Fallopian tubes: A pair of tubes that retrieve and carry the eggs from the ovaries into the uterus. Fertilization typically occurs within the fallopian tubes.

Fertilization: The fusion of the male's sperm and the female's egg to form an embryo.

Fibroids: Noncancerous (benign) muscular growths that form on the inside or outside of the uterus. They may cause no symptoms but could potentially cause abnormal bleeding or pain.

Flow cytometer: A scientific instrument used to measure various traits of individual cells.

Follicle: The saclike structure within the ovary that holds the egg. It ruptures and empties upon release of the egg in the process known as ovulation.

Follicle-stimulating hormone (FSH): A hormone that is made by the pituitary gland in the brain. It causes growth and development of eggs in women and sperm production in men.

Gamete: An egg or sperm cell.

Genes: The genetic material or DNA "blueprints" that code for specific traits, such as hair and eye color.

Genital herpes: A sexually transmitted disease caused by a virus that produces painful and very contagious sores around the external sex organs.

Gestational surrogate: A woman who is pregnant with an embryo that has been derived from the egg and sperm of people not related to her. Therefore, she has no genetic relationship with the baby.

Gonadotropin-releasing hormone (GnRH): A hormone secreted by a part of the brain (called the hypothalamus) that stimulates the pituitary gland to release FSH and LH hormones.

Gonadotropins: The type of hormones (such as FSH and LH) that are made by the brain's pituitary gland and control reproductive function in both men and women.

Gonorrhea: A sexually transmitted disease that may lead to pelvic inflammatory disease, infertility, and arthritis.

Hirsutism: Extra hair on a woman's face, abdomen, or chest caused by extraordinary high levels of male hormone, usually testosterone.

Hormone: A chemical substance produced within the body to trigger a specific activity in another part of the body.

Human chorionic gonadotropin (hCG): A hormone produced by the placenta early in pregnancy, used as the basis of pregnancy tests. This hormone is also given to fertility patients to trigger ovulation.

Human immunodeficiency virus (HIV): A virus that attacks the body's immune system and causes acquired immunodeficiency syndrome (AIDS).

Hypothalamus: A small area in the brain that works with the pituitary gland to regulate the producing and release of many hormones in the body.

Hysterosalpingogram (HSG): A test performed to evaluate the shape of the uterine cavity and to determine if the fallopian tubes are blocked. A fluid with dye is injected through the cervix and into the uterus; the fluid's pathway is tracked with x-ray.

Hysteroscope: A telescope-like instrument that is passed through the cervix into the uterus, so the doctor can assess the cervix and inside of the uterus for defects or disease.

Infertility: A condition whereby a couple has been unable to become pregnant after 12 months of regular heterosexual intercourse without the use of any form of birth control.

Insemination: The insertion of sperm into a woman's body or into eggs in a laboratory to achieve a pregnancy.

Insulin: A hormone that lowers the level of sugar (glucose) in the blood.

Intracytoplasmic sperm injection (ICSI): The injection of a single sperm directly into an egg cell for the purpose of fertilization.

Intrauterine insemination (IUI): A technique used to become pregnant, sperm sample is processed in the lab, inserted directly through the cervix and into the uterus using a thin catheter.

In vitro fertilization (IVF): A process in which eggs are removed from a woman's ovary and fertilized in a laboratory with a man's sperm, after which the resulting embryo is transferred to the woman's uterus for pregnancy or is cryopreserved for future use.

In vitro maturation: A process that allows eggs to mature in a laboratory instead of the usual method, within a woman's ovary.

Laparoscopy: A surgical procedure in which a slender, telescope-like instrument is inserted into the abdomen and used to view abdominal and pelvic organs and perform surgery.

Laparotomy: A surgical procedure in which an incision is made into the abdomen for the purpose of surgery to the abdominal or pelvic organs.

Lupus: An autoimmune disease that causes changes in the joints, skin, kidneys, lungs, heart, or brain.

Luteal phase: In the menstrual cycle, the time just after ovulation and until menstruation begins.

Luteinizing hormone (LH): A hormone that is made by the pituitary gland in the brain, which helps with ovulation in women and sperm production in men.

Menopause: The progression in a woman's life when her ovaries stop functioning and menstruation stops, marking the end of her natural fertility.

Menstrual cycle: A woman's process of bleeding, ovulating, and bleeding again. The average cycle occurs every 28 days, with ovulation usually occurring at the midpoint on day 14.

Miscarriage: The spontaneous loss of a pregnancy before the fetus can survive outside the uterus, usually occurring during the first trimester.

Molar pregnancy: The growth of abnormal placenta tissue within the uterus and usually the absence of a normal fetus.

Multiple pregnancy: A pregnancy in which there are twins, triplets, or more fetuses.

Neural tube defect: A serious birth defect that is due to the improper development of the brain, the spinal cord, or their coverings.

Nuclear transfer: A process in which the nucleus of an egg cell is removed and replaced with another nucleus from another cell.

Nucleus: The center part of the cell that contains the genetic material.

Oligospermia: A very low and inadequate amount of sperm in the semen sample.

Ovarian hyperstimulation syndrome (OHSS): A potentially dangerous condition caused by overstimulating the ovaries with medication, leading to painful swelling of the ovaries and fluid collection within the abdomen and lungs.

Ovaries: Two glands located on either side of a woman's uterus. They produce hormones and also contain eggs that are released at ovulation.

Ovulation: The release of a mature egg from its follicle from the outer layer of the ovary, usually occurring around day 14 of a regular 28-day menstrual cycle.

Ovulation induction: A technique used often in fertility treatments whereby various medications are given to the woman for the purpose of stimulating the ovaries and causing ovulation to occur.

Pap test: A screening test performed in a doctor's office in which cells from the cervix are scraped away and examined under a microscope to evaluate for signs of cervical cancer.

Pelvic exam: An examination performed by a doctor or another health care provider where the examiner's hands are used to examine the woman's internal and external pelvic organs.

Pelvic inflammatory disease (PID): A medical condition resulting from infection to the pelvic organs that can lead to blockage and scarring, especially of the fallopian tubes, leading to fertility problems.

Pituitary gland: The master endocrine gland that is located at the base of the brain, that together with the hypothalamus makes and regulates many hormones in the body.

Placenta: An important tissue of pregnancy that implants within the wall of the uterus and serves as an interface between mother and fetus, providing the fetus with nourishment and removing waste from the fetus.

Polycystic ovary syndrome (PCOS): A medical condition that occurs in a woman that involves increased levels of male hormones leading to cyst formation within the ovaries, lack of ovulation, and infertility.

Polyps: Small growths that develop and pouch outward from tissue. For example, uterine polyps grow from the tissue lining the uterus.

Preimplantation genetic diagnosis (PGD): A lab technique that uses DNA analysis to determine the genetic material with an embryo prior to embryo transfer.

Progesterone: A hormone that is produced in the ovaries and prepares the uterus for implantation and pregnancy. If pregnancy does not happen, the progesterone level drops off and menstrual bleeding occurs.

Prostate gland: A gland located near the male's bladder that contributes to ejaculation fluid. It is prone to infection that might affect his fertility.

Semen: A thick and cloudy fluid that usually contains sperm and is discharged from the male's penis during sexual climax.

Semen analysis: The microscopic assessment of semen to determine the number of sperm (sperm count), their shapes (morphology), and their ability to move (motility).

Septate uterus: An abnormality and birth defect of the uterus in which the uterus is divided into two distinct compartments.

Sexually transmitted disease (STD): One of several infectious diseases that are spread by sexual contact and include such ailments as chlamydia, gonorrhea, genital warts, herpes, syphilis, and human immunodeficiency virus (HIV, the cause of AIDS).

Sperm aspiration: A technique used to remove the sperm from part of the male's reproductive tract (for example, the epididymis, vas deferens, or testicle), usually for the purpose of fertility and reproduction.

Sperm washing: A laboratory method that separates the sperm from the seminal fluid.

Surrogacy: A situation where a woman carries a pregnancy and delivers a child for the intended parents. Surrogacy can be divided into gestational surrogacy, in which the surrogate does not contribute genetically to the baby, and traditional surrogacy, in which the surrogate does contribute genetically to the baby by providing her own eggs.

Syphilis: A sexually transmitted disease that is caused by the organism *Treponema pallidum*. It can cause major health problems and, in the later stages, even result in death.

Testicular sperm aspiration (TESA): An outpatient procedure performed on a male where sperm are aspirated from his sperm duct for use in an assisted reproductive technology.

Testicular sperm extraction (TESE): An outpatient procedure performed on a male where small and thin biopsy specimens are removed from his testicles and sent to the laboratory, where sperm will be removed and used during an assisted reproductive technology.

Testosterone: A predominantly male sex hormone that is produced by the testicles and is responsible for sperm production and certain male physical characteristics, such as muscle mass and facial hair.

Traditional surrogate: A woman who is pregnant with an embryo that has been derived from her own egg and the sperm of the intended father in order to carry and deliver a child for the intended parents.

Transducer: A device typically used during an ultrasound procedure. It emits sound waves that are translated into electrical signals so that an image appears on the monitor screen.

Ultrasound: A test in which sound waves are used to evaluate internal structures of the body.

Umbilical cord: A cablelike structure that forms during a normal pregnancy between the placenta and the baby and provides nourishment to and removes waste from the baby.

Uterus: A female reproductive organ that is made of muscle and is located within the pelvis. Its purpose is to contain the fetus as it grows and develops during pregnancy.

Vagina: A muscular and tubelike passageway leading from the outside of the body to the uterus. It is sometimes referred to as the birth canal.

Varicocele: An abnormal enlargement of the vein (varicose vein) near the spermatic cord. It may be a cause of fertility problems in the man.

Vas deferens: A pair of tubelike structures that carry the sperm from the male's epididymis to his ejaculatory duct.

Vulva: The area that comprises the external female genital region.

X-bearing sperm: Sperm cell that carries the X (female) chromosome. If it fertilizes the egg, the resulting offspring will be a female.

Y-bearing sperm: Sperm cell that carries the Y (male) chromosome. If it fertilizes the egg, the resulting offspring will be a male.

Zygote: Another term for a very early developing embryo. It marks the time from fertilization until implantation within the uterus.

REFERENCES

Chapter 1

American College of Obstetricians and Gynecologists. *Endometriosis* (pamphlet). 2001 November publication number AP013. Washington, D.C.: American College of Obstetricians and Gynecologists.

American College of Obstetricians and Gynecologists. *Evaluating Infertility* (pamphlet). 2000 June publication number AP136. Washington, D.C.: American College of Obstetricians and Gynecologists.

American College of Obstetricians and Gynecologists. *Gonorrhea, Chlamydia, and Syphilis* (pamplet). 2000 July publication number AP071. Washington, D.C.: American College of Obstetricians and Gynecologists.

American College of Obstetricians and Gynecologists. *Pelvic Inflammatory Disease* (pamphlet). 2004 September publication number AP077. Washington, D.C.: American College of Obstetricians and Gynecologists.

American College of Obstetricians and Gynecologists. *Polycystic Ovary Syndrome* (pamphlet). 2001 March publication number AP121. Washington, D.C.: American College of Obstetricians and Gynecologists.

American College of Obstetricians and Gynecologists. *Treating Infertility* (pamphlet). 2004 November publication number AP137. Washington, D.C.: American College of Obstetricians and Gynecologists.

American Society for Reproductive Medicine. *Patient's Fact Sheet: Smoking and Infertility* (pamphlet). 2003 November. Birmingham, Alabama. Available at asrm.org. Accessed November 17, 2006.

Medical Encyclopedia: Asherman's Syndrome. Medline Plus. Available at nlm.nih.gov/medlineplus/ency/article/001483.htm. Accessed November 17, 2006.

Mello, N. K., J. H. Mendelson, and S. K. Teoh. "Overview of the Effects of Alcohol on the Neuroendocrine Function in Women." In S. Zakhari, ed. *Alcohol and the Endocrine System*. National Institute on Alcohol Abuse and Alcoholism Research Monograph No. 23. NIH Pub. No. 93-3533. Bethesda, Maryland: National Institutes of Health, 1993. pp. 139–69.

Pajarinen, J., P. J. Karhunen, V. Savolainen, et al. "Moderate Alcohol Consumption and Disorders of Human Spermatogenesis." *Alcoholism: Clinical and Experimental Research* 20 (2) (April 1996): 332–37.

Raab, Diana. *Getting Pregnant and Staying Pregnant* 3rd ed. Alameda, California: Hunter House Publishing, 1999.

RESOLVE: The National Infertility Association. *Optimizing My Fertility—Risk Factors*. Bethesda, MD. Available at http://resolve.org/site/PageServer?pagename= lrn_oyf_rfac. Accessed November 16, 2006.

Sher, Geoffrey, V. Davis, and J. Stoess. *In Vitro Fertilization: The A.R.T. of Making Babies* 3rd ed. New York: Checkmark Books, 2005.

United States Department of Health and Human Services Centers for Disease Control and Prevention. *Known Health Effects for DES Sons*. Available at cdc.gov/DES/ consumers/about/effects_sons.html. Accessed November 17, 2006.

Chapter 2

American College of Obstetricians and Gynecologists. *Early Pregnancy Loss: Miscarriage and Molar Pregnancy* (pamphlet). 2002 May publication number AP090. Washington, D.C.: American College of Obstetricians and Gynecologists.

American College of Obstetricians and Gynecologists. *Repeated Miscarriage* (pamphlet). 2005 September publication number AP100. Washington, D.C.: American College of Obstetricians and Gynecologists.

American Family Physician. "Insulin Resistance Syndrome." Available at aafp.org/ afp/20010315/1165ph.html. Accessed November 18, 2006.

Duke University Health System, Duke Fertility Services. "Polycystic Ovarian Syndrome." Available at dukehealth.org/Services/Fertility/Resources/Diagnoses/ PolycysticOvarianSyndrome?search_highlight=polycystic%200varian%20 syndrome. Accessed November 18, 2006.

Karim, M. Y., and G. R. V. Hughes. "The Antiphospholipid Syndrome (Hughes' Syndrome)." Available at netdoctor.co.uk/diseases/facts/antiphospholipid.htm. Accessed May 25, 2006.

Raab, Diana. *Getting Pregnant and Staying Pregnant* 3rd ed. Alameda, California: Hunter House Publishing, 1999.

Sher, Geoffrey, V. Davis, and J. Stoess. *In Vitro Fertilization: The A.R.T. of Making Babies* 3rd ed. New York: Checkmark Books, 2005.

Chapter 3

American College of Obstetricians and Gynecologists. *Menstruation* (pamphlet). 1999 December publication number AP049. Washington, D.C.: American College of Obstetricians and Gynecologists.

Raab, Diana. *Getting Pregnant and Staying Pregnant* 3rd ed. Alameda, California: Hunter House Publishing, 1999.

Sher, Geoffrey, V. Davis, and J. Stoess. *In Vitro Fertilization: The A.R.T. of Making Babies* 3rd ed. New York: Checkmark Books, 2005.

Chapter 4

American College of Obstetricians and Gynecologists. *Evaluating Infertility* (pamphlet). 2000 June publication number AP136. Washington, D.C.: American College of Obstetricians and Gynecologists.

American College of Obstetricians and Gynecologists. *Hysterosalpingography* (pamphlet). 2000 November publication number AP143. Washington, D.C.: American College of Obstetricians and Gynecologists.

American College of Obstetricians and Gynecologists. *Hysteroscopy* (pamphlet). 1999 December publication number AP084. Washington, D.C.: American College of Obstetricians and Gynecologists.

American College of Obstetricians and Gynecologists. *Laparoscopy* (pamphlet). 1998 April publication number AP061. Washington, D.C.: American College of Obstetricians and Gynecologists.

American College of Obstetricians and Gynecologists. *Ultrasound Exams* (pamphlet). 1998 May publication number AP025. Washington, D.C.: American College of Obstetricians and Gynecologists.

Johnson N., P. Vandekerckhove, A. Watson, et al. "Tubal Flushing for Subfertility." *Cochrane Database Systemic Reviews* 3 (2002): CD003718.

Raab, Diana. *Getting Pregnant and Staying Pregnant* 3rd ed. Alameda, California: Hunter House Publishing, 1999.

Sember, Brette McWhorter. *The Infertility Answer Book*. Naperville, Illinois: Sphinx Publishing, 2005.

Sher, Geoffrey, V. Davis, and J. Stoess. *In Vitro Fertilization: The A.R.T. of Making Babies* 3rd ed. New York: Checkmark Books, 2005.

Chapter 5

Akmal, M., J. Q. Qadri, N. S. Al-Waili,, et al. "Improvement in Human Semen Quality After Oral Supplementation of Vitamin C." *Journal of Medicinal Foods* 9 (3) (Fall 2006): 440–42.

American College of Obstetricians and Gynecologists. *Good Health Before Pregnancy: Preconceptional Care* (pamphlet). 1999 September publication number AP056. Washington, D.C.: American College of Obstetricians and Gynecologists.

American College of Obstetricians and Gynecologists. *Guidelines for Diagnostic Imaging During Pregnancy* (pamphlet). 2004 September ACOG committee opinion number 299. Washington, D.C.: American College of Obstetricians and Gynecologists.

American Society for Reproductive Medicine. *Patient's Fact Sheet: Smoking and Infertility.* 2003 November. Birmingham, Alabama. Available at asrm.org. Accessed November 17, 2006.

American Society for Reproductive Medicine. *Patient's Fact Sheet: Weight and Fertility.* 2001 August. Birmingham, Alabama. Available at asrm.org. Accessed November 17, 2006.

Fischl, F., R. Riegler, C. Bieglmayer, et al. "Modification of Semen Quality by Acupuncture in Subfertile Males." *Geburtshilfe Frauenheilkd* 44 (8) (August 1984): 510–12.

Frisch, R. E. *Female Fertility and the Body Fat Connection*. Chicago: University of Chicago Press, 2002.

Gerhard, I., and F. Postneek. "Auricular Acupuncture in the Treatment of Female Infertility." *Gynecology Endocrinology* 6 (3) (September1992): 171–81.

Geva, E., B. Bartoov, N. Zabludovsky, et al. "The Effect of Antioxidant Treatment on Human Spermatozoa and Fertilization Rate in an In Vitro Fertilization Program." *Fertility Sterility* 66 (3) (September 1996): 430–34.

Glenville, Marilyn. "What Medicine. Natural Solutions to Infertility." Available at whatmedicine.co.uk/WomensHealthInfertility_903.htm. Accessed July 25, 2006.

Grodstein, F., M. B. Goldman, D. W. Cramer, et al. "Infertility in Women and Moderate Alcohol Use." *American Journal of Public Health* 84 (9) (September 1994): 1429–32.

Hatch, E. E., and M. B. Bracken. "Association of Delayed Conception with Caffeine Consumption." *American Journal of Epidemiology* 138 (12) (December 15, 1993): 1082–92.

Internet Health Library. "Aromatherapy and Infertility." Available at internethealth library.com/Health-problems/Infertility%20-%20researchAltTherapies.htm. Accessed July 25, 2006.

Parazzini, F., M. Marchini, L. Tozzi, et al. "Risk Factors for Unexplained Dyspermia in Infertile Men: A Case-Control Study." *Archives Andrology* 31 (2) (September–October 1993): 105–13.

Sher, Geoffrey, V. Davis, and J. Stoess. *In Vitro Fertilization: The A.R.T. of Making Babies* 3rd ed. New York: Checkmark Books, 2005.

Wilcox, A., C. Weinberg, D. Baird, et al. "Caffeinated Beverages and Decreased Fertility." *Lancet* 2 (8626–8627) (December 24–31, 1988): 1453–56.

Wong, W.Y., C. M. Thomas, J. M. Merkus, et al. "Male Factor Subfertility: Possible Causes and the Impact of Nutritional Factors." *Fertility Sterility* 73 (3) (March 2000): 435–42.

Chapter 6

Raab, Diana. *Getting Pregnant and Staying Pregnant* 3rd ed. Alameda, California: Hunter House Publishing, 1999.

Sher, Geoffrey, V. Davis, and J. Stoess. *In Vitro Fertilization: The A.R.T. of Making Babies* 3rd ed. New York: Checkmark Books, 2005.

Yarali, H., O. Bukulmez, T. Gurgan, et al. "Urinary FSH Versus Recombinant FSH in Clomiphene Citrate-Resistant, Normogonadotropic, Chronic Anovualtion: A Prospective Randomized Study." *Fertility Sterility* 72 (2) (August 1999): 276–81.

Chapter 7

American College of Obstetricians and Gynecologists. *Treating Infertility* (pamphlet). 2004 November publication number AP137. Washington, D.C.: American College of Obstetricians and Gynecologists.

Raab, Diana. *Getting Pregnant and Staying Pregnant* 3rd ed. Alameda, California: Hunter House Publishing, 1999.

Sember, Brette McWhorter. *The Infertility Answer Book*. Naperville, Illinois: Sphinx Publishing, 2005.

Sher, Geoffrey, V. Davis, and J. Stoess. *In Vitro Fertilization: The A.R.T. of Making Babies* 3rd ed. New York: Checkmark Books, 2005.

Chapter 8

American Society for Reproductive Medicine. *Third Party Reproduction: A Guide for Patients* (pamphlet). Birmingham, Alabama. Available at asrm.org. Accessed November 17, 2006.

Raab, Diana. *Getting Pregnant and Staying Pregnant* 3rd ed. Alameda, California: Hunter House Publishing, 1999.

Sember, Brette McWhorter. *The Infertility Answer Book*. Naperville, Illinois: Sphinx Publishing, 2005.

Sher, Geoffrey, V. Davis, and J. Stoess. *In Vitro Fertilization: The A.R.T. of Making Babies* 3rd ed. New York: Checkmark Books, 2005.

Wagner L. "Fertility of the Aging Male." *Progres en Urologie* 14 (4) (September 2004): 577–82.

Chapter 9

American Society for Reproductive Medicine. *Patient's Fact Sheet: Infertility Counseling and Support: When and Where to Find It*. 2004 January. Birmingham, Alabama. Available at asrm.org. Accessed November 17, 2006.

Raab, Diana. *Getting Pregnant and Staying Pregnant* 3rd ed. Alameda, California: Hunter House Publishing, 1999.

Sember, Brette McWhorter. *The Infertility Answer Book*. Naperville, Illinois: Sphinx Publishing, 2005.

Sher, Geoffrey, V. Davis, and J. Stoess. *In Vitro Fertilization: The A.R.T. of Making Babies* 3rd ed. New York: Checkmark Books, 2005.

Chapter 10

American Society for Reproductive Medicine. *FAQs About Cloning, Stem Cell Research, and ASRM's Position*. Birmingham, Alabama. Available at asrm.org. Accessed September 17, 2006.

Kentucky Center for Reproductive Medicine & IVF. "Preimplantation Genetic Diagnosis." Available at kcrm-ivf.com. Accessed September 17, 2006.

Pehlivan, T., C. Rubio, L. Rodrigo, et al. "Impact of Preimplantation Genetic Diagnosis on IVF Outcome in Implantation Failure Patients." *Reproductive Biomedicine Online* 6 (2) (March 2003): 232–37.

Sember, Brette McWhorter. *The Infertility Answer Book*. Naperville, Illinois: Sphinx Publishing, 2005.

Sher, Geoffrey, V. Davis, and J. Stoess. *In Vitro Fertilization: The A.R.T. of Making Babies* 3rd ed. New York: Checkmark Books, 2005.

Silber, Sherman. "Preserving Your Fertility." The Infertility Center of Saint Louis. Saint Louis, Missouri. Available at infertile.com/treatmnt/treats/preserving_your_fertility.htm. Accessed September 17, 2006.

Chapter 11

Raab, Diana. *Getting Pregnant and Staying Pregnant* 3rd ed. Alameda, California: Hunter House Publishing, 1999.

Sember, Brette McWhorter. *The Infertility Answer Book*. Naperville, Illinois: Sphinx Publishing, 2005.

Sher, Geoffrey, V. Davis, and J. Stoess. *In Vitro Fertilization: The A.R.T. of Making Babies* 3rd ed. New York: Checkmark Books, 2005.

INDEX

ABOUT THE AUTHOR

Susan Warhus, M.D., is a physician and a board-certified obstetrician and gynecologist. She cofounded the largest all-female practice in the state of Arizona. During her clinical practice, she had the pleasure of delivering more than three thousand babies. She is the author of *Countdown to Baby* and *Darn Good Advice—Pregnancy* and contributes to articles for various women's and health magazines.

Dr. Warhus is a member of the American College of Obstetricians and Gynecologists and the American Medical Association. She earned a master's degree in business administration from Arizona State University and worked in the pharmaceutical industry prior to obtaining her medical degree at University of Arizona.

She would love to hear from you and can be reached through her website: askdoctor susan.com.